Folk Housing in Middle Virginia

A STRUCTURAL ANALYSIS OF HISTORIC ARTIFACTS

Folk Housing in Middle Virginia

By HENRY GLASSIE

Photographs and Drawings by the Author

THE UNIVERSITY OF TENNESSEE PRESS

Books by Henry Glassie

A Guide for Collectors of Oral Traditions and Folk Cultural Material in Pennsylvania (1968). With MacEdward Leach.

Pattern in the Material Folk Culture of the Eastern United States (1969).

Forms Upon the Frontier: Folklife and Folk Arts in the United States (1969). With Austin and Alta Fife.

Folksongs and Their Makers (1970). With Edward D. Ives and John F. Szwed.

Folk Housing in Middle Virginia: Structural Analysis of Historic Artifacts (1975).

LIBRARY OF CONGRESS CATALOGING IN PUBLICATION DATA

Glassie, Henry H
   Folk housing in middle Virginia

   Bibliography: p.
   Includes index.
   1. Architecture, Domestic—Virginia. 2. Folk art—Virginia. I. Title.
NA7235.V5G55   975.5   75–11653
ISBN 0–87049–173–3

PUBLICATION OF THIS BOOK was assisted by the American Council of Learned Societies under a grant from the Andrew W. Mellon Foundation.

for Fred Kniffen

Preface

The lonely cold in ancient cathedrals chilled John Ruskin. He was fatigued by endless trips across Europe, distracted by illnesses of body and mind. The cathedral drafts set him shivering, but he kept sketching. His fingers must have stiffened in pain and then numbed; his back must have ached, but his notebooks thickened with measurements and lines, with traceries, crockets, finials, and startling Gothic fantasies. When he wrote or spoke, John Ruskin began with the architectural details that he had drawn with precision. But his discourse sailed from stones to speculation on the culture of the craftsman; his mind soared from chisel marks to the morality of the mason's society.

A century has gone by. The intellectual rage of Ruskin and his contemporaries lies unread, entombed in old volumes that bring cheap prices in second-hand bookshops. Unaware of their efforts, we must work to reinvent their goals. It took me a long time sketching before I could battle past wood and stone to begin considering the human beings who left material things as their only legacy. This book, a record of my effort, is not exactly a study of old buildings, or even old builders. It is a study of the architecture of past thought—an attempt to reconstruct the logic of people long dead by looking seriously at their houses.

Architecture studied for itself can fulfill a personal curiosity and provide a test of personal capacity. Architecture studied as an expression of personality and culture may provide us with the best means available for comprehending an authentic history. If a person's interest is in the timeless principles governing human behavior, the study of architecture is an unnecessarily complicated way for him to locate those principles. It would be better to watch human beings in action than to spend time trying to catch reflections of behavior in mute artifacts. If the scholar's interest turns to people he cannot observe, however, and if his interest is in the ways that people's minds have operated over long stretches of time, then artifacts can provide him with the best means to confront his interest. Many of today's cleverest and most creative thinkers have abandoned the field of history in a quest for human principles. It follows that when they lost interest in the past, they lost interest as well in the analysis of artifacts. By forgetting the past, these thinkers have been able to develop thrilling synchronic theories, and they have made it easier for unscrupulous men to co-opt the vast power of history, harnessing it to their own ends.

Like archaeology, art history, and cultural geography, the discipline of folklore is a natural center for the historical study of artifacts. Folklore has not totally lost its interest in the past, though that interest, lamentably, has been more in the history of things than in the history of people. Folklorists in America now generally count "material culture" as part of their subject matter, and folklorists in greater numbers—younger folklorists especially—are concentrating on the study of artifacts. As yet, however, their goals have been weakly defined. Understandably, folklore's progressives are little interested in artifacts; the past does not worry them. It is likely that their nonhistorical program will continue to mark folklore's high road into the future, but the way of the social sciences will not and should not become folklore's only path. Folklore's tradition of humanistic literary scholarship is probably due for a revival. Philosophy—phenomenology and existentialism, in particular—may become a future source for folkloristic ideas, just as anthropology and linguistics have been in the past. And more folklorists will probably take a look at historical possibilities. I wrote this book partially to help my discipline consider these historical possibilities.

Folklore is in a strange state, assessing its new-found

maturity in text books, anthologies, summaries, recodifications of old thought, and tentative pronouncements for the future. Much is being said, but little is being studied. Prescriptive essays do less good in the furthering of a discipline than do actual studies, and "theoretical" essays, trimmed with assorted examples, are too easy to write. For those reasons, though my purpose is to show how artifacts can be analyzed to get at history, I have attempted a tight little study rather than the outline of a method. I respond, emotionally and aesthetically, to folk architecture, and I was fascinated by the historical results of my analysis. Still, this study is a test and an explication of a method. I have meant to be rigorous, and to state openly the assumptions upon which it is founded, for it depends upon influences from several disciplines, as will be apparent from the footnotes (I have not been stingy with them) and the classified bibliography.

The reader will probably find some parts of the study more useful or familiar than others, depending upon his own disciplinary traditions. The historian, for instance, might wish to glance from chapter II to chapter VIII before working through the whole book. The person interested in structuralism, which is the book's theoretical mainstay, might wish initially to skip the chapters the historian reads and read those he skips. The person who has no interest in architectural history might want to pass by chapters IV and V and then refer to points within them when it becomes necessary for his understanding of the subsequent chapters. The architectural historian and the cultural geographer might relate most comfortably to chapters V and VI. However, this work is not exactly "interdisciplinary"; rather, it is the kind of openly synthetic attempt that is possible within the modern discipline of folklore. I wish to learn as much as possible from the objects I select to analyze.

The study is occasionally complicated, but the problem it addresses is complicated. A much simplified statement would require the omission of crucial aspects of the method and would be an insult both to the reader and to the human beings I am attempting to explain.

John Ruskin's architectural studies became the basis for an effective radical romanticism. Ruskin's friend William Morris, blue suit crumpled and hair aflame, could stand before a gathering of genteel socialists, manual laborers, or artists, and proclaim a future based on the analysis of the folk craftsman's art. Unlike the Victorian romantics, I have no social program, but, like them, I know that humble old artifacts have important messages for us if we can figure out how to read them. I am saddened that many of the best minds of our time feel no responsibility toward history, and that even the historian feels no responsibility toward most artifacts. Everyone knows that the bulldozer begets ugliness on the land, but fewer seem to be aware that it destroys history. When the land is blasted and paved over it will be easy for anyone to remake the old American in his own image.

I thought about doing this book for six years, and I thought intensely about it for the four years following the completion of *Pattern in the Material Folk Culture of the Eastern United States.* That book and this one treat similar material, and the older book contains some information that is useful within the arguments I have framed here. The theoretical bases of the two books, however, are entirely different. I finally wrote this book in the spring of 1972. When I had finished the first draft, I owed a number of debts.

I would like to thank those people in Middle Virginia who were especially helpful to me when I was at work in the field: Otis Banks, Lee Bradshaw, Mr. and Mrs. E. E. Brooking, B. B. Harris, Athylone Julia Lloyd, N. O. Rigsby, Ida Smith, and Mr. and Mrs. James Watson.

Many of my intellectual debts will become apparent in the footnotes, but I have learned more in conversations than I have from reading. My greatest debt will always be to Professor Fred Kniffen, to whom this work is dedicated. I also take pleasure in mentioning the names of these men who have helped me define my concern for the artifact: Ronald Brunskill, Jim Deetz, Estyn Evans, James Marston Fitch, Bunny Fontana, Alan Gailey, and Warren Roberts. Chips of this book were tried out at academic meetings of folklore, archaeology, and historical societies. Nice comments were made to me in those contexts by people who have probably forgotten that they were encouraging: Dick Dorson, Roger Abrahams, Elliott Oring, Joe Illick, John Walzer, and Anthony N. B. Garvan. It is possible that all of the men named in this paragraph will want to deny any connection with this book, but comments made by all of them were helpful to me while I was at work.

By February of 1973, when I was revising the manuscript, my debts had increased. The John Simon Guggenheim Memorial Foundation provided me with a very generous grant from June through December of 1972. Though the project I completed as a Guggenheim fellow was not the one reported here, the grant did allow me to do fieldwork in Britain, and this book was improved at many points by my first-hand experiences on the other side of the Atlantic.

Drafts of this work were buoyed by my friends, the faculty, staff, and students of Indiana's Folklore Institute. They provided me with as pleasant an atmosphere as can be found in these disagreeable times. Phil and Pat Peek brought me my own *ivri* from Isoko country, and from it I borrowed the energy to keep at it on some particularly tiring nights.

My family has always 'patiently indulged my fanaticisms. My grandmother, my mother, my father (the nation's most insightful, unsung critic of nineteenth-century American painting), my sister and her friend Jim—all helped me in diverse ways. My wife's parents, Mr. and Mrs. Irving J. Friedman, helped us with housing while the folk housing of Middle Virginia was being studied. Then there are Polly, Harry, and Lydia, without whose interruptions my scholarship would seem like work instead of the fun it is. Betty-Jo and the kids lived with me in the field. Betty-Jo nursed me back from an incredible case of poison ivy that I contracted because one especially important old house was covered with that God-forsaken weed and my choice was to not measure the house or to become totally covered with obnoxiously itchy sores. I chose the latter. Betty-Jo and John Vlach drank a lot of coffee while proofreading. She typed and retyped the manuscript and thought I was a little hard on the old Virginia heritage that we share. Actually I was surprised by the results of my analysis: the old Virginians were hard on themselves.

Contents

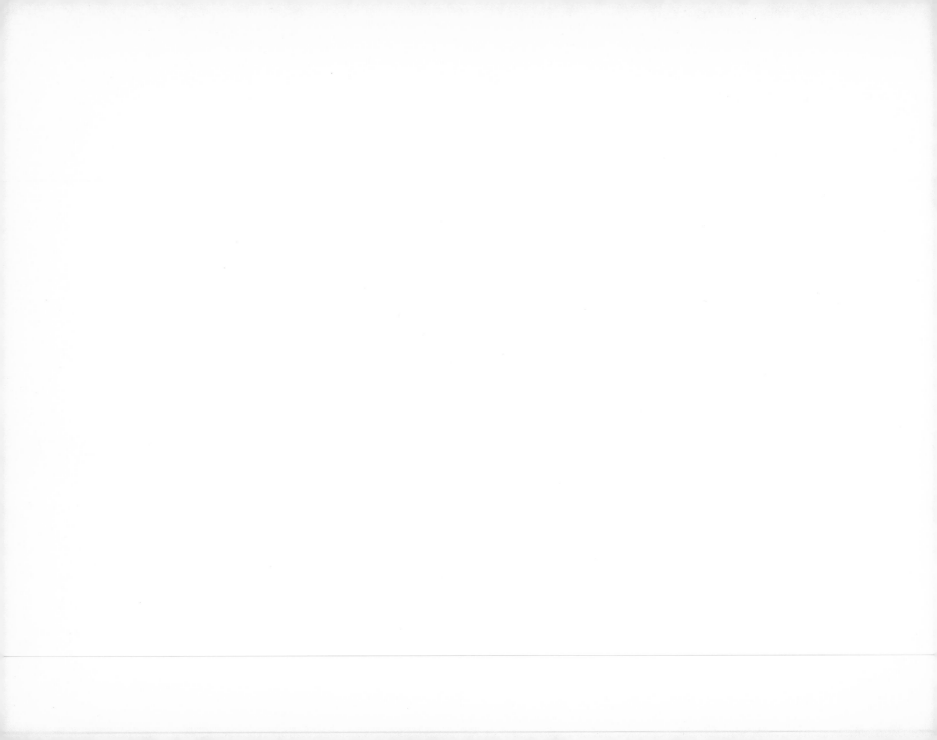

Figures

Fig. 1 SIGNS ON THE LAND.

4

I

A Silent Land

Slow wheels on the roads in Virginia summertime spin pink dust into the sky. It remains until long after quiet returns. The fields in winter, rough with fodder stubble and brittle under a sheet of snow, glide away into the black pines. Shattered only by the tree tops, the horizon is bleached soundless. It is that sort of country.

The skies come constantly into view. The land bears no features that hold the attention; it rises and falls flatly along the lines struck by small rivers, rows of tobacco or corn, fence posts or timber. The red clay on which most livelihoods and all moods depend is waxy and thick with too much rain, and it dries to dust with too little. At the end of a row, a farmer will stoop to take up a pinch of mud or dust, cocking his head back to take in the sky. Cloud streaks sailing back from the sunset bespeak fair weather, and a low metallic blackness indicates rain. The farmer will stand and stiffen, his hand curled over the top of his hoe, his chin resting on his knuckles. The face in the shade of his hat will not move as his eyes lower from the sky to the dirt and then level to follow a car passing through the dust. No nods are exchanged. When he was a young man, half a century ago, he plowed behind oxen for forty cents a day and carved tracks through the forests that had grown over the plantations of his grandfather's manhood. He had known and joked with everyone and gathered with his friends for dances. He still follows the moon's wisdom and attends to nature's signs, but things do not look good. Tractors pack the clay too tightly to let the young shoots struggle into the sun, and mules have become so expensive that he has to harness one to a two-horse rake to scratch the lumps out of his garden. And these younger generations. They stare sullenly out of automobiles, waiting to leave. They have lost the logic of the farmer's world.

Centered for some on the stores at Orchid, Inez, or Gum Spring, for others on white wooden churches in the woods, this land lies across the line separating Goochland County, formed from Henrico in 1727 and named for a colonial governor, and Louisa, formed from Hanover in 1742 and named for King George III's daughter. Located

Folk Housing in Middle Virginia

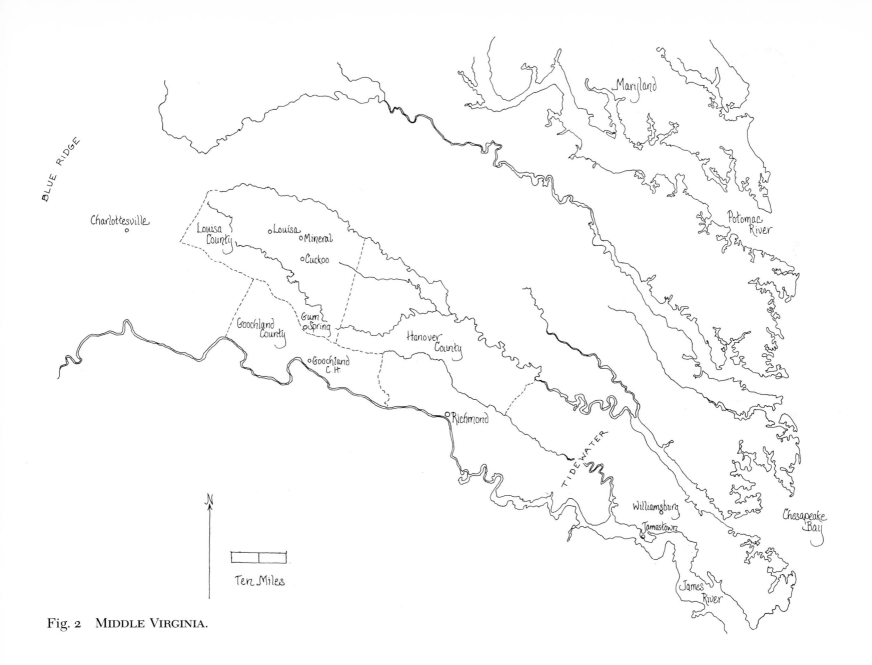

BLUE RIDGE

Maryland

Potomac River

Charlottesville

Louisa County

Louisa

Mineral

Cuckoo

Goochland County

Gum Spring

Hanover County

Goochland C. H.

Richmond

TIDEWATER

Williamsburg

Jamestown

Chesapeake Bay

James River

N

Ten Miles

Fig. 2   MIDDLE VIRGINIA.

just west of the fall-line, lolling between the Blue Ridge and the Tidewater, this land is called Middle Virginia. Roads reach out to prevent its isolation. The main road from Mineral to Goochland Court House cuts through, crossed by the highway that runs from Charlottesville to Richmond. Gum Spring is near the halfway mark. There travelers stopped to water their horses,[1] and drovers of cattle and turkeys broke the two-day trip from the Blue Ridge to the eastern markets. Lest travelers should lose it in the net of farm lanes cast over the red clay and piney woods, the highway was blazed by three strokes of an ax, whence its name: Three Chopt Road. The chops remain in the oak tree standing amid the boxwoods in front of the ruined Rackett house, where people on the road used to stop to pass the night. From beneath that oak the low-clustered shapes at Gum Spring are visible: the new highway and the old one part here, one carved straight through the landscape and the other wandering into the woods. Richmond lay only a half a day from here, if your horse were a traveler; and produce could be sent from Goochland by water down the James River. This land was not, and is not, isolated. It is a home for those whose living grows from the ground, but for the outsider the land is located too near the center of things to be more than a place to pass through.

People from across the Atlantic began breaking the land as the eighteenth century opened. In the 1790 census both Goochland and Louisa counties had a population of nearly nine thousand, and in each of the counties the majority of the people were black slaves (Fig. 3).[2] Before the Civil War exploded, the black majority had

		1790	1850	1880	1900	1930
Louisa	white	3880	6423	7409	7896	8468
	black	4573	9864	11531	8621	5341
	free not white	14	404			
Goochland	white	4140	3865	4058	3961	3839
	black	4656	5845	6234	5558	4114
	free not white	257	644			

Fig. 3 POPULATION OF LOUISA AND GOOCHLAND. The sources of these figures can be found in notes 2–4, p. 194.

increased.[3] Its decline began toward the end of the nineteenth century.[4] By the 1960 census 39.9 percent of the 12,959 people in Louisa were not white; of the 9,206 Goochland residents, 48.2 percent were not white.[5] In over a century and a half, Louisa County's population had increased by about a quarter and Goochland's by only 153 people.

The people's work was always agricultural. The enumeration of 1810 reported that Louisa had produced a couple of thousand dollars worth of clocks and watches, and had twenty stills in operation. A few carriages were made in both counties, but the main produce grew out of the land.[6] A decade later the census records that in the two counties 6,906 people were engaged in agriculture and only 465 in manufactures.[7] Thirty years later the number of people employed in manufacturing had decreased by more than one hundred. At the same time the two counties had produced 341,490 bushels of wheat, 653,676 bushels of corn, and 2,508,493 pounds of tobacco.[8] The 1880 census shows a further decline in the numbers working in manufacturing and a dip in agricultural output: 146,582 bushels of wheat, 513,719 bushels of corn, 2,578,114 pounds of tobacco.[9] After the Civil War the plantations contracted, and though there still are farms among the pines the young men are leaving cultivation to work in the whining sawmills that are cutting paths through the second-growth timber, spitting out low-grade boards and pallets. And they are leaving the sawmills for Richmond and Philadelphia. In the melancholy rhetoric of the fading Confederate, the author of one of the thin local histories writes, "The material wealth of Goochland was bountifully supplied by nature . . . but it is hoped and believed that it will never be said of Goochland, as it has never been said in the past, 'Ill fares the land; to hastening ills a prey, where wealth accumulates and men decay.'"[10] The fact is, the area rests at the rock bottom of the Commonwealth of Virginia's economy.[11]

The correspondence between Cornwallis and Tarleton refers to the "Three-notched Road," and Tarleton galloped through Louisa.[12] We are informed by historians that a lady who was loved by both John Paul Jones and Patrick Henry was born not far to the east.[13] And the Civil War flamed all around this area. Despite these brushes with importance no great event chanced to happen just here. The land never struck anyone as culturally exotic. People passed through.

There are documents, government reports, and small books from which a little can be learned, but there is not enough to allow a historian to write about this area—or about the many other areas that are like it primarily in being unknown. If this land and the people who made it have no place in the historical record, then the worth of the study of history must be called sharply into question. The written primary sources are too scanty, but there are fences in the forests and silent old houses set back from the roads. They are decaying and difficult to decipher, they demand tiring work in the field and complicated analysis, but they can be made to reveal the information upon which a strengthened historiography could be based. With brave exceptions, though, historians pass by such sources without a look. History moves on, leaving this land, like almost everywhere else, and these people, like almost everyone else, out of account.

II

A More Human History

History is a difficult pursuit.[1] It is, in fact, passing difficult, possibly impossible, and for that reason the vanguard of social science has been in full retreat from history for most of our century. Left in the path of that movement is a critique of history compounded of three interrelated charges.

The first charge is that of unexplained process. It is intellectually unsound to develop a narrative of change through time without first accounting for the system that is undergoing and enabling change. Thinkers at odds on other matters—Claude Lévi-Strauss[2] and Jean-Paul Sartre,[3] for example—concur that any method of inquiry must include a synchronic statement as a prelude to diachronic interpretation. Time must be stopped and states of affairs examined before time can be reintroduced, else the scholar will be unable to determine his object of study clearly. He may include too much or, more likely, too little in his research, and when the object of his study mutates he will be caught without an explanation for the change. The architectural historian who operates

without a totalizing definition of architecture may focus on isolated detail—an object too small. As a consequence, he often finds himself having to explain architectural change as a series of unconnected revolutions instead of the gradual development that he would find to be the case if he examined architectural wholes. Actually, proceeding to diachrony without acknowledging synchrony is impossible.[4] How can you study change before you know what is changing?

The second is the charge of elitism. The synchronic account of any past era cannot be assembled, because available records concern only a tiny minority of the people and phenomena that existed at any time. A method based on the document is prejudiced: fated to neglect the majority of people, for they were nonliterate,[5] and, within the boundaries of literacy, to neglect the majority of people, for they did not write.[6] Even today, in societies of nearly universal literacy, it is a rare soul who bequeaths to future historians a written account of his thought. The past becomes an anecdotal congeries. How can it be understood on the basis of the recent West alone? How can you study a society if you attend only to the expressions of a small and deviant class within the whole?

The last charge against conventional historiography is that of unscientific procedure. The records of people and events are the reports not of trained professionals striving to adhere to the troublesome ideal of objectivity, but of amateur information gatherers who often had axes to grind.[7] Appalled by the ethnocentrism of scientific ethnography, we still accept the random judgments of the casual travelers of olden times, even though their standards were not necessarily high; a reading of travel accounts reveals that their authors sometimes plagiarized from one another. We know that contemporary journalism is biased and inaccurate, and that the results of the latest census are questionable. What of past documents? How can the product of research approach truth when study proceeds from vaguely derived, uncontrolled statements?

Some have solved the dilemma presented in this critique by forgetting the past and turning their efforts to building laws out of the knowable present. Others have ignored not the severe responsibility of history, but the responsibility of logical methodology.

The latter regularly defend their actions as endeavors unencumbered by fashionable theorizing. But the historian must be a theorist,[8] if only unreflectively. Information is weighed according to tacitly held norms of significance: some bits of it are selected, most are rejected, and the useful data is then plugged into an established model—an act all the more scholastically pernicious because some who move in this manner seem to believe that they are getting from facts to pure truth without hypothesis. Unless theories are clearly formulated and brought cleanly to the surface, there is no way to defend against them. The scholar who believes that he works without theory, works with bad theory.

The model regularly employed by the historian is one cobbled out of a naïve functionalism ("naïve" because it is unformulated and lacks a causative mechanism), an optimistic sort of periodization (clearly a survival of ancient Greek theorizing[9]), and the concept, both unattractive and untrue, that "followers" automatically follow "leaders." Operating with such a model, the historian may create not a record of what happened in the past, but a serial array of literary scraps that give the reader the sensation of progress. History, as we are redundantly reminded by the orators of the oppressed (and by theoretical inconsistencies), is too much the genealogy of contemporary institutional power and too little the story of people. Judged and found undemocratic, history is forced into regular revisions and an embarrassing abundance of special studies programs.

The seriousness of the case has been recognized by historians and the labor of expanding the record is underway. The awareness is not new. There were the awful but valiant attempts by turn-of-the-century social historians. We are fortunate to have the modern works of spatially oriented students of history, such as W. G. Hoskins and E. Estyn Evans, and to have the passionate and intellectual *oeuvre* of Marc Bloch[10]—his quest for "a more human history." In recent American historiography there is hope in oral history,[11] historical geography,[12] historical archaeology,[13] and in that psychological or sociological or

9

anthropological or demographic new history excitingly set out by students of early New England.[14] All of these efforts are frontal attacks on the problems raised by the charge of elitism in the critique of history; they are studies of human beings. Of equal importance is the fact that problems of method and theory are being tendered a look. The methods of this new scholarship can be employed to answer simultaneously the objections of angry speakers and philosophical methodologists, but not if they are used to lead only to compensatory repairs. They must lead through disciplinary introspection to a complete overhaul. The goal of history must not be the chronicle of the *outré*, the obvious, and the violent; it must be a record of what happened. And there is no way to avoid the fact that the record will have to be built on sophisticated generalizing theories.[15] Without them the task is beyond doing, and history remains either an uncoordinated amassing of data or a linear linking of those maladjusted personalities who stand out from the crowd.

One step is taken toward solving history's problem—it is a contemporary problem with two main symptoms, one social and one theoretical—when close thought is directed toward the nature of the objects subjected to analysis. The answer for current events is ethnography: the analyst must construct his own objects out of observation. For the recent past, the best recourse is to interviewing. When a point is reached where observation is no longer possible, and the recollections that interviews capture become vague, then the analyst must turn to less direct sources. He may have access to a body of oral traditional history containing remarkably rich data on events long past.[16] The problem with traditional history, how-ever, is less that it may be wrong, like written history, than that, like written history, it tends to concentrate on a few striking personages and events at the expense of commonplace reality. While conducting extensive interviewing on the oral history of the troubled Irish border, I was offered fine, detailed information on bloody battles that took place as long ago as the sixteenth century. When I asked about the agricultural technology upon which life depends, I could get back only to the nineteenth century. Oral history, like conventional written history, teaches more about the narrator and his society than it does about the societies of the past. For the distant past the analyst will normally have to rely on artifacts. Some artifacts are overtly informational (books, for example, or letters), while others are not. The information on the artifact's surface may be perfectly accurate, although the likelihood of its accuracy obviously depends on what its maker knew and what he intended. If the document deals with the author's society, it is more apt to be accurate than if it deals with people he knows less well. The document that is unintentionally informative, such as the probate inventory, is less likely to be purposively falsified than one meant to sway the reader's thought.[17] The surface of the document, of course, cannot be accepted without question. People make mistakes. The historian has developed means for trying the reliability of an overtly informational artifact, thereby making it of some use, but stronger than these contextual tests are analytic procedures that force the scholar to search below apparent content to a level where falsification cannot occur.[18] Rigorously analyzed, the artifact is always genuine because it is an expression of its maker's mind. This move obligates the analyst to study only direct expressions, to use the artifact as a source of information about the maker rather than about whatever topic the analyst is addressing. If an expression is used to reveal its maker, then it can be used as material for the construction of schemes, rather than as mere stuffing for previously set schemes.

Using a piece of writing solely to analyze its author suggests answers to the first and third of the charges in the critique: written documents may be analyzed to construct a synchronic statement, and the analyst is dealing with direct and expert (though not easily understood) information when he is dealing with a person's own written projections. The middle charge remains unanswered: the written record is still the record of the few. What the few thought of some of the many might be discovered, but, properly, that is information about the thought of the elite, not about the thought of their subjects. The majority might be studied as phantoms in unintentionally informational documents or as distorted shadows of phantoms in the writings of the elite; or they might be studied through their own expressions.[19] Only this last choice yields at once potential answers to the full critique proffered by those who have abandoned the past.

In order to understand that vast majority of people who left behind no literate legacy, it is necessary to learn how to obtain information from the artifacts they did make, although these artifacts—potsherds, old houses, and the like—carry no information on their surfaces. This presents a difficulty because a subtle code must be cracked. The difficulty is fortunate, however, for there is little chance that the analyst will be spirited away by a superficial untruth.

Interpreters of mute artifacts, like interpreters of writings, are apt to indulge in half-cocked theorizing; the archaeologist, for instance, may assign an unexplainable artwork to a position within a sacred system. But there is the hope that the serious analyst of artifacts will not be tempted to believe that he understands what he does not. Theoretically, the historian would have to subject each word of his chosen text to semiotic analysis because the meanings of words are not rigid;[20] they slip and shift during even short periods of time. He does not do that, for it is not obviously necessary; it is only methodologically necessary. But when an artifact lacks simple semantics, the scholar does what he must do: he analyzes it as if he did not already understand it. This is the problem of ethnographic interpretation. Even speakers of the same language and members of the same stream of tradition must be treated as carriers of an alien culture when removed from the analyst by time or space. The historian must study the inhabitants of, say, eighteenth-century Philadelphia in a way comparable to that used by an anthropologist to study the people of a Micronesian atoll.

Of equal significance is the problem of psychological interpretation. The written record is a rationalization; it not only may be wrong, it is definitely shallow and incomplete.[21] Occurrences cannot be explained by appeal to consciousness alone, because the historic pattern is at least as much the product of the unconscious as it is of the conscious. Any serious attempt to comprehend history depends, then, partially upon theories of cognition.

It is not that literary commentary is valueless, but rather that its use is corroborative. Old writing cannot be used to construct the epistemologically essential synchronic record that will account for most people (writing is a rarity, the making of artifacts is universal); but once the synchronic account has been developed, the written record can return to utility as a qualifying supplement. A philosophically and socially valid history must come out of painstaking analysis of direct cultural expressions that the analyst can study at first hand. Many of these expressions will be documents; but when no documents are available, we must study other sorts of artifacts rather than consigning the great bulk of humanity to historical oblivion.

Two diseases have crippled and nearly killed the silent artifact as a source for history. Most historians, it seems, continue to view the artifact as only an illustrative adjunct to the literary narrative. Perhaps when the elite is studied, this is not an unintelligent course of research. A knowledge of Thomas Jefferson might be based on his writings and only supplemented by a study of Monticello, but for most people, such as the folks who were chopping farms out of the woods a few miles to the east while Jefferson was writing at his desk, the procedure must be reversed. Their own statements, though made in wood or mud rather than ink, must take precedence over someone else's possibly prejudiced, probably wrong, and certainly superficial comments about them. The historian's benign neglect of silent artifacts and their people is a reasonable, if shallowly reasoned, response to the

way that artifacts have most often been studied—obsessively, that is, as ends in themselves. Some archaeologists stop work when their findings are listed in site reports, and some connoissuers not only persist in treating the artifact as a unique wonder rather than as a material manifestation of culture, they even eliminate from scrutiny the things that do not measure up to their own taste. Maybe some of these things are "bad," but most of them are "good" things that the connoisseur has failed to understand.[22] The decision to eliminate some artworks from study makes as much sense as would the choice by a historian to read only books with pretty bindings or to study only old documents calligraphed in a lovely hand. Any artifact that can be provided with association in space and time, either by being accompanied by a document or better—as with gravestones or buildings—by being set into the land, is a valuable source of a great quantity of information.

When we have learned to read the silent artifact, history will not be an easier pursuit. But if artifacts, such as the old houses standing along dusty roads in Middle Virginia, can be read, then history will become a philosophically more plausible pursuit. The remainder of this book sets out a careful description and analytical interpretation of Middle Virginia's houses, digressing where necessary to explicate the method, in order to see how the mute artifact can be made to speak.

III

A Prologue to Analysis

It is no test of the scholar or his craft to invent a theory and pop bits of information into it. That is the sort of activity for which historians criticize other social scientists, and it is exactly that for which they, in turn, criticize historians. An *ad hoc* selection of data can provide no test of a theory. The test, rather, is to see whether the theory fits a natural body of material. A grammar, we are reminded by Noam Chomsky, must fit a natural language.[1]

In my own discipline, folklore, the newer structural or behavioral theories, like the earlier theories, have all been supported by artificially assembled sets of examples. New theories replace old ones not because the old are disproved, but merely because they lose favor. The newer theories, being new, gain adherents, but they are doomed to brief lives because they are never adequately tested. Modern savants will often chatter about theory, while avoiding the "craft-like"[2] work that sets Claude Lévi-Strauss aloof from his hasty imitators. Recognition of this fact led to a personal dissatisfaction with years I had spent in scattered architectural photographing and

measuring in the United States. Without assembling a natural corpus, it would be possible to assert anything and prove nothing.[3] It took a cold, wearing year of systematic research on barns in upstate New York[4] for me to realize that recording procedures must be painfully exact if the energies consumed in the field are to be considered well spent. I stopped, resolved to do it right, and entered the field.

In ordinary experience, the tendency of the person is to accumulate information randomly, incompletely, and then to order that information into conscious patterns that are specific, yet complicated and unwieldy. Normal perceptions are selectively small; normal concepts are large and weak. It is by constantly reexperiencing the same or similar things that a person's perceptions become adequate and his concepts become efficient, although generally these concepts remain unconscious and unarticulated. The problem of the scholar with a limited amount of time in an alien setting is to work rigorously against his natural proclivities. He must edit as little as

13

possible at the stage of perception, and he must labor to develop simple, powerful concepts.

The usual contemporary attempt to provide research with rigor, to conquer the difficulties inherent in the natural process of observation and conceptualization, is framed deductively. Studies, we are instructed, should begin and move forward with explicitly stated hypotheses that are continually tested and refined. Such studies are always methodologically admirable, but they may easily become trivial if the initial hypothesis was incorrectly formed with relation to the objects selected for study. An equally important trouble with the general demand for deductive research is that the scholar might like to approach a new problem, and yet find himself without enough information to form a useful first hypothesis. There must be, then, a strategy—it might be called neoinductive or quasi-phenomenological—that moves rigorously, not by means of hypotheses about particular cultures or things, but by means of theories of inquiry not tied to particular cultures or things.

Of the many difficulties involved in nondeductive endeavor, two are of particular importance, and we must take a look at them here.

If a scholar is not guided by hypotheses while gathering information, no matter how rigorously he works, it will be possible for him to interpret the data in any number of conflicting ways.[5] The researcher may labor long to accumulate a good corpus—all the folktales of a group, say—and then ruin his study by a premature leap into a discussion of how those tales exemplify preconceived social roles or ethical concerns. Because of this, the scholar who does not commence with hypothesis must defer interpretation until the collected information has been built into efficient, simple concepts that are natural to his corpus. Those concepts may then be compared to foreign ones, hopefully yielding particular interpretations and general principles.

The second problem is that if the analyst begins to build models without having a clear idea of what the models are going to explain, he could end up with models that explain nothing.[6] This is true, but if one builds only those models known to have explanatory capabilities, research may be reduced to a puzzle-solving reinforcement of academic norms,[7] and thus one may be unable to reach other than predictable, jejune conclusions.

Any serious study of culture must confront the goals of full, complex observation and powerful, simple conceptualization. If hypotheses about particular cultures are not introduced at the beginning of inquiry, they must be held off until systematic concepts have been formed. The scholar, gambling a bit, must begin, blind to interpretative possibilities, by means of a rigorous method.

When I went into the field, I went equipped only with the general idea that an understanding of history must depend on artifactual analysis, and that, of all classes of artifacts, architecture would be the most efficient guide to past culture because of its universality, tenacity, complexity, and fixedness. I set to work not with a theory for testing, but with a thoroughly tested method for recording information that could be used to mold the general idea into a theory. The method used to assemble information was organically folkloristic, being compounded of the methods of folklore, cultural geography, architectural history, and archaeology.

Fig. 4   THE SURVEY AREA WITHIN ITS REGION. The black spot in the white space surrounded by shading is the surveyed area. The white space is the region of which the area is being presented as a sample. The shading indicates the zone to which architectural affinities are next closest.

My first decision was to study in the Lowland South, the least known of the architectural regions of the eastern United States, and a desire for depth of time took me into the area west of Chesapeake Bay. Since 1961, I had crisscrossed that land and had an impressionistic sense of its characteristics. Twice (August, 1962; July, 1963) I had paused for photographing in an area that seemed to be in a good state of repair and representative of the region in which it was set. There, in the summer of 1966, I moved my family into a shanty to conduct a field survey. Although the survey was quantitatively restricted to that area, several weeks of that summer, as well as brief periods before and after (September, 1967, especially), were taken to range out of the area. So that while this study can be defended as true only for the countryside around the rural centers of Orchid and Gum Spring in Louisa and Goochland counties, Virginia, I believe that it can stand reasonably for the region east of the Piedmont and west of the Chesapeake in Virginia, and north of Albemarle Sound in North Carolina (Fig. 4). The survey, which took the months of July and August to complete, was an amplification and intensification of the procedures followed by Fred Kniffen in his classic study in cultural geography, "Louisiana House Types."[8] After a preliminary survey, I drew precise geographical limits around an area that seemed large enough to include all the varieties of architectural phenomena useful to study, yet small enough to be manageable for a person working alone. I then drove over every highway, road, and narrow lane in the area (Fig. 5), stopping to record every house no matter what its age. The total was 338. The recording included the following: the location of each house, regis-

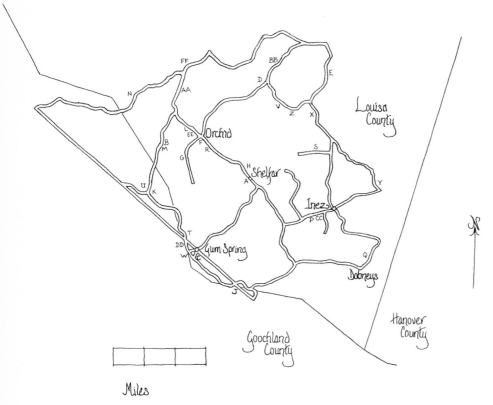

FF BB
E
D
N AA
V Z X
Louisa County
LEE EE
B Orchrd
M F S
G R
H Shelfar
A
U Y
K
Inez
P CC
T
DD Gum Spring
W C
Q
Dabneys

Hanover County

Goochland County

Miles

Fig. 5 THE SURVEY AREA AND LOCATIONS OF ARCHITECTURAL EXAMPLES. These are the roads that were surveyed—all the roads in the area. The letters locate the buildings chosen to illustrate the text.

tered with an odometer reading; the direction in which it faced; and a drawing of each of its sides. Ideally, photographs of every house would have been taken, in addition to the drawings, but expenses held photography to a minimum. I took about four hundred photos. The drawings of the exteriors of the houses were given a preliminary ordering. After this, I visited all the houses I could not understand, visited examples of every sort of house I thought I could comprehend from outside, and recorded notes on details and took exhaustive internal and external measurements.[9] After beginning analysis of the data, I returned to the area for a week in January 1970 to spot-check the accuracy of the original survey. It seemed fine.

Although the survey was sufficiently precise to enable a future scholar to restudy the area, the reason for all this care was a desire to understand past culture through architecture. Distrustful of tricky sampling means, and convinced of the inutility of surveys conducted entirely from within the armor of an automobile, I did not want inaccuracy at the simple level of data-gathering to hinder my interpretation. Within contemporary geography, some of it sadly mired in numerology, the reasons for such fieldwork have been occasionally misunderstood. It is not some strange way to come to demography; it is, as Fred Kniffen has written,[10] a way to get at past culture. The trouble is the old one of mistaken identity. Culture and society are, of course, not synonyms: culture is made of ideas, society is made of people. Were the goal to establish the historic origins and movements of populations, one might turn to statistical documents or to the names on the land: Banks, Dabney, Hicks, Bagby, Davis, Tinsley, Willis, Rigsby, Lacy, Ware, Waller, Hooker, Foster,

Meredith, Gorham, Parrish, Brown, Brashaw, Brooking, Atkinson, Robison, Fife, Shelton, Lloyd, Via, Chapman, Payne, and Carter. These names, which came out of the 1966 field notes (better than two-thirds of them were found in a quick glance at the area's eighteenth-century records[11]), are mainly English. That observation would hold implications for settlement history. The people, though, were also from Africa. The analyst has not been long at work before he finds the local architectural tradition to be basically British. However, knowing the origin of the people, or even of their architectural forms, does not empower any deep or correct predictions about the nature of a particular culture, much less the nature of culture in general.

It seems necessary to emphasize that artifacts are not studied to run a check on demography. Artifacts are worth studying because they yield information about the ideas in the minds of people long dead. Culture is pattern in mind, the ability to make things like sentences or houses. These things are all that the analyst has to work with in his struggle to get back to the ideas that are culture.

The work of mining the artifact for culture begins when the motionless stuff one touches is recognized as the product of an enormously complex and electric transaction in mind between two abilities. One is the ability to compose: "competence." The other is the ability to relate the composition to things external to it in its "context." The result of this interrelation is a person's actual "performance"—the product that can be observed by the scholar. The forces of this mental dialectic are usually visualized as levels. But when they are hierarchically arrayed so that competence is the lower level and context is the higher, they have tended to resist explanatory reintegration.[12] The reason is that while competence (sometimes reduced to "structure") has been considered to be internal, context (sometimes reduced to "function") has often been seen as external to mind. The creator might be imagined as thinking up some thing and then placing it in the world where it subsequently develops relationships to other things. Actually, an object is not simply composed and then related to external objects; a conception of the object is related to internalized ideas of external objects while the object is being composed. More aptly, the case is that of a synchronous, and sympathetic, negotiation between interlocking planes of thought. However, though we realize that both of these human abilities have simultaneous residence in thinking, it is most convenient for analysis to treat them as separable, sequential processes. Logically, competence is prior, for it is possible to imagine competence as action independent of context,[13] whereas any approach to the problem of a person positioning himself in context depends upon an understanding of his ability to generate objects. The development of an account of artifactual competence, then, is the minimum synchronic statement from which all analysis must proceed. This will be our first task.

The goal of analyzing for artifactual competence is to create a systematic model that accounts for the design ability of an idealized maker—a sort of artifactual "grammar."[14] This analogy does not loom up because of some mystic priority of language. Speech and artifacts are both expressions of culture. The theoretical implications of the study of any cultural expression should be suggestive for the study of any other,[15] and linguistics has been developed to a marvelous state.[16] Had I not been fascinated by the writings of Noam Chomsky, I would not have been able to approach the fundamental problem of artifactual competence. Among linguists there are debates about transformational grammar, and they will continue for years. Whatever the verdict in the courts of linguistics, the suggestive strength of Chomsky's thought within the relatively simple domain of architectural analysis is unquestionable, though Chomsky himself might be skeptical.[17] Having thus made public the source of my inspiration, I will turn away from analogizing and move on to my own historical, empirical task.

IV

The Architectural Competence

Middle Virginia comes first to the person who does not know it in vast expanses of gray and tan and blackish green, cut by rapid flashes, turning quickly from bright to drab. Curved oaks break amid the straight pines. Rigid blocks rise abruptly off soft fields. It takes concentration to distinguish wind-fallen trunks from faraway barns, to trace a fence line along the forest's edge, or to spot a distant house hidden within its pale of dark hardwoods.

The local child who will mature into a designer and builder of houses may feel an early confusion not unlike that of the stranger in his land. His visual sensations are not neat, for his world does not present itself as an ordered assemblage of geometric entities.[1] In such surroundings, however, the learning designer develops a set of pure and simple geometric ideas. As thinker, as perceiving, conceptualizing human being,[2] he shatters and rebuilds reality by dint of an inward capacity for sundering and ordering.[3] Without limiting his thoughts in terms of future need, he constructs ideas that are inherently useless but of enormous potential owing to their very

simplicity. He relates these essential ideas into a geometric repertoire much the way the learning speaker develops a set of phonemes or the learning musician develops a scale of notes. The designer's geometric repertoire is not composed of models of the sights of the phenomenal world. It is not a set of abstracted trees or faces, but a set of simple shapes abstracted beyond any connection with trees or faces. It is an unreflectively held repertoire of geometric entities, elegant summaries of features of shape, such as line or angle or curve.

The ability to design is intellectually grounded on the geometric repertoire. Competence proceeds from this set of geometric ideas, spiraling from the abstract to the concrete, from useless ideas to livable habitations. Static sections of this process have often been recognized as levels of typological abstraction. In the "syntagmatic" structural analysis of the folktale, for example, scholars have been able to present simplified descriptions of the shape of a narrative at different levels of complexity. But unless the levels are tied into a system by transforming rules—the mental procedures[4] used to move from level to level—then the levels are merely classificatory conveniences. Some scholars of the folktale have attempted to describe the transformations that lead to the form of a tale,[5] but a larger body of analysis has led only to inert abstractions.[6] Even without the benefit of advances in linguistics, it could be seen from the traditions of formalist method[7] that studies of form should answer questions of process.

The account of competence, then, cannot be a list of levels. It must consist of rules that might have been used to generate perceivable things. These rules are the structure that binds distinct elements into a synchronic system.[8] The set of rules, taken together, is the whole that is greater than its parts; the rules structure the whole. Once the designer's basic planning decisions are made, the structure is set and he becomes free to fret about specific relations within his story or building, while, deeply, the rules to which he is unconsciously committed prevent that focus on detail from producing anarchy. Were we to watch the house being raised, we would be observing technology. Were we to query the builder about it, he would respond in terms of techniques and use. But the seen and articulated rely upon the designing rules that make a house a whole. These rules, precisely like those in a grammar, are unconscious, but they are not unconscious in the sense that they are unknown. They are known, as their proper use proves, and they can be brought into consciousness through questioning or contemplation. Normally, they remain as the unconsidered principles that guide a person's actions throughout life.

Whether the analyst's rules are the rules in the designing mind is a question without an answer. If the rules that emerge during the attempt to indwell in other minds[9] account completely for observable phenomena, the chances are fair that many of them coincide, in truth, with the mental acts of the creators of the phenomena; and at least a possible, partial explanation for the phenomena has been constructed.

An instance of this problem of the reality of competence models is that my work has been influenced by the binary thinking that is one of the characteristics of contemporary scholarship.[10] The assumption is that thought proceeds by the isolation of contrasting or identical pairs. But is this a computer-age fashion or a genuine mental process? The linguists, Jakobson and Halle, defended the binary opposition as the child's first logical operation and as more than a heuristic device.[11] Conflict on the matter can be found in his works, but Claude Lévi-Strauss, who interacted with Jakobson when both were in exile during World War II, has turned the concept to great use. I feel that the ways of the imagination are far too complicated to be understood in binary terms, but when concepts are ordered for communication, the mind may, in fact, often handle only two things in a single move. The competence upon which expression—designing a house, framing a sentence—depends does not exhaust the varieties of mental process, but it is the problem of expression, of specifically channeled thought, that the model of competence is designed to solve. At least, binary thinking has aided in theory building.

We are now prepared to embark on our trip through the architectural competence. I developed the model in a way conceivably parallel to that used by the architects themselves,[12] except that I worked consciously and painfully where they worked unconsciously and with ease. Beginning by recording all the extant houses of a designated area, I developed sets of formal patterns that underwent a continual process of abstraction and synthesis. The purpose of these abstractions was not to eliminate information, but rather to generalize it. Once I had gotten to the bottom stratum of abstraction—a geometric entity—then I worked, trying and trying again, to develop sets of rules that would account in the simplest possible manner for the design of the houses.

Just as the rules used to generate language relate sound and meaning, so the rules used to generate artifacts relate form and use. The product of the employment of the rules should be a comprehensible statement or a usable artifact. In performance, the statement may go awry and the artifact may turn out to be useless. The speaker may lose his idea in a poorly formed sentence, the hearer may misunderstand a clear sentence, the viewer may not be able to assimilate the painting, the hunter may find that the rifle will not shoot. But these are an individual's mistakes, not the result of mistakes in the idealized competence. From the statement or artifact, the analyst may be able to get as clear an idea of sound or form as the statement's speaker or the artifact's maker, but from words or artifacts he will never be able fully and perfectly to reconstruct the statement's meaning or the artifact's "use." Different forms can be identical, but the meanings and uses different people associate with these forms can only be similar.[13] Thus, though the analyst's account may be complete and efficient, it must always be hypothetical. This is a reason for separating problems of meaning and use from the statement of the competence and holding them aside for separate analysis, even though thoughts of usefulness informed the actual competence at every step. This is one of those many times when rigorous thought requires artificiality. To enable understanding, the complex must be broken into simpler components and examined before being reassembled.[14]

Although simplified, the following statement of the architectural competence may appear to be complicated. If it seems too complicated to the student of architecture, all that can be said is that it is a process of this sort—or at least of this complexity—that he takes for granted when he generalizes about architecture. If nothing else, he may never again feel comfortable in discussing folk houses as the products of simple minds solving simple problems.

This statement of the architectural competence accounts fully for the data and is therefore useful for my historical purpose.[15] An account not of how a house is made, but of how a house is thought, it is set out like a program. It is a scheme, analogous to a grammar, that will consist of an outline of rule sets interrupted by prosy exegesis.

RULE SET I: FORMING THE BASE STRUCTURE

I.A.   *Selection of the Geometric Entity*. The entity chosen is the square.

In the way that a "carpenter reaches into his lumber room and finds a board that fits the particular corner he's building,"[16] William Faulkner found ideas for writing in his stored up experiences, and our architectural thinker rummages through his thought for an appropriate geometrical idea. In our area he chooses but one of the imaginable geometric entities, and that is the square.

I.B. *Transformation of the Geometric Entity.* The square is transformed to provide a scale of shapes.

That is easily said, but moving on to the next rule would leave behind the vaguest variety of generalization. Although it will cause us to digress from cognition into guesswork about behavior and the presentation of empirical data, the topic of transforming the square had best be addressed, for the idea behind this assertion is very specific.

As an admirer of Le Corbusier, who adumbrated his scheme, "the Modulor," with early artifacts that were apparently the products of an unconscious modular design,[17] and having absorbed an interesting paper that showed how Welsh folk houses could have been designed in a modular manner,[18] I expected to be able to read these houses in Virginia as combinations of squares and halves and quarters of squares. I had thought the result would please the shade of Jeanneret, but my measurements suggested a more complicated, initially bewildering, nonmodular procedure.

Rather than proportionally dividing and subdividing the geometric entity, the builder seems to have played with a unit of measurement. In most instances this unit was the yard, and to keep the discussion clear it will be assumed, for the nonce, that only the yard was used. The unit consisted of three feet, of course, but the usual procedure in manipulating the unit was apparently that of halving a whole. The yard was first halved into two cubits, and these halves were, in turn, halved into two spans; that is, the yard was subdivided into halves and quarters rather than thirds. It became very important for

me to understand the various systems of measurement in use in the area so that superficial differences in individual houses would not block an attempt to develop a single system for all of the houses. The numbers were very confusing. There was the possibility of a foot that does not convert to twelve inches (some early Pennsylvania German builders, for example, used a thirteen-inch foot[19]). However, a yard or yardlike unit seems to have been what the old Virginia builders used.

The plan of each house included a square, and all of the other dimensions of the house are determined by adding or subtracting units to or from the width of that square. One house, for example (Fig. 80), has a 13½ foot square: that is, its square is four yards and a cubit by four yards and a cubit, and the other dimensions of the house are found along a series including the dimensions of the square. Measured in feet with semicolons marking the divisions between the yard-units, this series is: 0, 1½, 3; 4½, 6; 7½, 9; 10½, 12; 13½, 15. In addition to the room that measures 13½ × 13½ feet, there is another that is 12 × 13½ feet, and the entry is 4½ feet wide. This plan presents no conceptual problems, for the basic square can be measured in yards and half-yards. However, most houses did not present squares that could be measured in yards, even though all of their other dimensions could be. Their series, while made up of yards and cubits, do not commence at zero. In feet, series A is: 1; 2½, 4; 5½, 7; 8½, 10; 11½, 13; 14½, 16; 17½, 19; 20½, 22; 23½, 25. Series B is: ½, 2; 3½, 5; 6½, 8; 9½, 11; 12½, 14; 15½, 17; 18½, 20; 21½, 23. As an example, it can be seen that the front rooms of house N (Fig. 36) were measured in terms of series A—17½′ × 16′, 7′ × 16′, 16′ × 16′—whereas the rear range of rooms was measured along the zero series—12′ × 13½′, 12′ × 12′, 12′ × 15′—as a set dependent on the front rooms. However, the problem of the determination of the original square is yet unsolved, because the series start not at zero, but at one or one-half.

The answer seems to be that the first step in laying out a house was to strike a line, measured evenly in terms of yards and cubits. We will have wandered still farther from our theoretical problem but come closer to the little problem at hand if we imagine our house carpenter hauling a stick out of his tool kit. The stick happens to be three feet long; it has a scratch at its center and another at the middle of each of its halves. Beginning at zero, he measures a number of sticks along a string. This line is marked at its center. He might then transcribe a circle using half of his line as its radius, its center as the circle's center. Or he might cross his original line with another, forming an X, and then sight along a right-angle square, which he could dredge out of the same kit. Either method would result in a square with the first line drawn as its diagonal. Whatever actually happened, it is true that the sides of the squares of most houses cannot be measured in yards, while the diagonals of those squares can be.[20] The measures used in our area included the 6½ yard diagonal to get the 14½ foot square; 7½ yard diagonal, 16 foot square; 8 yard diagonal, 17 foot square; 9 yard diagonal, 19 foot square. The size of the square, determined by the length of the diagonal, committed the planner to a specific series. That is, the 6½, 7½, and 9 yard diagonals commit one to series A; the 8 yard diagonal commits one to series B. To obtain a room larger than the basic conceptual square, units were simply added: a

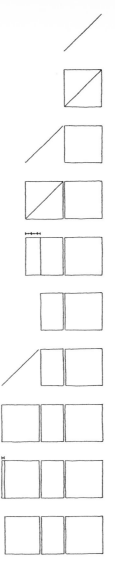

Fig. 6 Conjectural diagram of ground plan design. This is an account of the procedure for laying out the Rigsby house (house R: Fig. 41), beginning, at left, with the laying of a diagonal; it is based on a 19-foot square and a 3-foot unit.

nineteen foot square enlarged by a cubit would be 19′ × 20½′. To obtain a smaller room, however, measurements were not taken from the side of the preexisting square; instead, another square equal in size to the original was planned next to it and units were subtracted; a room smaller by a cubit than a 19′ square would be 19′ × 17½′. If measurements had been taken from the side of the first square, starting at zero, the room would have been 19′ × 18′ or 19′ × 16½′. This relatively complex protocol (Fig. 6) was probably followed to ensure that the square would be true and to allow the interior of the house to be planned around the variable thicknesses of walls.

While the yard was the most usual unit, others were used as well. The pace, an important traditional measure,[21] was also employed. It seems to have been used, as at house J (Fig. 32), in consort with some other unit, for the pace is part of a system of measurement that begins with a 17-foot square, and the 17-foot square cannot be obtained by multiples of units of thirty inches. The diagonal of the 17-foot square is 24 feet, which may have been measured as eight yards, though it could have also been planned as one and one-half 16-foot rods, or two 12-foot units or three 8-foot units or six 4-foot units—any one of which would be reasonable in terms of early measurement systems.[22] Another set of measurements may be rationalized most efficiently on the basis of a "yard" of 34 inches. Chances are that this was the system of a lone builder who made his own measuring sticks. Perhaps he had small hands and set up the stick as four spans, or maybe he sawed an inch off each end of a yardstick in order to cheat his customers. Who knows? But at the Old Moore Place (Fig. 31) there are doorways 2′10″ wide,

paneling 2′10″ high, chimneys 5′8″ wide (chimneys are usually two yards broad), and an overall plan comprehensible in terms of 34 inch units: the square is 15′7″ × 15′7″.

The unit varied, both traditionally and idiosyncratically it seems, but once the square was set planning became a matter of adding and subtracting units—30″ or 34″ or 36″, or halves of these—to yield a scale of transformations of the square. In many houses, for instance, the hallway is 2½ units (u) less than the square (s), so that when s is 19′ (19′ × 19′) and u is 36″, the hallway will be 19′ × 11½′; or when s is 16′ and u is 36″, the hallway will be 8½ feet wide. The hallway on this scale, then, is 7½ feet less than the square, no matter how big that square room is. For another example, in the hall-and-parlor house the hall is square (s), the parlor is a unit less than square $(s - u)$, so, if the hall is 13′ × 13′ and u is 36″, the parlor is 10′ × 13′ (Fig. 29); and if the hall is 17′ × 17′ and u is 30″, the parlor is 14½′ × 17′ (Fig. 32); or, if the hall is 15′7″ square and u is 34″, the parlor is 12′9″ × 15′7″ (Fig. 31). The point is that in traditional action the parlor of this house is not 12′9″ × 15′7″ at all; it is conceived in yardlike units: $4½u × 5½u$. And while the room may be measured as an independent volume, in traditional thinking it is bound to the rest of the house; conceptually the room is not $4½u × 5½u$; it is $s - u$.

This incursion into numbers—a venture I found as perplexedly engrossing as Uccello found his sweet perspective—has allowed us to transpose all of these diverse systems of measurement to one. Confusing differences of dimension in different houses have been eliminated, and we have come up with a precise way to

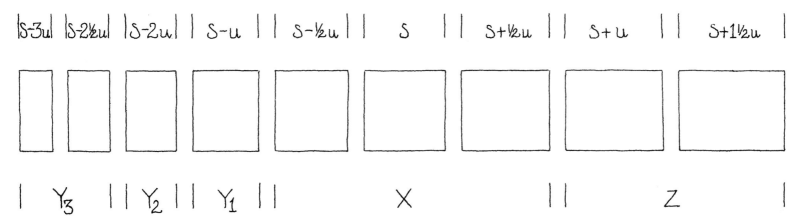

Fig. 7 SCALE OF SHAPES. Above the shapes are the designations for the transformations of the square. Below them are set out the classes of shapes. The shapes themselves vary in accordance with the square and unit that are chosen. This scale was figured out on the basis of: s = 15 feet, u = 3 feet. An example of a house planned along that scale can be found in Fig. 33.

compare actual houses. We have been allowed to abstract away from manifestations of individual behavior toward collective mind: several idiosyncratic systems have been reduced to a single cultural system. The square has been transformed into a scale of shapes divisible into three classes (Fig. 7), and we may move along to the next rule in Rule Set I:

I.C. *Addition*. The transformations of the square are selected and related.

I.C.1. The whole may consist of a single geometric entity: the whole is one square, in which case it must be either fully square (X) or a larger transformation of the square (Z).

I.C.2. The whole may consist of more than one of the transformations of the square: the whole is two or more of the geometric transformations, in which case one must be square (X) and the others may be square (X) or smaller (Y). Further:

I.C.2a. Not more than two different classes of shapes may be employed in the same whole (see Fig. 7 for the classes).

I.C.2b. Not more than three shapes may be employed in the same whole.

I.C.2c. When three shapes are employed in the same whole, one must be of a different class from the others (which by rule C.2a above must be the same), and it will be located centrally.

I.C.3.　Addition is always made symmetrically along the same axis, so that all parts of the whole will be exactly *s* in depth.

As a result of the application of these rules, a limited number of organizations of shapes could be achieved. In this locality, convention limited the architectural base structures to these: X, Z, XY2, XY1, XX, XY3X.

I.D.　*Invariability*. Throughout the operation, the base structures formed by rule I. C will not be changed.

I.D.1.　The base structures will not be reordered.

I.D.2.　Shapes of the same class will be treated identically.

These artifactual syntagms[23] must not be reordered; they must be maintained in the sequence in which they were originally formed and identical shapes must be treated identically. Practically, this means that for XX or XY3X houses, everything done to one X must also be done to the other. At this point we are at the lowest "level" of abstraction for actual houses. The abstractions, however, could be of things other than houses. A tombstone ornament might be generated as readily from an XY3X base structure as a house; indeed, seventeenth-century ship design seems to have begun with a comparable base structure.[24] This most abstract of levels—at which some formalistic analyses have both started and stopped—is the easiest to locate, but the structures that make it up are too powerful to be much more than (rather intriguing) curiosities.

RULE SET II: EXTENSION. The base structure is extended into space three dimensionally and equally.

The whole comes to occupy space, each of its individual shapes becoming components that are extended to the same height and, at that height, to the dimensions of the base. The base structure is now the plan for a three dimensional object. Although that object could as easily be a barn or a chest as a house, we have, in effect, the outlines for the first story of a building. The exact height of this extension is variable, being in reality between 6 and 12 feet, but the dimensions are conceptually reducible to one. The exact dimensions are a part of an individual's performance, and the important point is that all of the components achieve the same height in any individual house-to-be.

RULE SET III. MASSING AND PIERCING THE EXTENDED FORM. Extending the base structure requires that it be imagined as substance; this mental materialization obligates the employment of rules for massing and piercing.

This passage in the competence is a mundane corollary of the Cartesian position in a heady old argument:[25] it does not matter of what substance the house is made—of brick or wood or stacked bottle caps—but thinking it defines it in space, and that definition means walls, and walls mean holes through them. A note on terms might be helpful. We will use "massing" to mean imagining the existence of substance and "piercing" to mean imagining the existence of holes that allow passage through the substance.[26] It might be well to comment, too, that the use of the verb "to obligate" always implies that the designer has at that point no choice. Obligatory rules are frequently those (as is the case here) that connect different sets of rules.

III.A.   *Massing Rules: Partitioning*

III.A.1.	The Reality of Boundaries. All of the walls implied in the extended base structure are real.

There are architectural traditions where forms are composed of interpenetrating or assembled geometry, where each geometric idea is not given material existence—for example, a single room may be two bays long—but within the system of the Middle Virginia tradition, each idea becomes a realized formal component.

III.A.2.	The Location of the Boundaries. All of the walls are external to the components of the base structure.

All planning gives internal volumes. External walls run outside of the form, and internal walls do not steal space from the components; rather, the components are, in effect, prized apart to the width of the walls.

III.A.3.	Internal Subdivision.
III.A.3a.	X and Y components are not subdivided.
III.A.3b.	When the component is Z, internal subdivision is optional:
III.A.3b.1.	There is no internal partition.
III.A.3b.2.	There is an internal partition, in which case:
III.A.3b. 2a.	The partition is not centrally located.
III.A.3b. 2b.	The partition runs parallel to the shortest side of the component.

When a room is conceptually square (when it is an X, that is s, $s + \frac{1}{2}u$, or $s - \frac{1}{2}u$) or less than square (Y), it cannot be partitioned into small rooms, but when a room (which by prior rules I.C.2a and b must be the extent of the house) is larger than square (Z) it can be partitioned, but only asymmetrically; examples are wholes composed of $s - \frac{1}{2}u + s - 3u$ (Fig. 35), and $s - u + s - 2u$ (Fig. 34).

III.B.   *Piercing.* Partitioning requires piercing.

III.B.1.	Piercing Obligation. All partitions must be pierced.

This rule requires that at least one hole be punched through each wall of each component. There are several apparent exceptions to this rule. One of them involves the partitioning of a Z component. When an internal partition subdivides a Z component, the short sides of the small room that results are not pierced (see Fig. 35). This is, in actuality, not an example of a failure to adhere to the rule; rather, it is the proof of the observation that the Z component is a single module subdivided and not a composite of two modules. Subdivided or not, the Z component is treated (like X) as a unit. The little room within the Z house has only one wall of its own (its side walls and two end walls belong to the larger room), and it is pierced: it will get a door into the larger room. Other apparent exceptions are provided for in later rules. The most important of these exceptions is that the massed stairway is treated as equivalent to the massed chimney in design. This is so even though the chimney normally requires piercing in the form of a hole cut through the wall for a fireplace,whereas the stairway does not necessarily require a hole to be cut through the wall it blocks (see rules III.D.2c and E.3).

III.B.2.   Piercing Position. The piercing must be central.

III.B.2a.   When one opening is cut, it will be equidistant from the component's sides.

III.B.2b.   When two openings are cut, they will exhibit centrality:

III.B.2b.1.   by being symmetrically equidistant from the midpoint of the component's wall.

III.B.2b.2.   by having one opening determined as dominant, one subordinate, the dominant one being central, the subordinate one being centrally located between the dominant opening and the component's side. (The chimney dominates the door, the door dominates the window.)

III.B.3.   Piercing Relation. Piercing is dependent on the length of the wall that is pierced.

III.B.3a.   Lengths less than X can be pierced only once.

III.B.3b.   Lengths X or more can be pierced twice.

III.C. *Differential Piercing*. The piercing requires the openings to take shape.

The holes let through the walls must be of some configuration. The possibilities for these shapes—doors, windows, fireplaces—are limited.

III.C.1.   Entrance Position.

III.C.1a.   The front door is on the long side of the whole.

III.C.1b.   By rule III.B.2, the door must be central. It may be central in one of two ways:

III.C.1b.1.   by being central to the whole.

III.C.1b.2.   by being central to the component in which it is located.

III.C.1c.   The entrance will be located only in components taken from one of the classes of transformations of the square.

III.C.1c.1.   In XY_3X, the door is in Y_3.

III.C.1c.2.   In Z, X, XX, XY_1, XY_2 the door is only in Z or X components.

To this point, the rules of differential piercing have located the door on one side (the front) of the house, thus defining the ends as the shortest sides of the whole. The rules also establish that Z, X, XY_1, XY_2, XY_3X houses will have one door on the front and that XX houses will have two (by rule I.D.2). These doors, by prior rules, will be central to the whole façade or to the component in which they are located. Often they are both. For XY_3X this is the product of the mobilization of rules I.D, III.B.2a, 3a, C.1a, and 1b. 2. For other houses, the rules that enable this follow.

III.C.1c.2a.   For Z, X, XY houses and each X component, centrality is achieved either:

III.C.1c.2a.1.   by applying rule III.B.2a to door placement.

III.C.1c.2a.2.   by applying rule III.B.2b to door placement.

III.C.1c.2b.   If rule III.C.1c.2a.2 is applied, then:

III.C.1c.2b.1.   only one opening will be a door.

III.C.1c.2b.2.   the door will be positioned:

III.C.1c.2b.2a.   toward the center of the whole in wholes consisting of two components, or away from the chimney end of wholes of a lone component.

III.C.1c.2b.2b.   toward the end of the whole in wholes consisting of two components or toward the chimney in single component forms.

The group of rules under III.C.1c.2a is exceptionally confused. All of the design possibilities were given designations in order to facilitate reference back to this specific situation, for the confusion in the program accurately reflects a confusion in the Middle Virginia architectural competence.

III.C.2.   Fenestration of the Façade.

III.C.2.a.   All piercings of the façade that are not doors become windows.

Referring back to earlier rules, the façades of all Y_1 and Y_2 components must be pierced, pierced centrally and only once, and this rule turns those holes into windows. In some folk architectural traditions, such as that of south-western England (Fig. 78B), chimneys are occasionally located on the house's front. This rule prevents that possibility in Middle Virginia. Also by prior rules, Z and X components in Z, X, XY, and XX forms can have two openings, but only one door, so that those nondoors now become windows. The X components of XY3X houses by prior rules can have one or two central openings; neither of them can be doors, so they must be windows.

III.C.2b.   For XY3X forms:

III.C.2b.1. one window per X.

III.C.2b.2. two windows per X.

III.D.   *Second Massing.* Differential piercing requires a second massing.

Piercing is structured together with the massing of forms other than the walls—with chimneys and stairways in particular.

III.D.1.   Fireplace.

III.D.1a.   In accordance with prior rules (III.C.2a), the fireplace is located only on walls that run at right angles to the front.

III.D.1b.   In accordance with prior rules (III.B), the fireplace must be central to the wall on which it is located.

III.D.1c.   Any component smaller than Y_1 cannot include a fireplace.

III.D.1d.   Z, X, and Y_1 components receive one and only one fireplace.

III.D.1e.   In Z and XY forms, this single fireplace is not on an internal wall.

These rules set the chimney at the middle of a lateral wall and, therefore, also in the center of the end of most whole forms. These rules determine that houses with Z, X, or XY_2 base structures will have one chimney and that it will be located on the end of the house—the X end in the case of XY2. XY1 houses will have two chimneys, one on each end. XX and XY3X houses will have two fireplaces, though options are still open for their placement. There is also a lingering ambiguity about the Z house. So, more rules:

III.D.1e.1. The Z house that is subdivided by rule III.A.3b.2 may have the chimney:

III.D.1e.1a. in the room with the front door.

III.D.1e.1b. in the room without the front door.

III.D.1f. The fireplaces of the XY3X, XX forms are located according to these options:

III.D.1f.1. (Applicable to XY3X, XX): One central chimney with a fireplace opening into each X (one double chimney).

III.D.1f.2. (Applicable to XY3X, XX): A fireplace on the outside wall of each X (two chimneys).

III.D.1f.3. (Applicable to only XY3X): Fireplaces on the internal partitions that separate X and Y3 components, although these open only into the X by rule III.D.1c (two chimneys).

III.D.1g. The chimney dominates the other openings on the same wall.

III.D.2. Stairway.

III.D.2a. In XY3X forms, the stair is on a lateral wall within Y3.

III.D.2b. In other forms, the stair is:

III.D.2b.1. within X.

III.D.2b.2. directly accessible from X or the larger of the house's rooms.

In subdivided Z houses, rule III.D.2b.2 is followed by having the stair ascend in the smaller room with a door from the larger room located so as to open near it (Figs. 34, 35). This is another indication that Z houses are conceptually variant X houses with added partitions, not variant XY houses. The stair opens into the X component of XY houses, but in subdivided Z houses the stair is in what would be the Y component.

III.D.2c. The stair is treated as equivalent to a chimney in decision making.

III.E. *Second Piercing.* The second massing requires a second piercing—that of the lateral walls.

III.E.1. All internal partitions are centrally pierced with a door, unless:

III.E.2. The partition has a chimney (or a stair), in which case the door is displaced.

Because the chimney dominates all other openings (III.B.2b.2) and centrality controls all massing and piercing (III.B.2), the chimney will be central and the door or doors must be displaced (see Fig. 80), and even if the result is a twisting traffic flow through the house, the doors through the partitions that lack stairs or chimneys will be central, and not aligned with the doors that are displaced owing to the presence of a stair or chimney (See Figs. 41, 42).

The rules that have been established so far indicate that when there is a chimney or a stair on the end wall of a house there will not be a window, and that when chimney and stair are absent there will be a window. At this point in the process of design—and here only—the rules are broken often enough to suggest that special "variable rules" should be built into the system. Serious and intelligent objections have been raised to the incorporation of variable rules into models of linguistic competence,[27] but the rules that follow are not an attempt to account for endless idiosyncratic deviation in performance. There are "ungrammatical" houses. The rules that follow define a point of tension within the architectural *langue*: what appears as a confusion, that is, seems actually to have been a part of thought and not a consequence of the statistical compilation of data. Of these rules, only III.E.3a.2 is a novel breaking of established rules, as III.E.3b.2 could be formed (as it probably was) by analogy with III.B.2b.2. They follow:

III.E.3.   End Fenestration.

III.E.3a.   Ends of houses without chimneys (or stairs) are:

III.E.3a.1.   pierced according to prior rules; that is, lacking a chimney or stair, there is a central window.

III.E.3a.2.   not pierced according to prior rules; that is, there is no opening, even though there is neither stair nor chimney to block the wall.

III.E.3b.   Ends of houses with chimneys are:

III.E.3b.1.   pierced according to prior rules; that is, there is no window.

III.E.3b.2.   not pierced according to prior rules; that is, there is a window located between the centrally located chimney and the side wall.

III.F.   *Rear Piercing.*

III.F.1.   The rear piercing is identical to that of the front.

III.F.2.   The rear piercing differs from that of the front by having a window where a door appears on the front.

III.F.3.   The rear piercing differs from that of the front by having one central opening where there are two on the front.

III.F.4.   The rear piercing differs from that of the front by having no opening where there is one in the front.

The complete structure of the first floor of the house has been determined, and the relations between its features are set. Up to this point all of the major sets of rules and all of their major subsets—I. A, B, C, D; II; III. A, B, C, D, E, F—have been obligatory. Following are four rule sets that are optional: Expansion Backward, Massing and Piercing the Backward Expansion, Expansion Upward, Massing and Piercing the Upward Expansion. In many architectural traditions more expansions would be possible; here, however, the extended base structure can not be more than doubled in any direction.

RULE SET IV: EXPANSION BACKWARD. The extended base structure is doubled to the rear.

In the traditional competence this is possible only with XY3X base structures. All others remain conceptually one room deep.

RULE SET V: MASSING AND PIERCING THE BACKWARD EX-

PANSION. The backward expansion requires the application of rules for massing and piercing.

V.A. The backward expansion is massed and pierced identically to the front range of rooms.

V.B. The backward expansion is massed and pierced differently from the front rooms, but requires no rules not already a part of the system.

RULE SET VI: EXPANSION UPWARD. The extended base structure is doubled upward.

Just as it would be possible to expand any base structure backward, though it was done only with XY3X structures, it would be actually possible to expand any of the base structures upward, although in this area houses planned on Z and XY2 base structures are invariably only one story high.

RULE SET VII: MASSING AND PIERCING THE UPWARD EXPANSION. Upward expansion requires massing and piercing.

The rules for massing the upward expansion, like those for the backward expansion, do not comprise an independent set; rather, they relate the expansion to the completed singly extended base structure and are, therefore, but a series of dependent variations on the rules of the first story (Rule Set III).

VII.A. *First Massing: Partitions.*

VII.A.1. The partitions are the same as those of the first extension.

VII.A.2. The partitions vary internally from those established by the partitioning of the first extension.

VII.A.2a. Lower partitions are omitted in the upper story (rule III.A.1 is suspended).

VII.A.2b. The upstairs receives partitions not present in the lower floor (rule III.A.3a is suspended).

VII.B. *First Piercing.*

VII.B.1. All upstairs openings are located over lower openings.

By this rule, if there is no lower opening there can be no upper opening, even where the rationale for eliminating the lower opening is lacking upstairs. A stair running up beside an end wall of the first story would prevent a window from appearing on the wall, and, though the stair does not continue to climb up that wall in the second story, there is still no window there.

VII.B.2. Upper Piercing.

VII.B.2a. The upper piercing is identical to that of the lower story, although doors transmogrify into windows.

VII.B.2b. The upper piercing is different from that of the first story:

VII.B.2b.1. When the façade of a lower X has two openings, the upstairs has one.

This opening, by rule VII.B.1, will be located directly over one of the two lower openings.

VII.B.2b.2. on XY3X houses all of the windows of the first floor have second-story windows directly over them (according to VII.B.1 and 2a) except that there is no opening over the door.

VII.B.2b.3. on the end of the house there is no window over a window located on the first floor.

VII.C. *Second Massing*. With the exceptions for which previous provisions have been made, these rules are identical to those employed to mass the first extension.

Our trip through the darkness of cognition is nearly done. The floor of the mentality where the base structures were discovered lies below and behind, and the bright, if false, light of the real world has begun to filter back to us. Here we must turn from optional back to obligatory sets and subsets.

RULE SET VIII: ROOFING.

VIII.A. *Roof Massing*.

VIII.A.1. The ridge of the roof is aligned transversely to the entrance.

The structure that relates the entrance and the ridge line is a powerful connective. These features lie near opposite ends of the design process when it is treated as a sequence, but they are part of a single, invariant decision in design—a given in the culture—that serves as a unifier for the system.

VIII.A.2. The roof is symmetrical over the entire mass.

This helps to define everything under the roof as the product of a single set of mental activities.

VIII.B. *Piercing the Roof Mass*.

VIII.B.1. The sides of the roof mass are not pierced.

VIII.B.2. The front side of the roof is pierced.

VIII.B.2a. (Applicable to one-story houses): The roof is pierced symmetrically by one dormer for every X or Y_1 room on the first floor.

VIII.B.2b. (Applicable to one-and two-story XX or XY_3X houses): The roof is pierced centrally by a single dormer.

VIII.B.3. The ends of the roof mass are not pierced.

VIII.B.4. The ends of the roof mass are pierced:

VIII.B.4a. by two windows symmetrically.

VIII.B.4b. by one window, offset.

These rules are employed in the design of houses where the chimney prevents a central window. The chimney blocks the center of the attic's end, but the attic is not served by a pierced fireplace; therefore, two small windows can peek out beside the chimney or one can be displaced next to it, as provided for in rules III.B.2b.1, 2, and E.3.b2.

VIII.B.4c. by one central window.

By utilizing rule III.B.2a, a window can be inserted into the middle of the end of attics in houses with internal chimneys or in houses two rooms deep, for neither of the chimneys would emerge at the gable's apex.

We have now reached the level of the type, a relatively shallow and comfortable level of abstraction. Some have failed to drive even this deeply and have developed artificial taxonomies based on random surface features that may hold an *ad hoc* local utility but tell nothing about the human mind that designed the artifact and are inefficient, at best, when used as aids to historical or semio-

		X	Z	XY_2	XY_1	XX	XY_3X
height	one story	✓	✓	✓	✓	✓	✓
	two story	✓			✓	✓	✓
depth	one room	✓	✓	✓	✓	✓	✓
	two room						✓
chimneys	central					✓	✓
	end	✓	✓	✓	✓	✓	✓
	paired						✓

Fig. 8 SUMMARY OF TYPOLOGICAL DIFFERENCES.

tic interpretation. These artificial groupings of features are often called types in archaeology, whereas the full mental model, which I am terming a "type," is called a "template."[28] But a valid classificatory scheme should

34

embrace only types that could be defended as templates. If the analyst conceived the type as a late stage in a model of competence, the problem of conflicting typologies would be near its solution, for types would necessarily become complete, rather than fragmentary, formal descriptions.

Our goal is broader than the development of a natural taxonomy for artifacts, but such a taxonomy is one of our by-products. Even those who have pondered artifactual morphology and who have not confused form with construction techniques and materials, nor been snared even closer to the surface by formal encrustations, have often erred in establishing types. Tacitly, at least, they have been aware that different systems are used to generate the artifact's shape, the means and materials with which the shape is given existence, and the details that the shape orders. However, by failing to consider the artifact as a manifestation of an involved design process they have frequently missed some of its crucial relations. Artifactual analysis must spring from a full account of the thing's being. The neatest map of the distribution of types is worthless if the types were incorrectly defined to begin with. The most sophisticatedly computerized quantification of the wrong data proves only that the computer can count: it is scientistic superficiality squared.

Each basic type is a structure of structures, a summary of relations. In our area there are seventeen basic types and, before we move on to more complicated and shallower levels of the competence, these will be listed. The list is useful only internally to distinguish between types. It states the necessary and essential distinctive features of each of the types, but it leaves aside the stronger relations that tie all of the types into a single system, such as the transverse structure of ridge and entrance and the specific structure of door to chimney to stair to window to component.[29] For identification in the field and for comparative purposes, both the disjunctive and connective aspects of a type's form must be considered. The most striking differences having been charted (Fig. 8), the actual types, minimally identified, may be registered.

1. X: one story
2. X: two story
3. Z: one story
4. XY_2: one story; one end chimney
5. XY_1: one story; two end chimneys
6. XY_1: two stories; two end chimneys
7. XX: one story; two end chimneys
8. XX: one story; central chimney
9. XX: two stories; two end chimneys
10. XX: two stories; central chimney
11. XY_3X: one story; one room deep; central chimney
12. XY_3X: one story; one room deep; two end chimneys (central hallway)
13. XY_3X: two stories; one room deep; central chimney
14. XY_3X: two stories; one room deep; two end chimneys (central hallway)
15. XY_3X: two stories; one room deep; paired central chimneys (central hallway)
16. XY_3X: one story; two rooms deep; four end chimneys (central hallway)
17. XY_3X: two stories; two rooms deep; four end chimneys (central hallway)

Overtly, I have shied at taking the last of the steps in the structural paradigm presented by Lévi-Strauss.[30] I have refrained from comment on general laws. But we have, so far, taken the first steps firmly: the rules are unconscious (or at least they are articulated only by their employment), and they structure the separate into the systematic. The system is not a broken series of relations between independent parts, but a structure manifoldly interrelating all parts and all wholes. As the structure heaves toward the concrete, complexity increases, but the types are not weakened in their interrelations and their submission to the system's totality. The level of abstraction shallower than the level of the types is that of the subtypes. Here forms further proliferate, but these complications increase instead of diminishing the system's control.

When planning a house, the folk designer is conscious of the "levels" of the type and the subtype. When he decides to build a house that we identify as a subtype, he is aware of its relation to the full existence of the idea as a type. The "deeper" levels in his competence are unconscious. But because they are there, the person of innovative inclination, or the person with a novel problem to solve, can resolve to these lower levels, breaking types into individual structures in order to create new forms without going outside of his competence. The situation is similar for other expressions that we conceive of as having been "generated." One tale-teller might memorize a tale, but because the tale was initially generated (and therefore incorporates a generative structure), another raconteur might not memorize the tale, but take its structure, or aspects of that structure, to create a new story. A speaker's statement likely includes some sentences that are generated and others that are repeated as lengthy lexical entries, but the remembered sentence has within it a structure of the same sort that the generated one does. The generated sentence, then, is the one on which syntactic theorists must concentrate. Similarly, some speakers do not employ the passive voice and embedded constructions that have caused linguists to seek more complex and powerful explanations for the syntactic ability. Yet the theory of language must account for the most complex and creative possibilities open to the speaker. Some house-builders never tackled a design problem tougher than that which related the subtype to the type. Others did. They created new things, and the theory that accounts for those new things seems best founded on the idea that the house, even the house that was repeated rather than generated, incorporated a generative potential as an unconscious structure summarized in the type. If the more difficult problem is solved, the solution of the simpler problem will probably follow.

Most designers were not creative, just as most speakers do not utilize the language as fully as they are theoretically competent to do. However, most designers do seem to have modulated comfortably between the type and the subtype. They readily used the rules of subtypification to generate, by simple subtraction, a small clutch of formal variations on the basic types. They could do this, however, only by sticking (probably nonreflectively) to the rules that were bundled into the structure that is the type.

RULE SET IX: SUBTYPIFICATION.

   IX.A.   *Limitations*. Types consisting of one component (X or Z) may not be divided.

   IX.B.   *Possibilities*. Types consisting of two or more components may be divided, in which case:

   IX.B.1. The division can take place only along boundaries that exist between components.

   IX.B.2. The resulting form must include at least one X.

   IX.B.3. All of the prior rules of the system must be enforced.

These simple steps empower the designer to eliminate certain components from certain base structures. He can eliminate one X from both the XX and XY₃X forms. Taking an X from XX yields the X form that has already been generated on its own. From rule I.D.2 on, one half of the XX form would equal an X form. There is one important characteristic of systems, such as that of the architectural competence, that makes this act of subtraction more complicated than it seems at first glance. For clarity, the competence has been strung out to appear as if it consumed clock-time, but the system cannot be measured by time's passing. It consists of relations so strong that, while the culture's system may be conceived to start at Rule Set I and follow to IX, the individual's system may be less efficient. It may start at any point, take any route, and yet come to the same end—the whole design for a house— much as different explorers, so long as they share a cartographic tradition, may arrive at closely similar depictions of an island, though their patterns of travel over it differ completely and their drawings of it began at different points. No matter in what "direction" the rules are read, they will structure the system. This property of synchronic systems is generally called reversibility. Be-

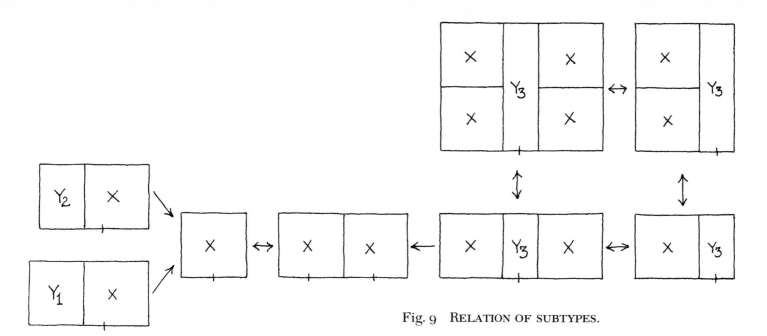

Fig. 9 RELATION OF SUBTYPES.

cause the rules are reversible, and because the rules that rest deep in the mind must be adhered to during the subtypification process (IX.B.3), shapes can be added as well as subtracted. An X can be added to an X to arrive at the XX form. Subtypification, though, cannot be conceived of as thought restricted to the level numbered IX. The employment of one rule requires the employment of all the rules. The rules of the other levels remain in effect. In the instance of the XX house, there must be reference back to Rule Set I because, if there were not, there would be no assurance that the addition of one X to another, even if they were identical, would result in an XX form properly structured in terms of the tradition. The rules for subtypification do not provide for the creation of new components, so that reversing the subtraction process with an X form could not result in, say, XY1. An X can be

dropped from the XY3X form. This XY3 subtype demands no new rules. Again, by reversing the rules, the full form may be regained. Any Y component is also removable; XY1, XY2, and XY3 forms can, then, change to the X form and XY3X can become the XX form (the rules under III.C.1 would trade a door for a window in each X). Thus, new subtypes that amount to approximately two-thirds of types 12, 14, 15, 16, 17—the central-hallway houses—are created and other types are interrelated as subtypes of each other. Just as one- and two-story houses (by Rule Set VI) and one- and two-room-deep houses (by Rule Set IV) can transform reversibly into each other, the subtypification rules have created another synchronic web of interconnecting transformations rather than a linear construct of increasing complication (Fig. 9).

Unlike functionalism or historicism, structuralism,

with its attractive goal of completeness, leaves no debris. All information is converted into usable data. The system of architectural competence outlined thus far is that from which a house's basic structure is generated. To understand fully the houses that squat about on reality's landscape, this must be seen as only one part of the total architectural competence. This part is, however, the basic formal system upon which other aspects of the total competence are dependent.

In a brilliant paper delivered shortly before his death, Melville Jacobs argued that structural students of the narrative had concerned themselves with only the "gross architecture" of the tale, and that the tale that is heard manifests this plus many other structures.[31] Up to this point we have been concerned exclusively with architectural "gross architecture." We have not yet completed a statement that can fully account for real houses. If Jacobs' twenty-one sorts of structures are herded into classes and translated into terms appropriate to artifactual analysis, the end product may be seen to require, in addition to the system of gross architecture, a technical system (the process by which nature's substances are altered to serve man's ends), as well as formal systems that provide the gross structure with details and with two kinds of dependents (appendages and ornamentation).

All of the rules of the gross architectural system control only relations. They deal not at all with the elements being related. These elements or details are the products of their own systems of relations. These systems commence, too, with the selection and organization of geometric entities; the entities are moved through transformations until they become complex shapes. The details are analogous to the motifs that are plugged into the structure of the narrative. The villainy slot in a tale's syntagm, for example, might be filled with an evil stepmother, a dragon, a capitalistic politico, or any number of other wicked forces. The details are the forms that the basic structure relates. The basic structure, for instance, sets up the relation between the door and the ridge line of the roof, but it does not dictate what type of door or what type of roof. The door might be single or double, paneled or battened; the roof might be gabled or hipped. To extend James Deetz's suggestive vocabulary,[32] the types of details could be ordered into a limited lexicon of *alloformemes*—sets of alternative details that are formally distinct but that function equivalently within the structure. The walls and windows, stairways and chimneys are related to each other by the gross structure, but the walls may be of different widths (their materials are determined by the technical system); the windows may have from one to eighteen lights; the stairways may be open or closed, straight or curled; the chimney may include one or two or four or no fireplaces, it may be external or internal, it may have one or two sets of shoulders. We are now at one of many points where erecting too trim an analogy between linguistic and artifactual structures becomes shaky. If geometric entities are parallel to phonemes and formal details are parallel to words—and those comparisons strike me as apt—the trouble is that "sentences" generated by the gross architectural competence are built up out of the same inherently useless minimal organizations of features that words are. It would be as if to understand the sentence one had to return to the phoneme in the way one does to understand the morpheme; language's levels[33] are different. At another plane of comparability, if the gross system produces words, then the first of the dependent formal systems produces bound morphs. Such analogizing is both endless and inexact, and it would be better to come to these dependent structures in terms that suit them more comfortably.

The dependent forms, such as porches and ornamental gewgaws, exist outside of the process that unifies the gross architecture and the formal elements. Unlike the gross structure and the elements related by the gross structure, they are wholly optional. The house must have a door and the door must be related to the other features of the room into which it breaks, but the door does not have to be flanked by Corinthian columns. The dependent forms are secondary, and as students of architecture[34] and structural analysts of riddles[35] and tales[36] have recognized, secondary forms are those that can be removed without disturbing the primary basic structure. The dependent forms are of two kinds, each again the process of transforming geometry.

One class of dependent forms is analogous to the opening and closing formulas of tales. These are the appendages: (front) porches and (rear) additions—either sheds or ells—that, even if they were built at the same time as the house, are always conceptually separable. They are not enfolded into the form. In many areas, porches, sheds, and ells are enclosed by a symmetrical cover, but that is not true of our little piece of Virginia. There are rules that relate these appendages to the basic form, determining their locations and the modifications they engender. Specifically, a door can be cut to join them if there is no opening, or a window can be made into a door. The other of the dependent systems produces ornamentation—decorative details of internal woodwork, external paint, and the like—that compares with the flourishes of non-narrative rhetoric in oral literary performance.

The old house that rots in the sun at the surface, then, was the product of the gross system plus the product of the detailing systems, possibly appended and ornamented, and materialized by means of the technical system. The maker had to be in control of this systematic complexity, and the analyst trying to understand him has to be able to develop a full account of it. Anything less leads from artificial taxonomy to ersatz interpretation.

In structuralism some have seen a sterile exercise. The mote of truth trapped in that criticism opens questions about the value of producing a system such as that which has been described. One answer bubbles out of the fascination that solving any problem provides. Scholarship is one of the arts: the act of scientific classification, like any other art, is a test of the spirit that may be gauged on its intrinsic merit as an exploration in an arbitrary medium. The more orthodox answer is predicated on the acceptance of the academic aphorism that classification is not its own end, that the scholar's labor must tell not of its author, but of its author's objects and subjects. Indeed, some of what passes for structuralism may be a bit pointless, but the development of a system of rules is not. It is a compassionate attempt to explain the structure of alien thought. A single system has been developed which proves that from the humblest and simplest to the most elaborate and sophisticated, all the old houses down in Middle Virginia were products of the same mind at work.

The competence that generated the small house was not simpler or cruder than that which generated the large house. The man who built the smallest, "crudest" house was not a poorer designer than the one who built the largest, most "important" house. He was poorer.

In his earlier writings, Noam Chomsky intriguingly defended studying syntax hermetically.[37] His writings were theoretically impressive and a welcome antidote to the excesses of behaviorism. They remain especially suggestive to those who study things, such as ancient pottery brought out of the earth, for which no semantic is available. However, grammar is but one part of the act of verbal communication.[38] A person can utilize his compe-tence in playful personal expression, but mostly he uses it to relate himself to his context. Architecture could be considered in solely formal terms as an object, and the nature of the mind revealed by the foregoing system could be interpreted, but real houses had to turn the rains and stop the winds and act as signs for their inhabitants.[39]

So instead of pausing to contemplate architectural "syntax," I wish to push on to meanings, using the model of the architectural competence, first as a foundation from which to quantify the surface, then as a measure for change, and finally as the main girt of an interpretive frame joining the maker's ability to his context—all toward the end of wresting history from the artifact.

V

Counting Houses

Structuralism is social scientific modernism. It is modernist in its concern with principled abstraction rather than particularistic realism. The structuralist's interest is in process more than product, in hidden law more than manifest shape, in relations more than entities, in the universal, the unconscious, the simultaneous, the systematic. Thus structuralism provides the social scientist with an entree into his own times, a period pioneered by physicists and artists. Claude Lévi-Strauss, anthropological structuralism's most illustrious exemplar, finds an anticipation of his research in the music of Wagner,[1] but more obvious anticipations of his methods can be found in the writings of great moderns. The mythic sense of time that Lévi-Strauss explicates can be found applied in Faulkner's *Absalom, Absalom!*; meanings unfold in *Finnegans Wake* in a manner strikingly like that Lévi-Strauss discovers in South American Indian narratives; and Paul Klee codified many of the structuralist principles in his essays on the artist's practice.[2] At the same time, structuralism, owing to the training and genius of its fathers, incorporates much of the best of traditional Western philosophy; this is most evident in the attention it accords to the nature of mind. Both Chomsky and Lévi-Strauss have related their thought to that of the great philosophers of the seventeenth and eighteenth centuries.[3] Thus structuralism is a convenient local channel through which the social scientist can make reference to enduring problems.

It is, therefore, no surprise that structuralism is currently fashionable. In some areas of research this fashion may be fashion only. When conducting ethnographic work in a living situation, I find that structuralism is but one useful guide in the accumulation and interpretation of information. However, structuralism seems to me to be a genuine improvement over the older methods available to the student of autonomous objects. Its method enables the analyst to locate an unexpected abundance of information in discrete things—things floating free of their contexts—and it enables him to relate apparently unconnected phenomena into systems. Such a method is of

41

special benefit to those who are forced to begin their study with discrete, autonomous objects (as the historian, the literary critic,[4] or the archaeologist must) and to those who elect to start with autonomous objects (as the folklorist, the humanistic anthropologist, and the historian of modern art often choose to do).

For the student of a thriving architectural tradition, structuralism may be only one of many useful methods, but for the student of isolated old houses, structuralism is the best available strategy for interpretation. Although I have found structuralism to be of great assistance in my analysis of old houses, I do not feel bound to adhere totally to structuralism's tradition. Specifically, I wish to extend the method in two directions that are normally not part of the structuralist's procedure: I wish to approach the problems of history and quantification.

Structuralism might be seen as posthistorical. Its overt search is for the *intemporelle*, for unchanging universals, but that does not mean that it is opposed to historical research. Claude Lévi-Strauss is opposed to the philosophical primacy of the time dimension, and he is dismayed by the self-conscious societies that burn their way through history. But he does not assert that the cool, clocklike, timelessly functioning society has no history. He does not do history, but he has cautioned his colleagues that "a little history . . . is better than no history at all."[5] Perhaps, just as it is logically prefunctional,[6] structuralism is theoretically prehistorical, and not chronologically posthistorical.[7] It can be a method for the historian, too. And the benefits would be mutual, as time is the test for the timeless. The need for an examination of structuralism against historical realities has been pointed out by Jean Piaget in his calm and positive critique.[8]

Structuralism might be seen as postempirical.[9] It encounters the concrete and returns to it regularly, but its goal is not descriptive. Quantification, which is an index to contemporary empiricism, is seen by the structuralist as an endeavor of little worth. Before beginning his sparkling interpretation of thought in New World myth, Lévi-Strauss disavowed a need for all the texts.[10] All of the texts could not possibly be assembled, but it was for other than bland practical reasons that a vain attempt was not mounted. The hunt is for deep principles, and these are more apt to come from the close analysis of a few things than from an endless quantification of superficialities.[11] The things that can be measured, the discourse convincingly runs, are not the important things.[12] Still, the wise counsel of an elder historian—that if you can count, you should count—has continued to prove beneficial for me.

The request for quantification need not be taken as a plea for the variety of statistical deception that dresses trivia or intuition in a mathematical cloak. It may be a request for openness, a request that ideas be tested. The architectural competence was initially worked out with a few houses, but eventually it was tested on every house in the area, which caused the model to be much modified. It would not have been necessary to study all of the area's dwellings to construct the model of the design competence. Only one could have been chosen so long as it was the right one (it could only have been house N, Fig. 36) and the analyst were a lucky genius. But, in fact, including all of the houses made the task easier. With numbers to scrutinize, variables were readily isolated, principles popped out, and shallow realism could be avoided. Further, the counting enhanced the model's plausibility and increased its utility. All of the system's rules were used, but some were used only rarely. The ability to determine which were commonly used will allow us to come closer to interpreting the historical mind than could the unquantified statement of competence.

The rules in the competence will now be viewed as the steps taken to design the actual houses of the area. This will be accomplished by presenting a set of diagrams (Figs. 11, 13, 15, 17, 21). The diagrams provide the exact measure of systematic interrelation and typological tolerance in this architectural tradition, as well as a complete structural description of each of 156 real houses. To illustrate the model it would have been best to draw a single diagram, but that would have become woefully hard to read. Thus there are separate diagrams for separate base structures. The elaboration of the base structure is accounted for by presenting the applicable rules in boxes. Under the boxes, in circles, may be found the exact number of houses to which the rules in question apply. The diagrams most openly portray the configurations of rules connecting specific types and a specific base structure. Other of the system's relations unfortunately have been obscured, and to answer some questions the reader will have to follow the diagrams horizontally. If, for instance, one wished to know how many one-story and how many two-story houses there are, one would need to scan across the diagrams, counting the number of houses to which Rule Set VI applied. One would find a little over twice as many two-story as one-story houses.

Two comments need to be made about the figures. The

Fig. 10 TYPE 1, HOUSE A. This late eighteenth-century house, which once stood alone, is now built into the end of a much modified later dwelling. It is a perfect representative of the minimal housing unit: square, it has one central opening per wall; a front door, a rear window, a window on one end, a chimney on the other. The stair winds up in the left rear corner.

first is that the rules do not fit all of the houses perfectly. A few of these houses are treated as exceptions. In the diagrams they are bracketed and moved off to the side to avoid the rules that do not apply to them. The other houses counted, but not included in the diagrams, will be

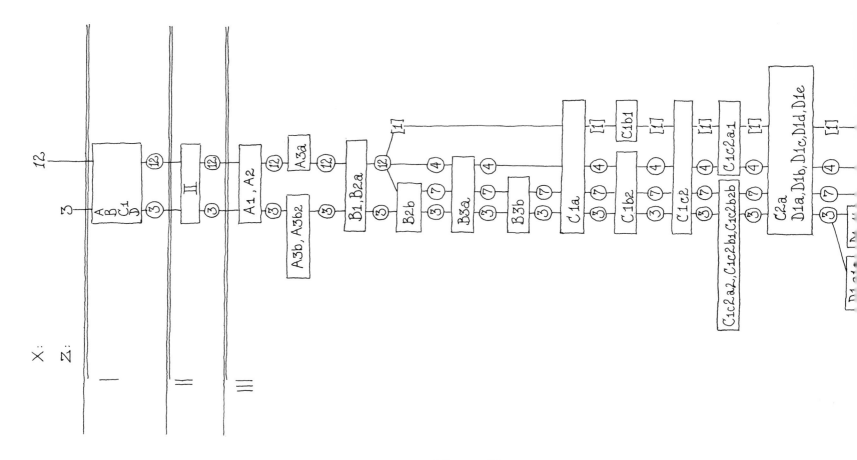

Fig. 11   DIAGRAM OF THE TRANSFORMATION OF THE X AND Z BASE STRUCTURES INTO TYPES 1, 2, 3. In the diagram, the numbers in the rectangles refer to specific rules in the architectural competence. The numbers in the circles are numbers of real houses to which the rules in the rectangles apply. The numbers in brackets are the numbers of "ungrammatical" houses moved aside in order to avoid the rules that do not fit them.

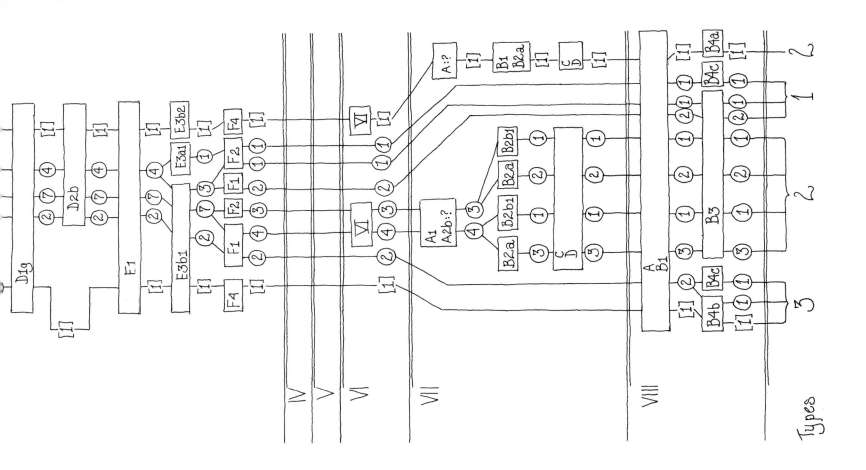

45

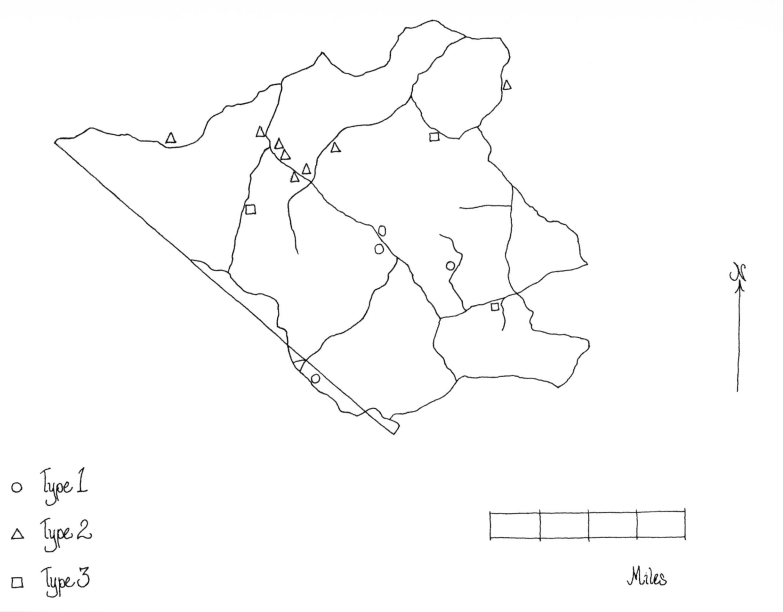

o Type 1

△ Type 2

□ Type 3

Miles

Fig. 12 Distribution of types 1, 2, 3.

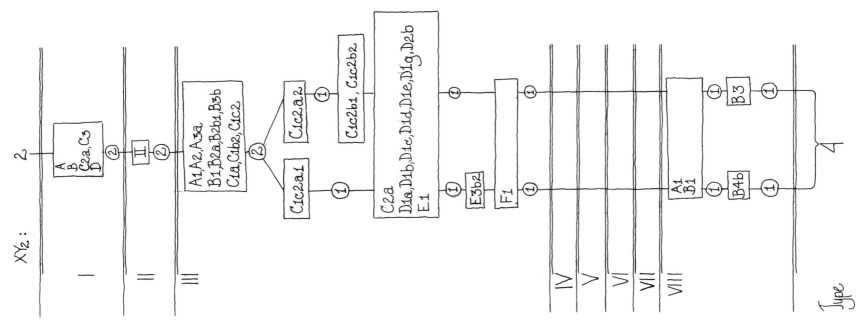

Fig. 13 DIAGRAM OF THE TRANSFORMATION OF THE XY₂
BASE STRUCTURE INTO TYPE 4. See Fig. 11 for an explanation of
the diagram.

described as a class once the diagrams have been presented.

The second comment is that some aspects of some individual houses remain unknown. When I knew that a rule applied in general but was unable to find out the exact number of houses to which it actually applied, a question mark was registered in the rule box and no changes were made in the quantities. This situation arose because asking to see the upper floors of people's houses seemed discourteous. I did, however, query people about upstairs layout, and there were many abandoned houses that I could inspect completely, so I did get a good idea of second-story plan.

Each house is counted but once, although some houses are, in fact, composites of different houses built at different times. In those cases the main house is the one considered. Other, generally later, houses that were parts of composite dwellings were studied in order to test the rules against them, but they are omitted from this enumeration so that the final tally will equal the number of

47

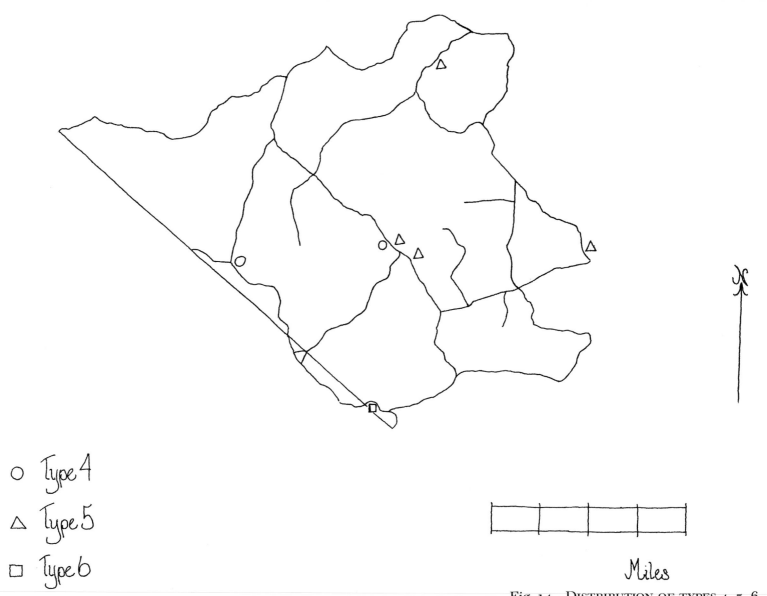

○ Type 4

△ Type 5

□ Type 6

Miles

Fig. 14 DISTRIBUTION OF TYPES 4, 5, 6.

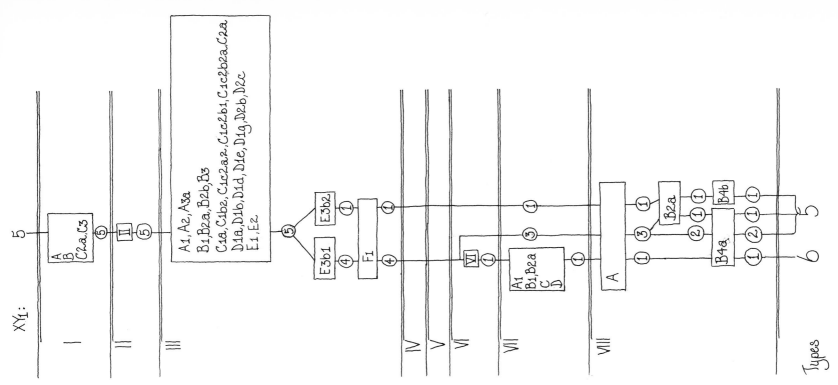

Fig. 15　DIAGRAM OF THE TRANSFORMATION OF THE XY1
BASE STRUCTURE INTO TYPES 5, 6. See Fig. 11 for an explanation of the diagram.

houses extant at the time of the survey. Examples of such composite houses are the Watson house (Fig. 34) and the Brooking house (Fig. 33); there were only four others for which a comparable decision had to be made.

The following enumeration provides a summary that will serve in many ways. It has already given the theory of the competence a tough test. Immediately, it provides

a precise and full report of the traditional domestic architecture of a small area. It will become the basis for architectural comparisons so that the area it represents will not remain isolated, but can fill the role I intend for it. The area was carefully chosen to be geographically representative. By comparison it will become historically representative. What can be said about the mind behind

Fig. 16 TYPE 10, HOUSE B. A good example of a later nineteenth-century, two-story XX house with a central chimney.

the house in this small area will be found to hold implications about thought over a broader area and about change in thought through time.

THE ENUMERATION

X, Z (Figs. 10, 11, 12, 34, 35, 45, 79): There are fifteen houses generated out of a base structure consisting of a single geometric entity. There are twelve houses with a single X base structure. Of these, eight are two-story houses (type 2: Fig. 34) and four have one story (type 1: Fig. 10). Type 1 has occasionally been called "the square cabin" in the literature of folklore and cultural geography. Three of the houses were generated from a Z shape; all of these are one-story houses (type 3: Fig. 35).

XY_2 (Figs. 13, 14, 33, 79): There are two houses with an XY_2 base structure. Both are one story high (type 4: Fig. 33) and both are now parts of larger houses (Fig. 79). This type has been referred to as "the rectangular cabin."

XY_1 (Figs. 14, 15, 31, 32): Five houses commence with an XY_1 base structure; four are one-story dwellings (type 5: Fig. 31); one is two stories high (type 6: Fig. 32). Type 5 has been called both the "hall-and-parlor house" and "the Tidewater house" by students of traditional architecture.

XX (Figs. 16, 17, 18): There are sixteen houses with an XX base structure. There are six central-chimney, one-story houses (type 8), three with a central chimney and two stories (type 10: Fig. 16), two of a single story with end chimneys (type 7), and five two-story houses with end chimneys (type 9). The XX one-story houses are among the types drawn together under the designation "double-pen house." Double-pen houses with central chimneys (type 8 is one of the possibilities) are often called "saddlebag houses" in the literature.

XY_3X (Figs. 19, 20, 21, 22, 23, 24, 28, 36, 37, 38, 41, 42, 43, 44, 48, 75, 77, 80): The full form and its two-thirds subtype are treated together throughout the sequence (Fig. 21). The decision to eliminate an X from the base structure would have been made at the beginning of the design process, but the remaining components of the extended base structure continue to be handled as if the missing component were present. Requiring no special rules, the partial form exists dependently as a reference to the full form. The builder and user fill in the missing X conceptually, much as the speaker and hearer make an utterance lacking a verb phrase into a sentence by gathering meaning from surrounding sentences to complete it mentally.

One hundred and eighteen houses were generated out of the XY_3X base structure. Two of them have central chimneys; one of these has one story (type 11: Fig. 80), one is two-story (type 13: Fig. 19). The rest of the houses have central hallways. Of these, twenty-eight are one room deep and one-story high (type 12); one of these is an XY_3 subtype (two-thirds subtype of 12). Eighty-two central-hall houses are one room deep and two stories high. Of the sixty-five full examples, fifty-four have chimneys on the ends (type 14: Figs. 41, 42), ten have them flanking the hall (type 15: Fig. 48), and one is mixed, having one chimney on the end and one flanking the hall. There are seventeen XY_3 subtypes; one of them is a two-thirds subtype of type 15; the others are examples of the two-thirds subtype of type 14 (Figs. 20, 43, 44).

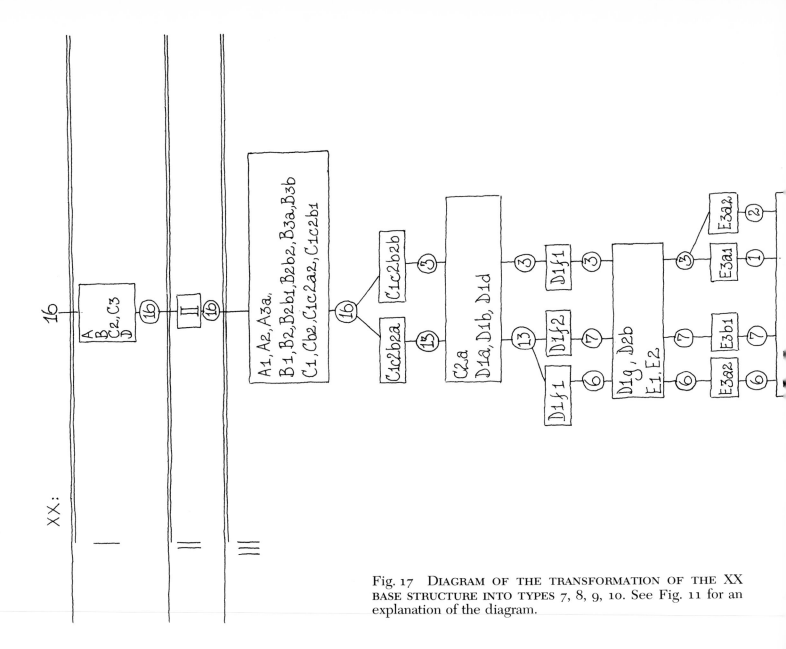

Fig. 17 DIAGRAM OF THE TRANSFORMATION OF THE XX
BASE STRUCTURE INTO TYPES 7, 8, 9, 10. See Fig. 11 for an
explanation of the diagram.

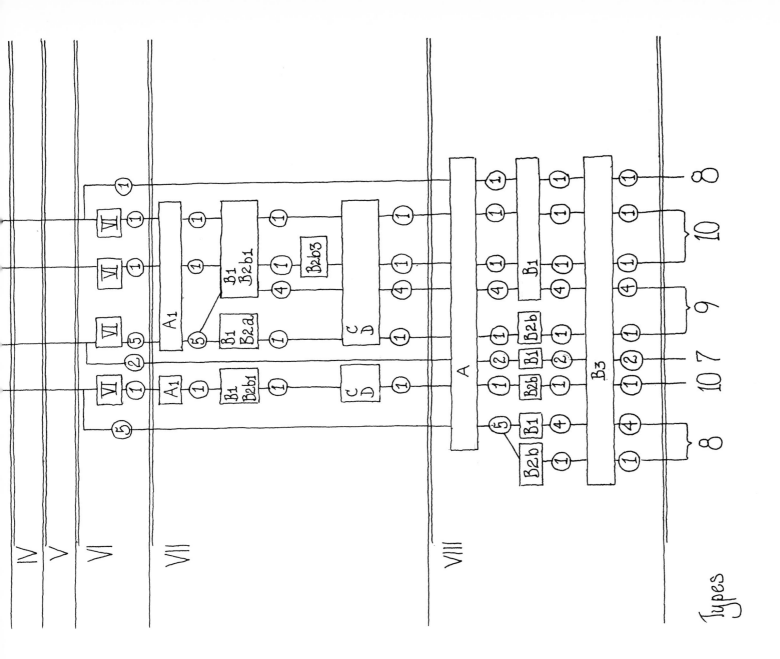

53

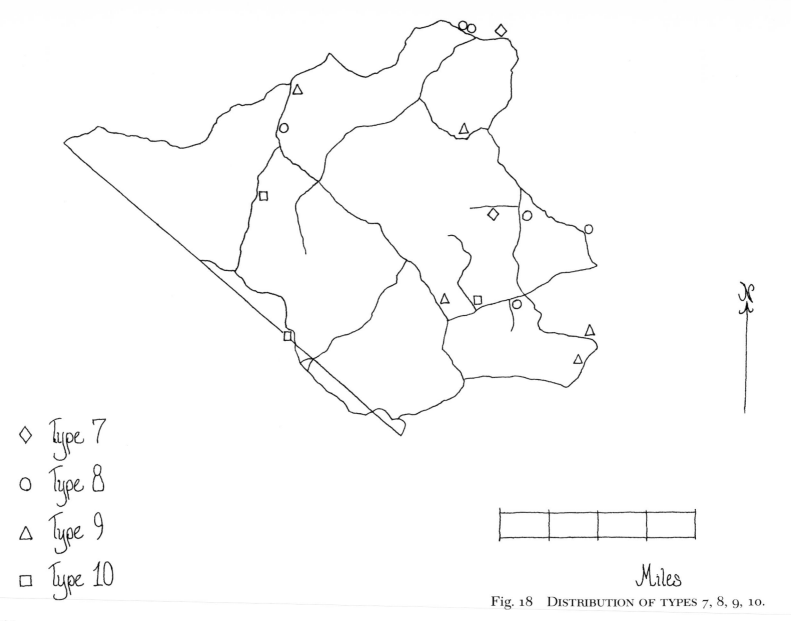

◇ Type 7

○ Type 8

△ Type 9

□ Type 10

Miles

Fig. 18   DISTRIBUTION OF TYPES 7, 8, 9, 10.

Fig. 19   TYPE 13, HOUSE C. Apparently built after the Civil
War, this XY3X central-chimney house has two shed additions
on the back.

Fig. 20   TWO-THIRDS TYPE 14, HOUSE D. This partial materialization of the dominant central-hall I house concept was probably built toward the middle of the nineteenth century.

Types 14 and 15 are most conveniently collected under a single designation as variants of the type Fred Kniffen named "the I house,"[13] though in his terms the two-story XX and XY1 houses would also be considered I houses. There are six houses that are two rooms deep; half of these are two-thirds subtypes; one of these is the only one-story, two-room-deep house in the area. Thus there is one example of a two-thirds subtype of type 16 (Fig. 38), two examples of the two-thirds subtype of type 17, and three full examples of type 17 (Figs. 36, 37). These two-room-deep, central-hallway houses (types 16, 17) are generally classed together as variants of the Georgian house type.

Jetsam (Fig. 25): The total of habitations in the area includes 182 other houses. Eight of these are contemporaneous with the 156 counted houses; they are innovations which will receive their due shortly. The rest are houses that are the products of an architectural system different from the one outlined, a system carried into the area, mostly since the beginning of our century, on blueprints, in how-to-do-it manuals, and in fast-buck catalogues. Some of the rules of the traditional competence could, of course, be employed in the building of these houses, but they mark a disruption even more striking than the introduction and acceptance of a foreign language. Most of these nontraditional houses, 161 to be exact, are modern dwellings—bungalows, solid-brick ranchers, a few mobile homes. The remainder consist of two turn-of-the-century blueprint homes of an urban sort, and eleven early twentieth-century houses with pyramidally hipped roofs, window-door-window façades, and two-window ends; four are two stories high, seven have

one floor. In a shallow sense, these are transitional in that they display the ordered openings suggesting a type 16 or 17 house, but their plans were not products of the traditional competence.

Some of these blueprint houses bear an external resemblance to traditional houses, but internal inspection reveals that they were built after imported plans rather than designed according to the old system. The alien new language was spoken, perhaps, with the accent of the old vernacular, but the break was dramatic. The old competence failed, and by World War II it had been replaced by a totally different means of house planning. The builder, no longer needing to develop his own competence at all, had only to follow plans in which some distant designer's competence was summarized. The plans might have come from anywhere; though the houses built from them may manifest a competence, there is no reason to assume that these competences fit into a single system. The local competence was gone.

The break was abrupt. It was not only a break in a tradition, but a break in the responsibilities and capabilities of the house carpenter. He lost his designing role and became solely a builder. My historical and theoretical purposes suggest that I stop with the death of the old competence. I will now eliminate from further consideration the later houses of the area. Although this means that I will be dealing almost exclusively with houses built before World War II, this is not the result of the establishment of an arbitrary cut-off date. Rather, I am choosing to concentrate on only those houses generated out of the traditional competence, and I am choosing to ignore houses built according to purchased plans.

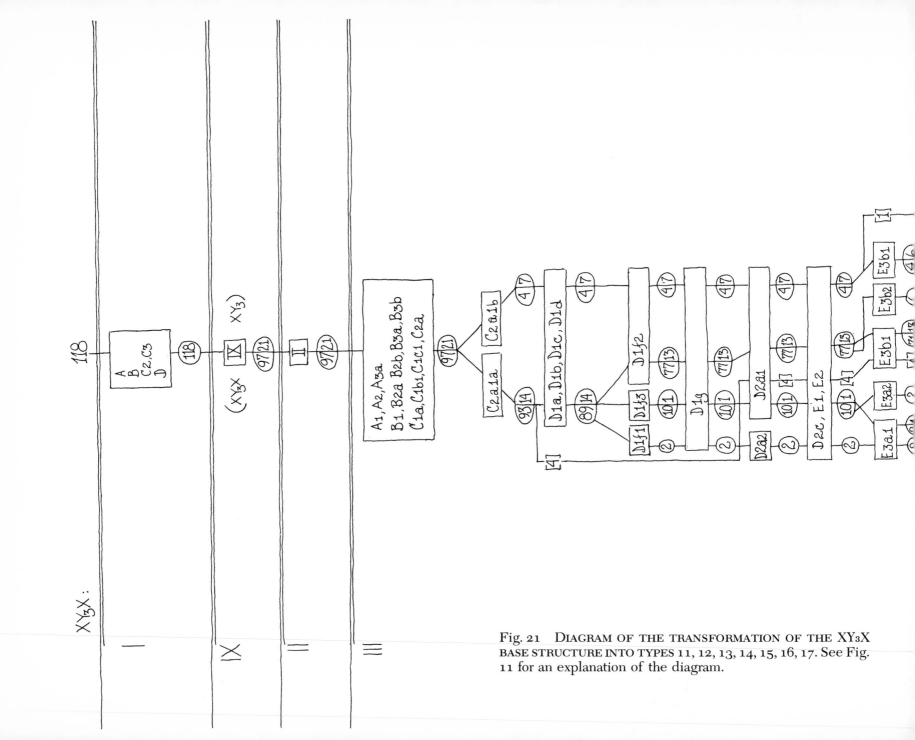

Fig. 21   DIAGRAM OF THE TRANSFORMATION OF THE XY₃X
BASE STRUCTURE INTO TYPES 11, 12, 13, 14, 15, 16, 17. See Fig.
11 for an explanation of the diagram.

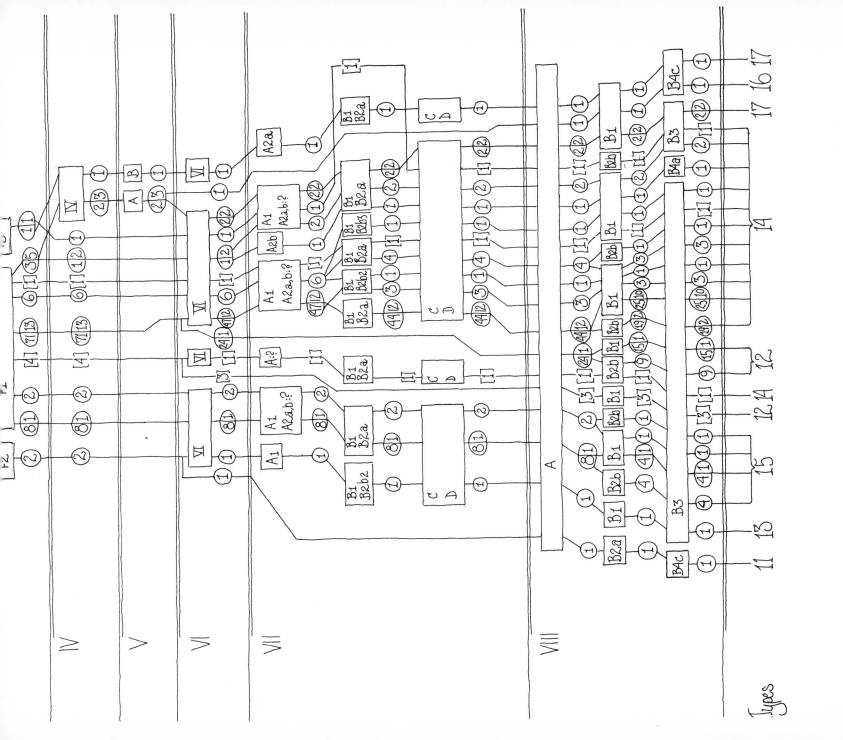

Types

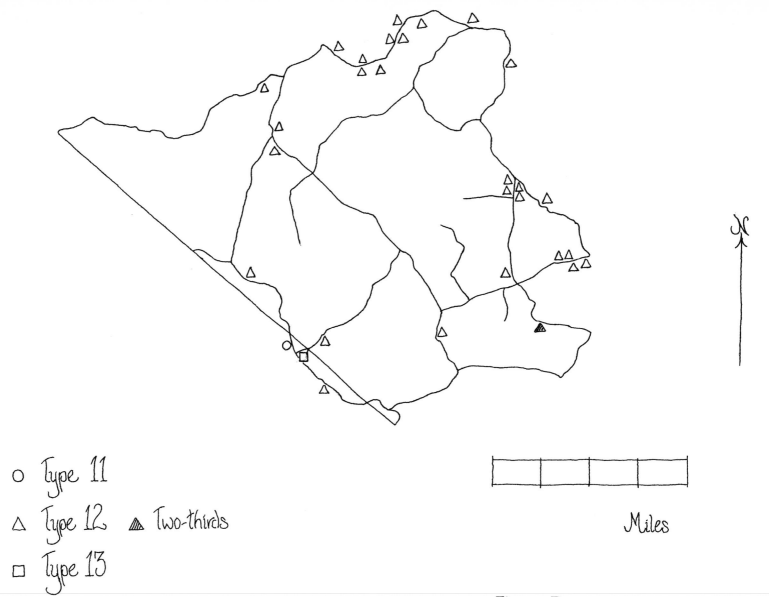

○ Type 11

△ Type 12   ◭ Two-thirds

□ Type 13

Miles

Fig. 22   DISTRIBUTION OF TYPES 11, 12, 13.

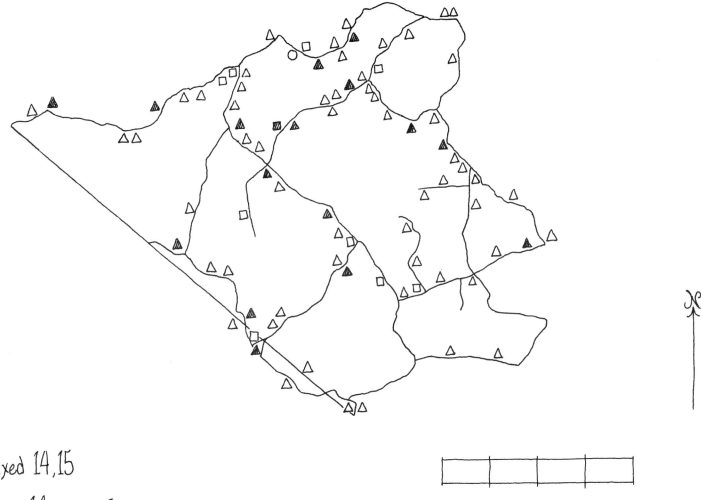

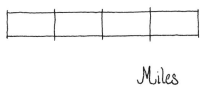

Miles

Fig. 23   DISTRIBUTION OF TYPES 14, 15.

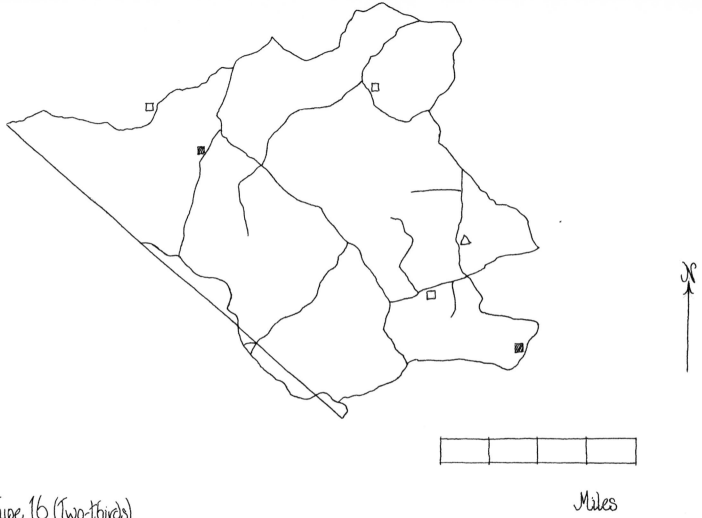

△ Type 16 (Two-thirds)

□ Type 17   ▨ Two-thirds

Miles

Fig. 24   DISTRIBUTION OF TYPES 16, 17.

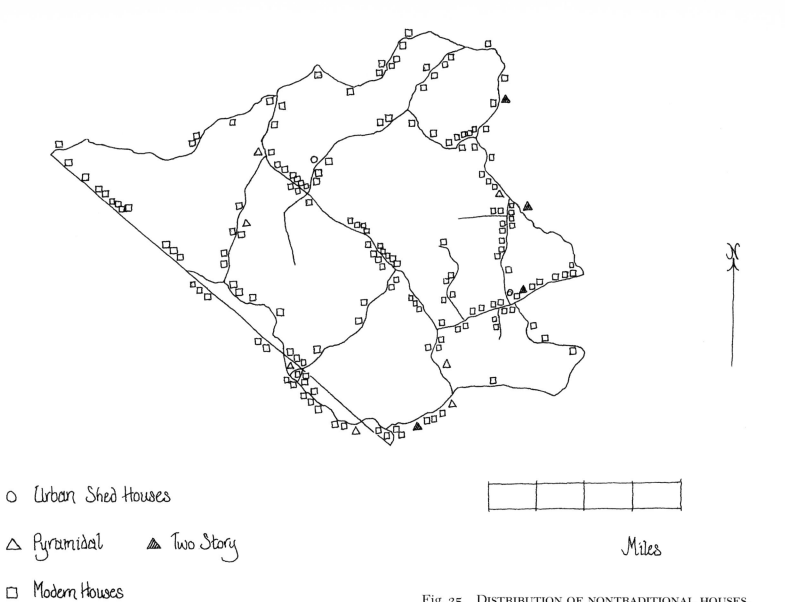

○ Urban Shed Houses

△ Pyramidal   ▲ Two Story

◻ Modern Houses

Fig. 25 DISTRIBUTION OF NONTRADITIONAL HOUSES.

Miles

63

Type	Total			Type	Total
1	4			12	27
2	8			12 (2/3)	1
3	3			13	1
4	2			14	54
5	4			14 (2/3)	16
6	1			15	10
7	2			15 (2/3)	1
8	6			14-15	1
9	5			16 (2/3)	1
10	3			17	3
11	1			17 (2/3)	2

Fig. 26 TYPOLOGICAL TABULATION.

We have now assembled an exact quantitative profile of the area's traditional house types (Fig. 26). Our goals will take us quickly across this stage, but in passing it must be commented that such an enumeration should be a step in any serious comparative endeavor.

This enumeration summons up some of the decrepit generalizations of architectural history and suggests they be laid to rest. The region of which our area is a core sample has been characterized as a land where hall-and-parlor houses are common but I houses are not. This notion has led scholars to look to Pennsylvania for the provenance of the I house of the Upland South.[14] The fact is that in our area there are four hall-and-parlor houses (type 5) and eighty-two central-hall I houses—a ratio I would defend as true enough for the Chesapeake country in general. It is sometimes written that the South took to the Greek Revival style with more vigor than did the North.[15] Virginia is in the South. The temple-form house, which is densely distributed from the Berkshires to the Western Reserve,[16] is the formal symbol of Greek Revival acceptance. The grand total of temple-form houses in our area is zero. Our tight conclusions (complemented by years of random roving over the countryside) lend support to Peirce Lewis' "guess that the average county in east-central New York has more high Greek Revival domestic architecture than does, say, the entire state of Alabama."[17]

Such quibbles may hold little interest outside the small circle of people who study old houses, but another complaint carries more general significance. It has been said of the South (and of eastern Virginia) that it lacks the middling sort of farmhouses that typify the rural North[18] and that no houses are to be found there save the grandi-ose mansion and the humble hut.[19] A somewhat simpli-fied reworking of the area's traditional typology reveals this break-down of housing size:

one-room: 8
two-room: 76
four-room: 77
six-room: 3

Many, probably most, of the smallest early homes have been reclaimed by nature, and any prejudice in the enumeration should favor the larger houses. It turns out that the grandest mansions, of which there are not many, are about the same size as the run-of-the-landscape Pennsylvania German farmhouse. There were, in Vir-ginia, palaces like Westover and Mount Airy, to be sure, but the Yankee and Quaker merchants erected compar-able monuments to their commercial wiles. One must jog blindered past hundreds and hundreds of humble wooden farmhouses before coming across one (statisti-cally insignificant) gem in the South or in the North. The big house on the plantation in old Virginia tends to be a little smaller than the modest farmhouse of the North—an observation that should call to mind the plain folk of the Old South revisionists[20] and replace any image of architectural opulence and despair with one of workaday plainness.

VI

The Mechanics of Structural Innovation

Like the practitioner in any social scientific or humanistic discipline, the folklorist who studies old houses may let his mind wander in different directions. He may find himself in a relatively philosophical mood, pondering the ways of human beings, regardless of historic specifics, or he may follow a relatively historical path through thought about the characteristics of a particular culture, society, or person. As he muses on his study, the house becomes not an object to measure, but an example of some principle in operation or the home for some fancied past family.

It is a commonplace that the scholar seriously questing for truth will attend tightly to sensate objects, to old houses or to the actions of persons in communication. And he will necessarily relate his own thought to those objects in order to test the reasonableness of his notions. It may be less obvious that the health of a discipline like folklore requires the scholar's own thinking to oscillate from the philosophical and theoretical to the human and actual. The social scientist's art is different from that of the physical scientist. Social theory is formed in relation to real phenomena; it must explain the phenomena, of course, but together the theory and the phenomena must improve our understanding of the human beings who caused the phenomena to exist. To get at history from houses, the fieldworker must begin at the houses themselves, at nail heads and window sizes and room arrangements. On becoming an analyst, that same person must come to grips with theories of history and models of change *and* with social and human facts.

The main theoretical justification for the time spent in field study of artifacts is that the fieldworker will discover things of differing ages that can be organized to provide the best possible data on the nature of change across large spans of time. Typically, the historically oriented scholar holds little interest in such theorizing and attempts to come directly to an understanding of actual people. This is humanistically laudable, but it has left much of historical scholarship exposed to the charge of unexplained process. After finishing the historian's work, we may feel let down in that we have much information about people but little understanding of their actions. In order to understand change rather than merely document it, in order to understand how much is actually changing when an apparent revolution occurs, the humanistic historian must think about theories of innovation. Conversely, if the theories utilizing objects such as houses are to be more than a test of the analyst's own facilities, if they are to be relevant to the human beings of whom the objects are but a shadow, principles of human behavior and mind must help us in our understanding of real human situations. Houses cannot teach us much about history unless we use them to build models of change that clarify our thought about the people of the past.

Not surprisingly, those who approach culture with models of balance and those who come with models of change evaluate the fact of change differently—yet they often wind up accounting for it similarly. The extremist of functionalism may count all change as the sum of equivalences that serve to maintain cultural institutions. The extremist of historicism may admit nonchanging essences into being only to dismiss them as trivial. But both of them, by trading in loose-knit generalizations backed by different metaphors robbed from biology, have been unable to explain how change takes place. Change, reduced to a list of periods or functional equivalents, becomes a chronology of things rather than a process. Even when in the presence of change, the positivistic social scientist may opt, oddly, for a reduction of process to static sections which are later subjected to comparison in an attempt to regain time. And even the unusual anthropologist who has maintained an interest in process through time has often stopped short of fluidity. He may

reasonably identify process as systemic alteration, but if he looks at process as influence on the system's elements, rather than as changes in the rules that relate the elements, and if he sees synchrony as a static pattern—a still photo—rather than as an atemporal process, then he is left thinking "of process as a very rapid succession"[1] of static images. He sees a movie rather than reality. Understanding change, it seems, must involve facing up to the reality of two very simple observations: there is no culture save that carried in individual minds; and those minds, when metaphorically reified, are not vessels where facts are stored, but instead are unstoppable mechanisms for the processing of facts. Positing a designing mind behind the architectural reality lets the analyst explain architectural change. We may unbind synchrony, letting it fly into time.

The person who will be the maker of houses travels through architectural experiences from the beginning of his life. The experiences that bounce from walls, through space, and along the corridors of his senses are accumulated randomly, but they are systematically ordered, so that when it comes his time to act he is not a copyist but a fluent practitioner. Perhaps, like the learning singer of epics[2] or chanter of sermons,[3] he passes through an apprenticeship of imitation. But at maturity, like the best of epic singers, he is reliant not on one original, but on a competence constructed out of numerous originals. He labors within tight lines of correctness, but his design competence allows for a variable range of actions. The houses he makes are similar each to the other, but never are they identical in every particular. Houses that look the same turn out to be different in small ways. A window conceptually in the exact center of a wall may be, in fact, a few inches one way or the other. When the architectural competence directs that a door be placed symmetrically, the carpenter's actual performance generally results in a door that appears to be symmetrically positioned; but when the tape measure is consulted it reveals that his performance only closely approximated the directives within his unconscious design ability. This constant minor variation in real phenomena blurs the clarity of the surface, confusing him who would be a copyist, confounding him who would simplistically account for cultural processes. As the painter Klee said the artist must do,[4] both the maker and the scholar are forced to abstract away from the perceived—away from tiny differences to profound similarities.

Operating entirely inside the bounds of the traditional design competence, the maker will engender vast superficial variation. Innovations, too, can come from one who makes no alterations in the system's individual rules, but who, for some reason, unconventionally reorganizes them by breaking whole types down into individual clusters of rules. In the diagrams of the competence model (figs. 11, 13, 15, 17, 21), not all of the houses which were bracketed as a consequence of nonconformity were exceptions to the system's sections; they were exceptions to the specific configurations of rules that led to certain types. One two-story house of a single room per floor (Fig. 27) is perfectly "grammatical," except that it was a blending of distinct configurations. It has the front window-door-window piercing of a house generated from an XY or XY$_3$X base structure rather than the window-door piercing appropriate to a house with an X base structure.

Similarly, the gable of one two-thirds (XY$_3$) subtype of a type-14 I house was pierced as if the house were two rooms deep; on both floors of the gable end a window was placed on each side of the chimney. This synthetic practice is common on early houses, like this one, in southern New Jersey and Maryland's Eastern Shore,[5] but within our area this was the lone sample. These two houses were the only ones with more than two openings on one wall of a module—the only ones that broke rule III.B.3.[6] The rule that requires an upstairs opening to be located directly over a lower one—IV. B.1—was broken in the example of a two-thirds I house subtype built onto the back of Meredith's Store in Orchid (Fig. 28). The front windows of the upper and lower rooms are both internally central, but on the first floor there are two, where on the second there is but one. The rules for the individual modules were correctly followed, but the rule for relating the modules to each other was not. Four houses with central hallways—three of type 12, one of type 14—have one chimney positioned so that it is on the rear rather than the end of the house, but in every instance this chimney serves an ell so that it was properly positioned—but positioned properly with regard to the ell rather than to the main pile of the house. This was a rather common practice from the Deep South up into the southern Midwest. All of these houses were simple innovations. To plan them, no ideas needed to be drawn from without and nothing had to be invented. Their builders had only to have the capability to break types apart and note similarities between formerly distinct configurations,[7] or they needed the capacity to isolate relational requirements so that one might be elided. Then they could

68

Fig. 27   TYPE 2 HOUSE WITH XY₃X FENESTRATION, HOUSE E. The Slayden house. A frame house covered with brick imprinted asbestos, this late eighteenth-century house is 19 feet square. It would be expected to have one rather than two windows per floor in the front. Note that the low wing, built about 1900, has the door and window arrangement of the older house.

Fig. 28　Two-thirds type 14 house with ungrammatical fenestration, House F. The Meredith house. The house is built continuously with W. W. Meredith Gen. Mdse. A seam to the left of the door separates the house from the store. It has Victorian touches that date it about 1885.

proceed with the usual sequence of rules until reaching a juncture where one rule or bundle of rules—a set of relations that might be named an architectural image or passage—was subtracted and a comparable preexisting rule or passage was inserted into its place. After this the sequence was carried on as if nothing had happened.

One house (Fig. 29) does not appear in the diagrams and has not as yet been counted. Its base structure is XY1. The stair goes up in the X as it should, but there is only one chimney; other houses generated out of an XY1 base structure have two. This chimney and the entrance are in the same room, but it is the small room rather than the large one, and when the chimney and the entrance are in the same room in the area's other houses, they are in the larger of the two rooms. All of the other houses that turned out to be rare within the Middle Virginia study area were ones familiar to me from research in other areas. This house is unique in my experience, however, and perhaps no others were built like it. It might have been built by someone whose grasp of the competence was weak, for it seems inconvenient, lacking as it does any source of heat in the larger room. More likely it was built for some special purpose, because its details and basic layout were handled with precision. But whether or not that purpose is ever discovered, it can be said that it was not snipped from the whole cloth. Only a few of the rules used in its design were new. Its architect only had to modify his competence by suspending rules III.C.1c.2 and III.D.1d. This mental act left lacunae in the configuration of rules that generated type 5 out of the XY1 base structure. Our builder's creative endeavor, then, in-volved only making new rules with which to complete the configuration.

It is neither continual variation in performance nor minor internal innovation that has caused the confusion in the development of theories of change. The puzzle is, how does a system that seems to favor replication generate new things? What is the origin of the novelties that George Kubler, the art historian, calls prime objects?[8] Even the biologist, who has been able to demonstrate how mutations are conditioned, has been hard put to explain exactly how a new species comes out of an old one.[9] Establishing a formal series leading from the old to the new is not an explanation; it is to studies in time what static classification is to synchronic theory. In artifactual research this sort of classificatory diachrony is frequently found in outlines of the sequence of art historical "styles" or archaeological "types." "Style" and "type" are identically and tautologically defined as assemblages of temporally variable features. The Gothic Revival follows the Greek Revival as surely as black-on-white follows red-on-cream or Queen Anne follows William and Mary. But the process of which that arrangement is the phenomenal residue is quietly forgotten. To explain change, scholars often resort to evolutionary metaphors. Generally, students of architecture have not actually borrowed the evolutionary hypothesis from biology; rather, they have stiffly applied an ancient model of progress: objects are arrayed from the simplest to the most complex on the assumption that this ordering recapitulates chronology. The work of J. Frederick Kelly is regularly belabored in this regard,[10] but some of the evolutionary stages he

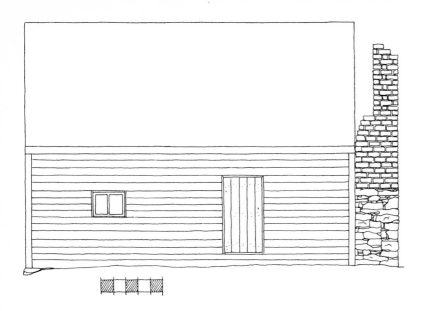

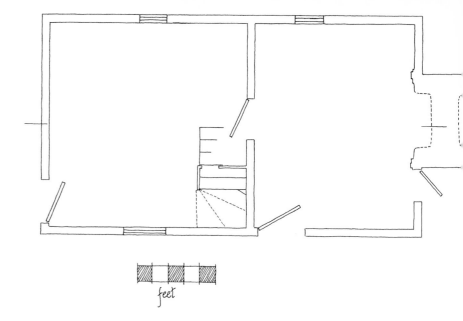

feet

Fig. 29 UNIQUE HOUSE, HOUSE G. This eighteenth-century house was designed from an XY1 base structure that was uniquely pierced. It originally had a shed appendage on the chimney end. While this book was in press I took some friends to visit the study area. All that remained of the Rackett house (Fig. 43) was a low mound in the brush, but the Parrish mansion (Fig. 36), which was in disrepair when I had last seen it, was being tastefully refurbished. The roof of house G had collapsed, and vandals had ripped the interior boarding off in the larger of the house's two rooms, revealing that there had once been a chimney on each end of the house. This house, then, was closer than I had thought to being a hall-and-parlor (type 5) house, though the position of the front door remains unique. Our unknown builder was even less creative than I had given him credit for being. See also Figs. 52, 53A, 57A, 67.

outlined in his *Early Domestic Architecture of Connec-ticut*[11] were real, even if others were, in fact, only internal synchronic transformations. Kelly's old book erred chronologically, but its theoretical faults have survived to be compounded in many new works[12] in which forms are ordered, with drastic distortions of morphology as well as chronology (and weird dislocations of logic), from simple to complex. To return to the biological analogy that the architectural evolutionist exercises, it would be rather as if man were at an evolutionary stage between that of the monkey and that of the elephant.

The pattern of culture in time is first apprehended as a slow curve traced by artifacts, plotted across time's map. The pattern seems to be a confusing succession of novelties, often of little relation to each other. But these things are the spoor of thought. They are human products, the manifestations of plans, and are therefore theoretically comprehensible to human beings.[13] The reason for this comprehensibility is the gentle paradox that, although material things may be old or new, old ideas are not old and neither are new ideas new.[14] The old idea, even when repeated in unaltered form, is not the same idea that it once was, for it is repeated in novel contexts. New structures are always transformed out of old structures, and even if its design is very complex, the new artifact is the result of melding ideas drawn from old artifacts. The process of design upon which the artifact, whether archaic or novel, depends is one of decomposition as well as composition. Simultaneously, the mind breaks down percepts and builds up concepts. The scholar and the maker are both analysts, comparativists, and, for that reason both of them can create and comprehend change.

With some sense of the mental mechanism involved, we can turn to a sketch of architectural change as it happened in Middle Virginia.

The establishment of the architectural sequence for our area will not depend on a search for more or less primitive forms. Dates are often glibly given on the basis of a building's gross form or its ornamentation. Such schemes are always primly efficient because they are never tested. The more we learn about architecture, the less reliable we find form and even decorative detail to be for dating. The main aid for arranging buildings in time—when, as is generally the case, documentary evidence is unavailable—becomes, then, technological scars, the marks of sawblades on boards and the kinds of nails driven into timbers. Nails have long been recognized as especially helpful.[15] The old siding of the Parrish mansion (house N; Fig. 36) was attached with rose-headed hand-wrought nails. The siding of the Rackett house (house T; Fig. 43) was put on with hand-headed cut nails. In sequence, boards were applied to other houses with machined cut nails and then wire nails. I have serious reservations about the common utilization of such marks for absolute dating. There were no naileries in Goochland or Louisa counties in 1810.[16] It is difficult to weigh the effect of the absence of local naileries in the interpretation of the fact that the Rackett house's nails suggest a date for the house of about 1810. But within a small area, the track or technological change can be followed to suggest rough absolute dates and a plausible local relative chronology. It may be fairly stated that house T is newer than house N.

There is no denying the need for chronology, but it

Fig. 30 ENGLISH HALL-AND-PARLOR HOUSE. This house, located at Hawbush Green, Essex (August 1973), is closely similar in form to house H (Fig. 31), with which it is also a close contemporary. It is an exact historic prototype for American hall-and-parlor (type 5) houses.

seems that a fetish for precise dating has lured many scholars away from matters of importance, sending them off on enervating, counterproductive peregrinations. As Marc Bloch has written,[17] the obsession with exact dating often leads to the erection of time periods that are neat but arbitrary, instead of instructive and natural. Concern with the datable has frequently served to distract archaeologists from large patterns, causing them to focus on minutiae.[18] Much more important than the fact that things like nail heads or screw points can be used to date a house,[19] is the fact that they *must* be. The truly important aspects of a house—the volumes it provides for its human inhabitants—do not fit into clean little temporal segments. History's "decisive question," wrote Von Martin, "is whether inertia or change predominates."[20] The answer that comes clearly from artifactual analysis is that little things change swiftly but big things do not. Continuity more than change is the human condition. If organized around the goal of isolating variable, datable detail, rather than around the goal of comprehending patterns of stasis and change, a discipline is doomed to the study of trivia.

The thread of chronology is picked up in the area before the middle of the eighteenth century. At this time the plan of the basic house consisted of two rooms, one square (X) and the other less than square (Y). This "hall-and-parlor" form was the British norm in the sixteenth and seventeenth centuries; it was found widely as an independent dwelling[21] (Fig. 30) or as the major part of a house incorporating a service wing from which it was separated by a cross passage.[22] The hall-and-parlor plan was built into a Cornish longhouse as early as the thir-

teenth century,[23] and at the time of the colonization of the New World it was, to cite demographically relevant areas, encysted in the longhouses of Wales[24] and Devon (Fig. 60).[25] The earlier of the hall-and-parlor houses in Britain often had but one chimney and one floor, but by the beginning of American settlement the hall-and-parlor plan generally included two fireplaces and was often built with a full second story.[26] In the countryside around Gum Spring and Orchid, if the smaller room were large enough (Y_1), each room had a fireplace. At the opening of the eighteenth century this was the usual plan of small homes in England and the British sections of New England, the Mid-Atlantic, and Southern colonies.[27] If the smaller of the two rooms, the parlor bedroom, were smaller than the square room by more than two units (Y_2), only the large room had a chimney. This smaller, single-chimney plan was found during the colonial period in many of the areas from which people emigrated to Virginia: northern and western Ireland, Wales, and England.[28] This form has not been previously recognized as a feature of the Chesapeake landscape; it is, however, found (though never commonly) through the Tidewater, and it is a trace element of the diffusion of British culture out of the Chesapeake country, as well as from Scotch-Irish Pennsylvania along the Appalachian axis[29] and into the southern Midwest.[30] In our area the larger of these plans (XY_1) could be built in a single-story expression (type 5; Fig. 31) or it could be two stories high (type 6; Fig. 32); the smaller (XY_2) was always a single-story dwelling (type 4; Fig. 33). The one-story houses all have a loft, the floor joists of which are framed in at the plate (Figs. 52, 69). The square form could be conceptu-

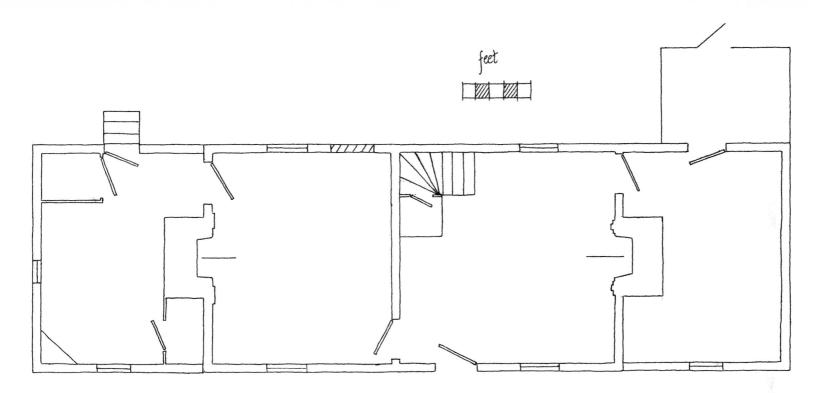

feet

Fig. 31 TYPE 5, HOUSE H. The Moore house. From left to right its rooms are now called "the junk room" (shed), "bedroom" (parlor), "living room" (hall), "kitchen" (shed). The back door leading out of the parlor has been blocked off. There was originally a small porch on the front. Although folk estimates of age may not be reliable, it is interesting that several local people pointed this out as one of the area's oldest houses. In many areas the people of the American countryside have little interest in chronology, dismissing all old buildings as "over one hundred years old," but that is not true of Middle Virginia. Ida Smith, who lives in this house, said it was "over two hundred years old" in 1964; in 1966, she said it was exactly 260 years old. It is surely a house of the earlier eighteenth century. See also Figs. 74, 84A.

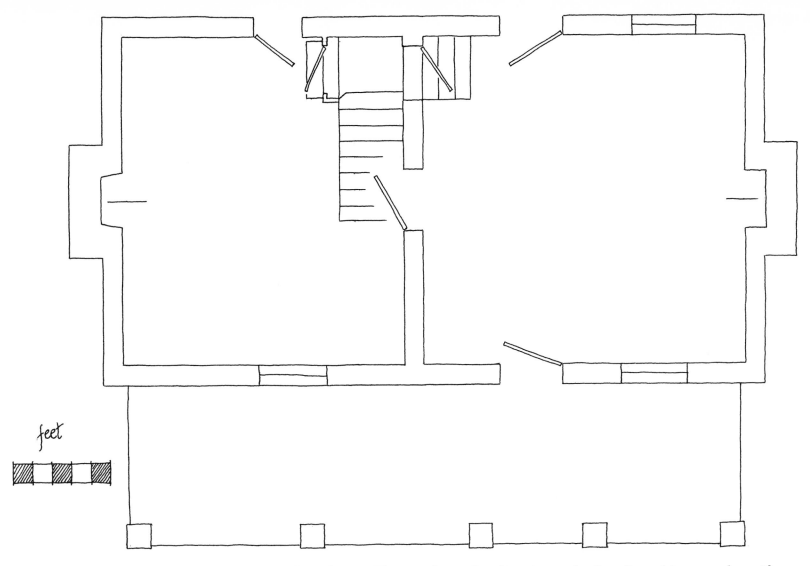

feet

Fig. 32   TYPE 6, HOUSE J. The Greater Dabney house. This rear view indicates the breadth of the missing ell. The two-room plan carries into the second floor and the basement. The porch is modern. Like most earlier houses, this house, built about 1800, has pitsawed rafters framed into couples with an open mortise joint, stiffened by halved-in dovetailed collar beams (see Fig. 52). This, the usual roof framing of the Middle Virginia tradition, was used also at houses G, M, N, V.

80

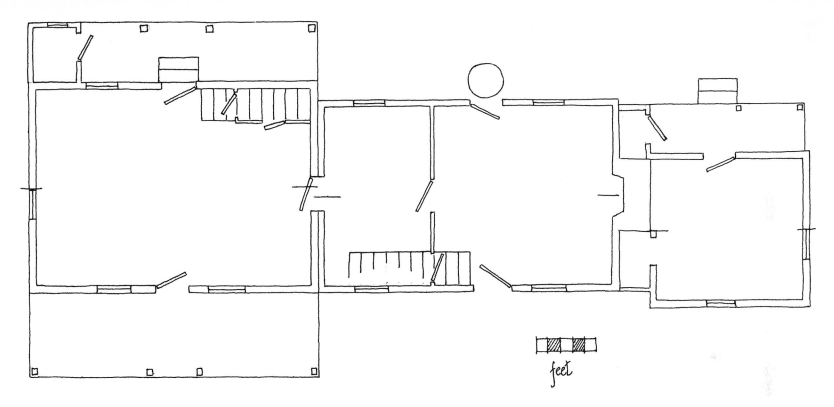

Fig. 33 TYPE 4, HOUSE K. The Brooking house. The central (eighteenth-century) part of this three-part house is an example of a type 4 house. This was once a post office and the focus of a settlement called Brookingville, which included, in addition to the house, a mill. The second stories were added; originally the house had lofty ceilings. The room to the left is an unpartitioned Z house of the nineteenth century. The room to the right is a perfect, though very late, example of an X house. See also Figs. 65, 72A.

83

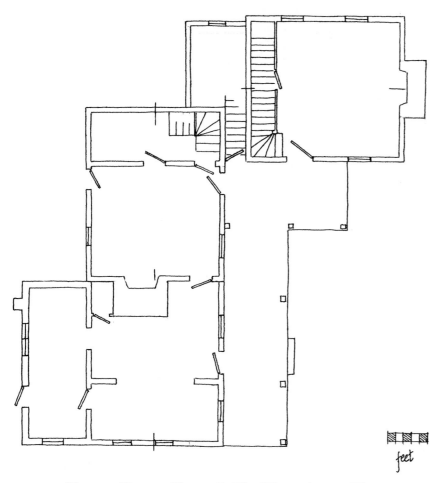

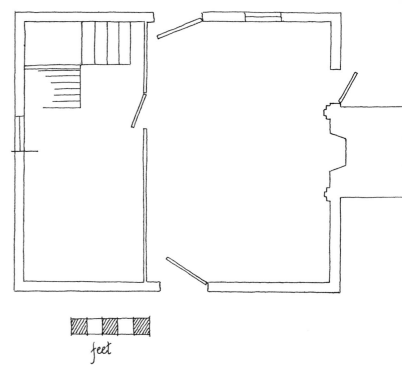

Fig. 35 TYPE 3, HOUSE M. The Parrish house. This small, mid-eighteenth-century house of sawed logs apparently had, originally, a shed built off the chimney end. When the area was visited again in 1970 all that remained of this house was the chimney. See also Figs. 57B, 64, 70A, 71C, 72B.

Fig. 34 TYPE 2, HOUSE L. The Watson house. The two-story section is a late eighteenth-century X house. A partitioned Z house of mid-eighteenth-century vintage is part of the loosely connected wing. The second section of the wing, with its flat roof pitch, is a recent variant of the Z form. Mr. and Mrs. James Watson said the house is two hundred years old. It was once inhabited by a Judge Simms, from whom it passed to a family named Smith.

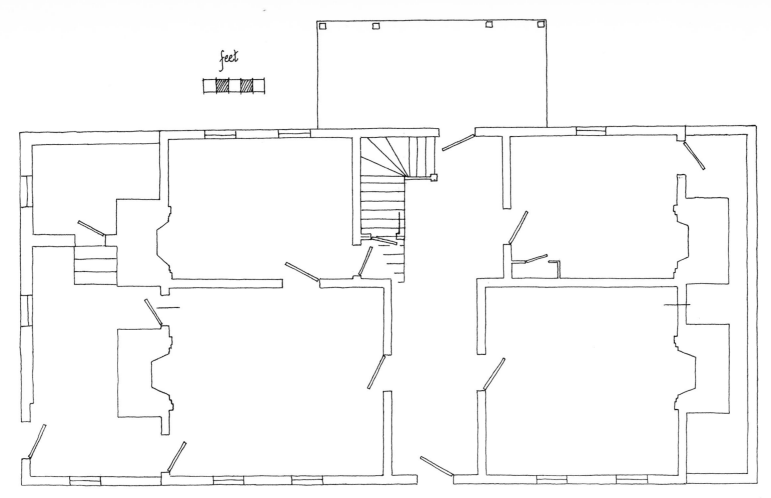

Fig. 36 TYPE 17, HOUSE N. The Parrish mansion. An early example of a Georgian house, this is the "old family home" of Mrs. Isbell, who lives near it. She remembers as a child finding lovely pieces of pottery while hoeing in the garden over the location of the overseer's house to the side of the mansion. She said it was built by an Englishman (perhaps the person who introduced the Georgian concept into the area) and that it was the seat of an eighteen-hundred-acre farm. The old people, she said, dated it to 1711, and told her that it was the oldest house and first post office of Louisa County. Everything about its fabric suggests a date fifty years later; it was probably the second house on the farm. If the 1711 date is correct, however, it would be a fascinating indicator of the ways of innovation, for this embodiment of the Georgian idea would have been available to local builders for half a century before it influenced local design. Possibly they had it, but did not use it until it was necessary for some deep purpose. See also Fig. 57C.

feet

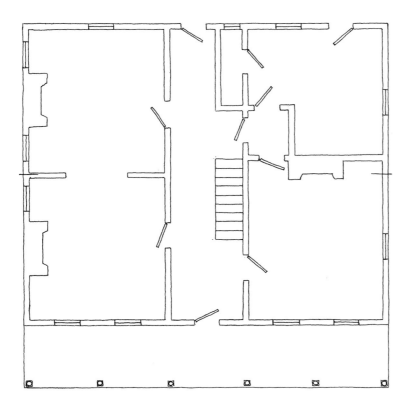

Fig. 37   TYPE 17, HOUSE P. This house of a Georgian form comes closer than house N to following eighteenth-century design, although it was built about 1845. It has a hipped roof, the left rooms are equal in depth, and those of the right share an internal chimney. Note that placing the chimney internally allows for the symmetrical arrangement of the end windows.

ally broken away and built as a one- (type 1; Fig. 10) or two-story house (type 2; Fig. 34). If it were a one-story dwelling, it could be enlarged (Z) and then subdivided so that its two rooms approximated the full plan of the larger houses: one large room with the front door and a chimney and a small room at one end (type 3; Fig. 35). That is a complete, if simplified, inventory of the domestic architectural repertoire of the middle of the eighteenth century.

The mid-eighteenth-century Middle Virginia builder may have been content that his X–Z–XY competence could answer his needs and those of his client. Then suddenly, about 1760, he was faced with a new house type. The course the new idea took into the area would not be possible to trace, because the alternatives were too many. But local thinking was knotted into nets tying it into the thought of eastern Virginia and, ultimately, London. No matter how homogeneous they are, little communities include innovators. There are members of the community whose personal bent or wealth or mobility or nonagricultural occupation places them in a peripheral position so that they may accept outside novelties, but whose primary affiliations are internal so that they may become local advocates for those novelties.[31] A local builder may have traveled to the East, there to see a house, or, more likely, many houses. Possibly an Easterner or a new arrival from England requested that an alien house be built. A book carrying plans and elevations may have been bartered for some barrels of Indian weed. However it happened, a local man perceived a new form—the Georgian house type (Fig. 47). It was not everywhere a new form; its sources are easily located in sixteenth-century Italian design, and builders in the English world had been employing it for nearly a century.[32] But here it was brand new. When compared with the old ideas with which it was competitive, the new idea was found not to be entirely foreign—a fact which facilitated its acceptance and suggested, via a reinforcing dialectic, innovative possibilities.[33] Its façade was pierced with five openings instead of three, but the door was located centrally between the windows. Although the door led into a formal hallway, in the old houses there had been an unmarked channel for direct passage from front to back (Fig. 32), and the cross passage was a typical feature of medieval British housing.[34] The entrance of the new house was still structured transversely to the ridge. The new type was two rooms deep, whereas the earlier houses were a single room deep, as was usual in the domestic building of the British Middle Ages; yet the new type was symmetrically roofed like the old houses. The new image (new, but not too new) was broken apart and compared with the forms that the old competence could generate; a new system was then developed that enabled the builder to design both the old and the new forms. But not only could the builder design houses of the old (1–6) and new (17) types, he could generate a set of compromises (types 11–16), which lay logically within the new system as reversible transformations between the old and the new.

The new idea was not materialized without modifications. Builders continued to design houses of the old types, and when they planned houses of the new "Georgian" sort, they designed them in accordance with the rules of the old competence. The shapes of the new base structure were taken from the traditional scale (Fig. 7), so that the hallway, like the old Y_1 and Y_2 volumes, was the result of subtracting units from the square. Its Y_3 dimensions left it narrower than the hallway of the Georgian type as offered in the builder's manuals of the day or as materialized on the grand plantations farther east.

The earliest extant specimen of the Georgian type 17 house built in our area (house N: Fig. 36) exhibits further deviations from its academic model, for the model was not passively accepted; it was actively, comparatively drawn through the structures in the folk architect's mind. Its front rooms, instead of being identical cubes, are of different sizes (s, $s + \frac{1}{2}u$); its rear rooms are laid out as dependent appendages to the front rooms (as if they were part of a shed addition) rather than as an independently equal pile; the stair and chimneys are like those of earlier local houses.

Only three examples of the new, two-room-deep, two-story, central-hall, full Georgian type 17 (Fig. 37) are extant in the area, and the sum total of houses generated entirely out of the original pre-Georgian competence is only twenty-one (types 1–6). All of the other traditional houses come from within the system's limits as defined by these early and late houses.

The new competence, developed to enable the planning of both the Georgian type and the early hall-and-parlor type, automatically included the rules for the generation of other types. The maker, by developing a single system to design both the new and the old, became competent to produce not only the new and the old, but also many syncretistic types which, by being partially older than the novelty, were, as a matter of fact, newer

than new. This mental event occurred with varying but comparable results in many parts of the rural Anglo-American world from the last quarter of the seventeenth century to the third quarter of the eighteenth. In Kent, England, the central-chimney I house yielded to a Georgian house with two central chimneys, which could be constructed as if it were two of the old houses shifted into parallel alignment.[35] The same thing happened in New England.[36] A fine study by S. R. Jones and J. T. Smith[37] reveals that the introduction of the Georgian type led to houses being built in Wales that were very similar to those that came to characterize the country around Chesapeake Bay.

Out of the old system, by way of Rule Set IX —the rules for subtypification—came the ability to fragment a form, to build a partial representation. Three houses were built in a form that amounted to the Georgian novelty with one of its thirds eliminated. This two-thirds Georgian subtype was an especially common housing solution in urban contexts—in Richmond, for instance.[38] As a rural home it is found with regularity through southern Pennsylvania,[39] northern New Jersey,[40] southern New York State, and Long Island's southern shore. In our area,

Fig. 38 TWO-THIRDS TYPE 16, HOUSE Q. In plan this late eighteenth-century house is two-thirds of the Georgian form. Its single story is fully "raised" on a brick basement. Note the differences in form and height between the original eighteenth-century chimney to the left and the nineteenth-century replacement to the right.

however, it is not common. One of the three houses of this kind here was built as a one-story house (Fig. 38). This was possible because the old rules empowered the planning of one- or two-story expressions of identically extended, massed, and pierced base structures.

The common compromise between the old and the new was positioned more equidistantly within the builder's competence. By reversing new rules at exactly the point where the tradition and the novelty were in greatest conflict (Rule Set IV, the backward expansion rules required by the Georgian type), an innovation was generated that consisted of the front half of the Georgian type. Basically, it was one room deep, like all of the early types, but it incorporated the new central hallway. Thus was born the central-hall I house, the most common type from the old Tidewater, across the Southern Mountains, out through the Bluegrass, and into the lower Midwest (Fig. 39).[41] Only one of these full central-hall I houses—the Rigsby house (Fig.41), a contemporary of the oldest Georgian house of the area (Fig. 36)—displays the five-opening façade of the Georgian type. The balance (a total of sixty-four) were products of the application of the old piercing rules to the new extended base structure. Each element is singly and centrally pierced. The new I house has the window-door-window façade of the early houses, except that, by virtue of the new base structure, this piercing operation had been brought into exact symmetry. The Georgian piercing, consisting of five openings per floor on the façade and two per floor on the ends, was accepted into the folk architectural traditions of the North, but the old pattern of three openings on the façade and none on the ends continued to be dominant in both

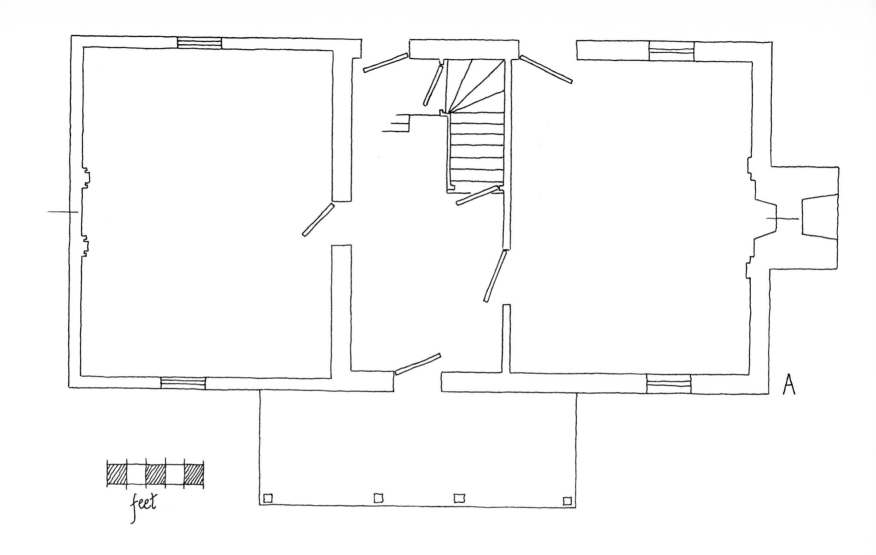

feet

A

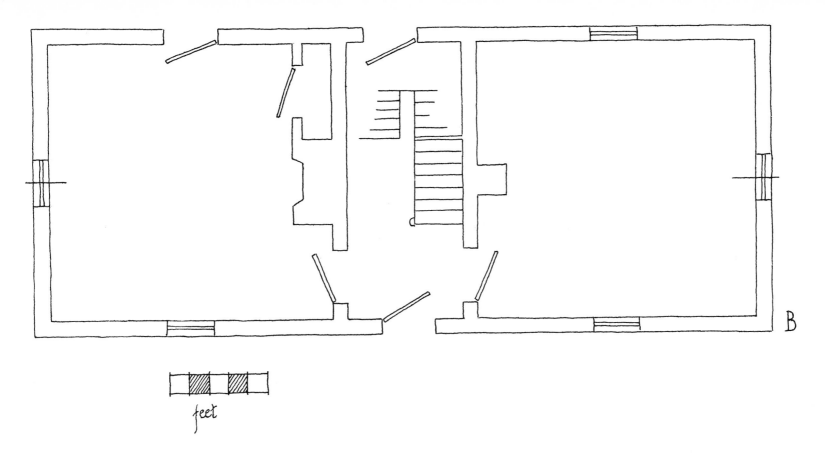

feet

Fig. 39 THE CENTRAL-HALL I HOUSE, WEST OF THE BLUE RIDGE. *A*. This house consists of a two-thirds central-hall I house built of logs, to which a room was added at the left, bringing the house up to the full form. It is located in the Valley of Virginia, between Mint Spring and Middlebrook, Augusta County (July 1963). *B*. Frame I house with chimneys flanking the hall. It is situated south of Falmouth, Pendleton County, Kentucky (December 1969). Both these houses had rear appendages; those on *A* are missing; those on *B* were left out of the drawing to make comparison easier.

94

the Lowland South and in rural Britain. In general, the eighteenth- and nineteenth-century folk houses of Scotland and Wales, as well as England (Fig. 40), display the blank gables and window-door-window façade so familiar to the student of Tidewater housing traditions.

The Rigsby house (Fig. 41) illustrates another early action. In many areas, the Georgian hallway was inserted between two rooms, analogous to the rooms of the XY_1 houses of our area, to create a plan that might be translated as XY_3Y_1.[42] The Rigsby house was drawn out of an XY_3X structure; however, one of its X components is exactly square (s), whereas the other is halfway to Y_1 ($s - \frac{1}{2}u$). We discover in it, then, a five-opening XY_3X form that is, when more precisely stated, $s - \frac{1}{2}u$, Y_3, s. This was one of the system's possible compromises, but the three-opening s, Y_3, s more symmetrical form became set as the local norm (Fig. 42)—the new type, at once older and newer than the alien novelty.

The rules for subtypification let the builder omit a room to create the XY_3 subtype of the central-hall I house. Of these, three were the partial expressions of the five-opening forms (Fig. 43)—window, window, door—but most of them (fourteen) exhibit the window-door incomplete façade of the three-opening central-hall I house (Fig. 44). The X forms came to be planned as one-third of the XY_3X five-opening I house (Fig. 34) and were pierced

accordingly, but this produced a circular nonchange—a reinforcing identity with earlier practice. The house generated out of a Z base structure, however, was modified so that instead of standing as a miniaturized version of the XY_2 type 4, it came to bear the same relationship with the XY_3 subtype 14. Rather than having a centrally positioned door leading into a squarish main room (Fig. 35), the door was displaced farther from the chimney and brought the visitor into a hallway where he would find a door opposite and an open stairway (Figs. 45, 46), just as he would if he had entered an I house. At the greatest distance from the Georgian novelty, and yet allowed by its internalization, were houses of the XX base structure. Neither of the rooms of the XX house was altered, but the new system integrated them axially into a single type consisting of the XY_3X base structure from which the Y_3 element had been dropped (Fig. 16).

No revolution other than that stimulated by the Georgian mode occurred in our area until the twentieth century, when the old system was smothered under blueprints. However, while there came no external disruptions to force a general reorganization of the traditional architectural competence between about 1760 and 1920, small statistical changes did occur. Two of the nineteenth-century changes were lagging responses to the Georgian novelty. One was a minor structural innovation; the other was an expansion of the lexicon of detail. Both seem to have come about because the old-fashioned mansions of the East continued to function as models for local builders—another of the many practices which serve to mess up tidy formal chronologies.

Once the new competence was operating smoothly,

Fig. 40 ENGLISH HOUSES. These houses at the entrance to Chitterne, Wiltshire (June 1972) illustrate the usual British piercing pattern: blank gables, window-door-window façades.

96

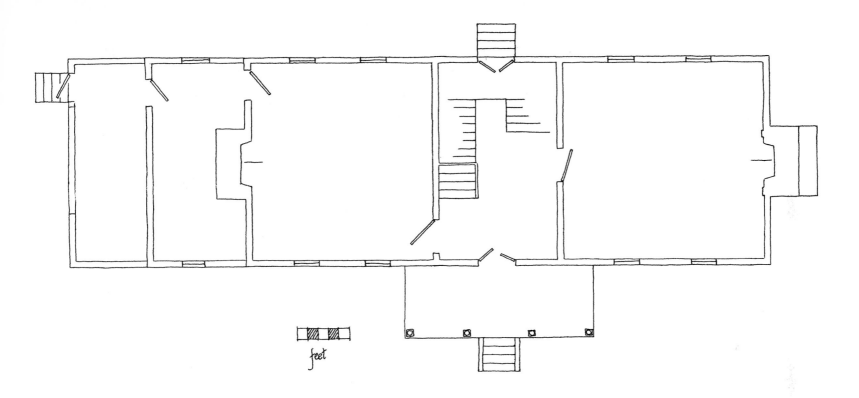

Fig. 41 TYPE 14, HOUSE R. The Rigsby house, built about
1770. The basic house has a central hall with an entry porch and
a room at each of its sides. Two shed additions have been made
onto its left end. N. O. Rigsby, its cordial owner, said it was built
by a "no account fox hunter" named Shelton, who kept a school
for boys in the house. The upstairs was divided into small
rooms for dormitories. It was later owned by a Colonel Chapman. Once it had a separate kitchen, a store, and slave cabins by
it. See also Fig. 73.

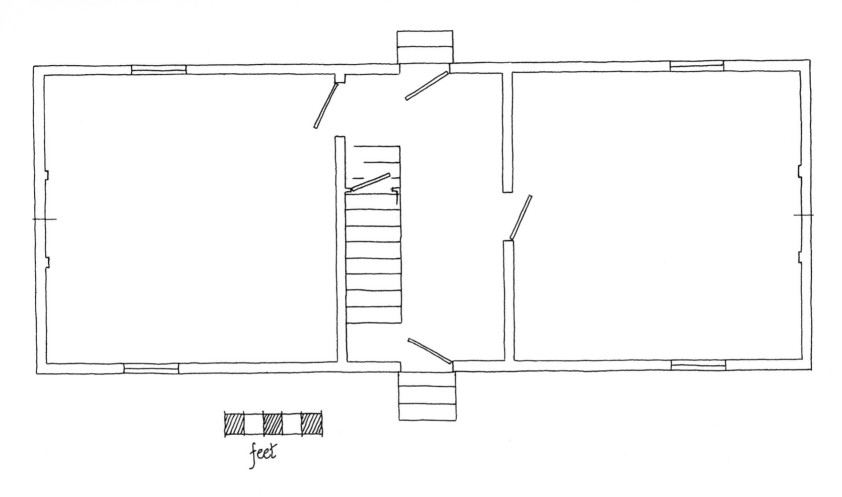

feet

Fig. 42 TYPE 14, HOUSE S. This is a later nineteenth-century example of the central-hall I house. The photo shows the characteristic tall, thin, blank gable. Its façade is drawn in Fig. 84B. See also Fig. 56.

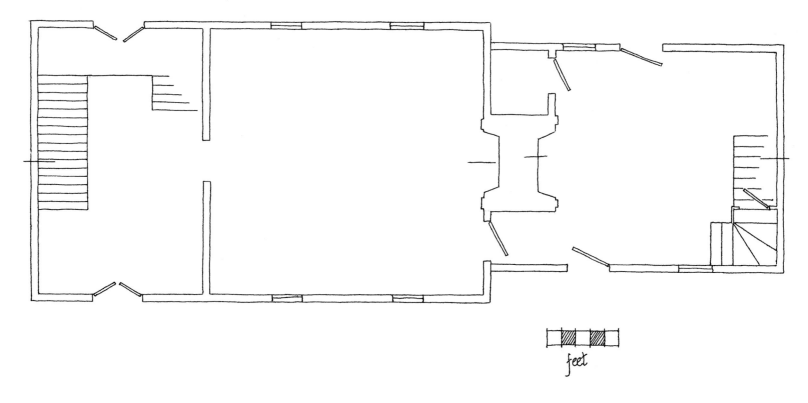

feet

Fig. 43   Two-thirds Type 14, House T. The Rackett house. Built about 1815, this house was an inn on the Three Chopt Road. The square room to the right was a kitchen. In bad shape when it was first visited, it had nearly collapsed by 1970. Originally it had two log cabins for slaves behind it. See also Fig. 53.

Georgian features that were initially rejected could be assimilated. The finest Georgian palaces of England or eastern Virginia often had the chimneys centrally located on internal partitions between the front and rear rooms so that they poked above the ridge in a pair (Fig. 47). The acceptance of this image by a Middle Virginia I house builder would have required placing the chimneys on the house's rear and breaking old rules. Builders in the southern Piedmont of North Carolina did just this, but the answer to this problem in our area was to locate the chimneys centrally on the walls flanking the hallway. This gave the general appearance of the Georgian chimney massing, though actually the chimneys were closer to one another than in the alien prototype (type 15: Figs. 48, 77). This innovation was used in the design of eleven central-hall I houses—one of them an example of the two-thirds subtype—but the great majority of the nineteenth-century houses and all of those of the mid-eighteenth century, whether double pile in plan or only one room deep, were fitted with chimneys on the end walls after the manner prescribed by the system of the early 1700s. Shifting the chimneys to internal partitions freed the ends of the house for a window per floor, but, though it broke the strong rule requiring a piercing for each wall, only two houses were planned to take advantage of this opportunity. Most people left the end blank as if a chimney were there (see rule III.E.3a.2). The hip roof was the second Georgian feature adopted by Middle Virginia builders in the nineteenth century. All of the oldest houses of the area have gable roofs, but during the nineteenth century, while most builders were still capping their dwellings with a gable, twelve central-hall I

houses, one XY₃ two-thirds I house, and one two-story XX house were built with hipped roofs instead. One builder of a one-story house—the only XY₃ one-room-deep, one-story house in the area—used it too.

Traveling through eastern Virginia in the late eighteenth century, a Louisa County farmer would have seen many houses, half a century old, with the five-opening façade, double-pile plan, paired internal chimneys, and hip roof that signaled the Georgian totality.[43] At Williamsburg, for example, he might have been impressed by the Brafferton Building at William and Mary College, or the Wythe House. Some elements of buildings like these he quickly absorbed, but it was not until the next century had begun that the farmer from Middle Virginia, or the man who built his house, figured out how to work paired chimneys into his competence and decided to add the hip roof to his repertoire.

All of the earliest central-hall, one-room-deep houses were I houses; they were two stories high. During the last quarter of the nineteenth century one-story central-hall houses began to appear. For the first time the rules allowing for one- and two-story versions of the same extended, massed, and pierced base structure—rules that had been used in the early times for XY₁ houses and which had been kept in use for XX houses—were applied to one-room-deep XY₃X houses. One-story central-hall houses were not unknown farther east in the eighteenth century, and they were common from the Georgia-Carolina coast[44] through the Deep South,[45] into the southern Midwest, and from thence to the Mormon West.[46] But after about 1760 came a century during which one-story houses were rarely erected in this area. During the De-

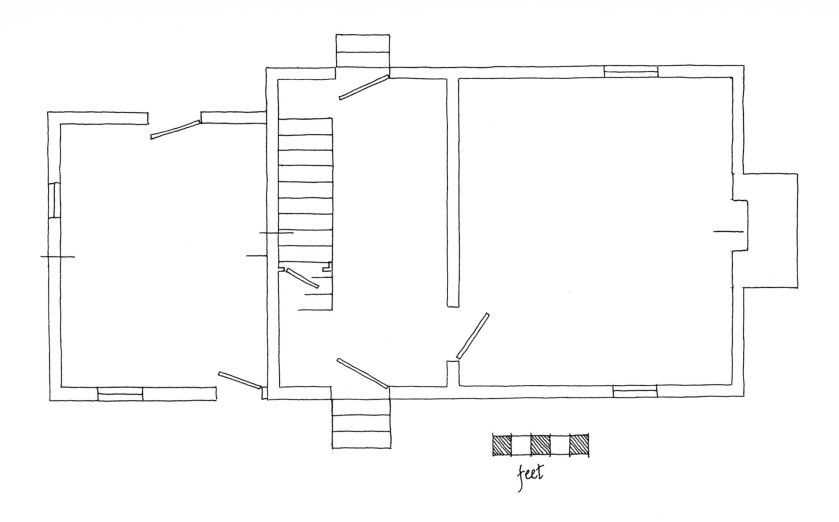

feet

Fig. 44 TWO-THIRDS TYPE 14, HOUSE U. This is a later nineteenth-century example of the subtype of which the Rackett house is an early example. The room to the left was a later addition.

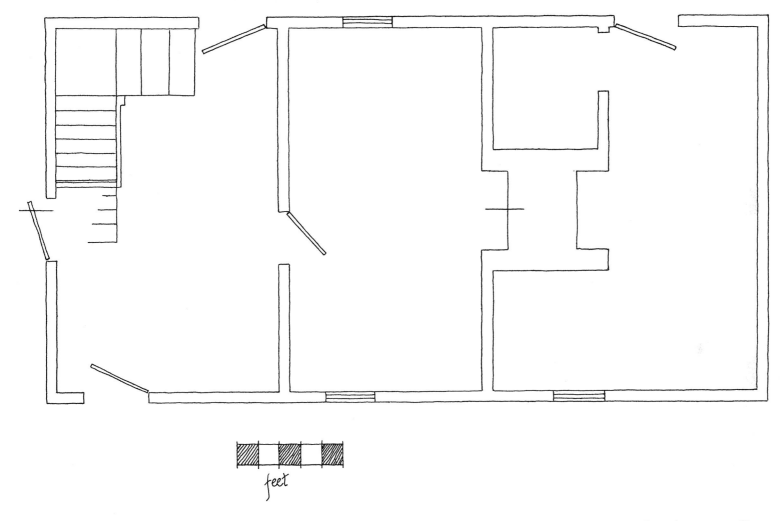

feet

Fig. 45 TYPE 3, HOUSE V. The Lesser Dabney house. The oldest stone in the family graveyard accompanying this house is that of Samuel Dabney (1752–1798). Probably Sam Dabney was the "old Dabney man" whom modern people credit with the erection of the house. It causes us to rearrange our thinking a bit when we realize that this house, though very small, was quite elegant back in the eighteenth century when it was new. It seems that the house originally had a shed on both ends. See also Figs. 53C, 68, 69, 71A.

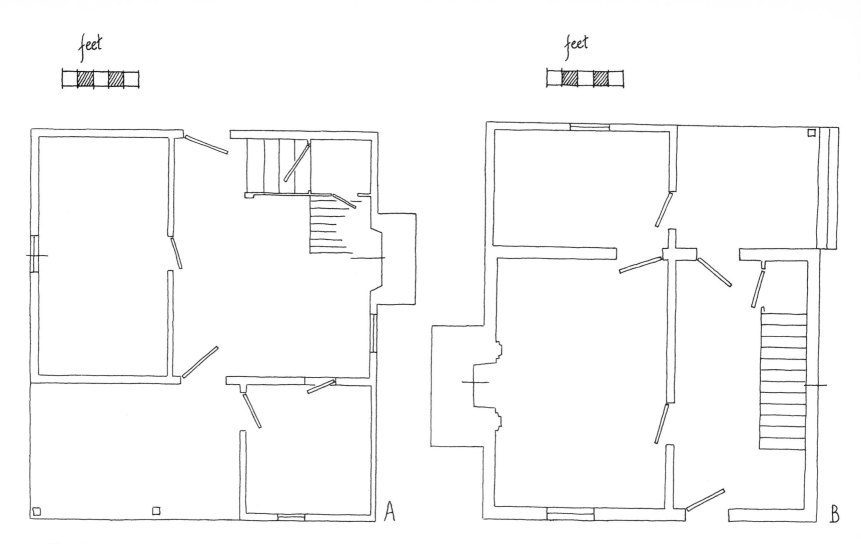

feet

feet

A

B

Fig. 46   TYPE 3 HOUSES. Type 3 is a previously unrecognized American folk architectural variety. It is nowhere a common house. As a buttress for the notion that the survey can stand as representative for its region, these geographically peripheral houses are offered. They illustrate the same change in the internal arrangements of houses generated out of a Z base structure that is to be found in our area. A. Frame house with a front porch and shed; located west of Fremont, Wayne County, North Carolina (September 1967); compare with Fig. 35. B. V-notched log house with a back porch and shed; located west of Linden, Warren County, Virginia (May 1969); compare with

Fig. 47   THE GEORGIAN HOUSE. With its hipped roof, internal paired chimneys, and elaborate treatment of the fenestration of the hallway area (in this case, narrow windows beside the door and upper windows), this house comes close to being a materialization of the Georgian ideal. It is located in Inkpen, Berkshire, England (June 1972).

Fig. 48   TYPE 15, HOUSE W. This nineteenth-century frame
central-hall I house has been clad in asbestos.

Fig. 49   THE LAST OF OLD VIRGINIA ARCHITECTURE, HOUSE X.

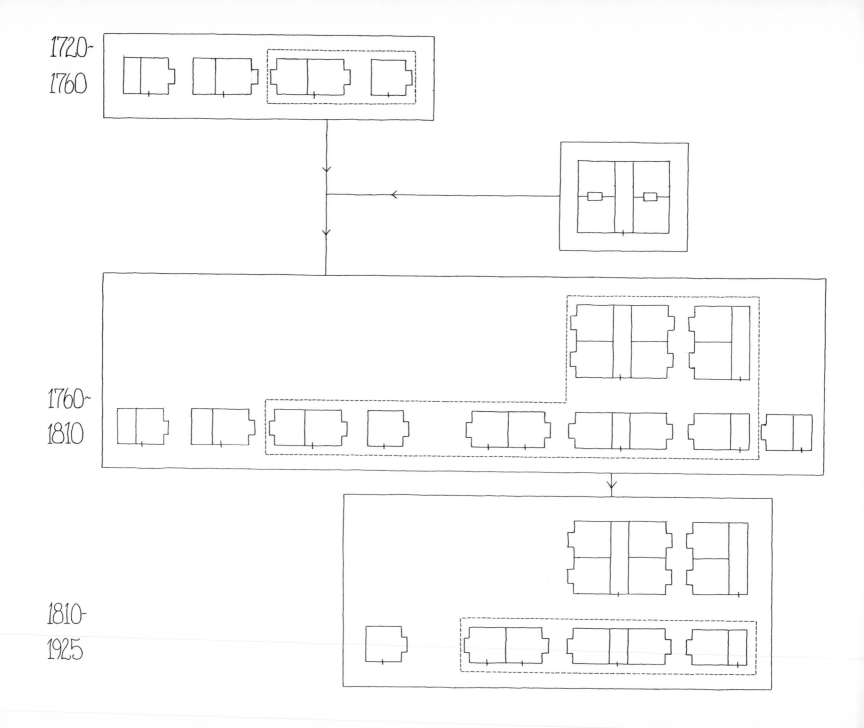

1720~
1760

1760~
1810

1810~
1925

pression of the 1930s the traditional competence was utilized to create a humble innovation, a single-story XY house that had a flue for a stove located on the internal partition (Fig. 49). The seven examples of this, the system's last gasp, bring to completion the enumeration of the folk houses of the area.

Toward the beginning of *Innovation*, H. G. Barnett comments that it is easier to explain artifacts as things than as ideas, but he flails that strawman to dust through the rest of his readable volume.[47] It is impossible to describe change in terms of things. It is not culture's discrete behavioral or material manifestations that change; what changes is the ideas that are culture. What changes is not the individual products of the competence, but the rules in the competence.[48] Taking a look at things alone, we might set up three architectural periods for our area. The first stretches from the beginning of European settlement to about 1760 and is characterized by houses with XY base structures. The second lasts from about 1760 to 1920 and is characterized by houses with XY_3X base structures. The third, characterized by bungalows of sundry nonfolk sorts, is that of the present. Those periods are statistical conveniences, a static series that sidesteps change. Houses, of course, do not "evolve"; what evolves is the ability to design houses.

Fig. 50 EVOLUTION OF THE ARCHITECTURAL COMPETENCE. The diagram includes plans of all the forms in the repertoires of the three different phases. The statistically important forms are enclosed by broken lines.

If we concentrate on the two periods during which the traditional architectural competence existed, we find no break in the ability to design houses until our century. The image is one of a contour of constant variation from the earliest times until the advent of the blueprint house. The traditional competence did, however, endure one revolution, taking place between 1760 and 1810, which may be used to divide the competence, historically, into three phases (Fig. 50). During its first phase the design competence consisted of all the rules necessary to generate house types 1–6 out of base structures X, Z, XY_2, XY_1, Adding to this competence the ability to design the Georgian type 17—that is, entering the second phase—required the addition of only rules I.C.2b and c; III.C.1c.1, C.2a.1, D.1e.1b, D.1f, and D.2a; IV; V; and VIII.B.2b. Most importantly, these rules added the XY_3X base structure and permitted doubling at the rear of the house. All of the rules of the competence of the first phase remained in effect.

The new competence not only provided for the design of types 1–6 and 17 (the type that caused the expansion), but also for types 7–16, the XX base structure being a chance development through subtypification of the XY_3X base structure. The competence of the expansive second phase enabled the design of the old types, the new types, and all of the compromises between. It was the competence of the second phase, 1760 to 1810, that was worked up into the program presented in chapter IV.

During the third phase of the traditional competence that spread through the nineteenth century, some of the old forms, it seems, were found to be redundant. They were equivalent competitors of the new forms, and the

XY1 and XY2 base structures fell into disuse. Although the rules in the competence of the first phase may well have been developed to enable the architect to generate houses from the XY1 and XY2 base structures, the only rules that became obsolete with their elimination were III.D.1e and D.1e.1a. These old rules were not broken; they were simply no longer necessary.

The house by Frank Lloyd Wright, writes Lewis Mumford, is dropped in isolation as a gesture of its maker's arrogance. It "challenges us by risking failure instead of courting safety—or courting perfection—by refining an old form," and "though it dazzles us by its brilliance, it sometimes fails to invite our love, because it offers no halfway place between rejection and abject surrender."[49] Some may hope to masquerade the "novelty" as a thing unbound to antecedent or social need. But the folk architect is no gambler; his work is continuous in planes of place and time. His innovation is inevitably a truce with time, a compromise in social assertion. A close analysis of the folk maker's product leads to a clear view of him modestly tinkering with given ideas that he can predict will be acceptable to those who must use them. A search for the sources of the genius of a Wright depends upon an intricate analysis, but even an impressionistic depiction of the folk architect's building reveals it to be a mediation between rejection and submission. It is the perfectionist's compromise: young enough to be arrogant, old enough to be loved. Looking at its exterior, one sees symmetrical lines and ornamental details placed there to tell the viewer that the house shelters people who are aware of the latest fashions and have money and strength enough to accept them. But upon moving inside, one finds familiar comfortable volumes to calm any fear of aggression that might have been taken from the façade.

Put simply, around Gum Spring the pattern of compromise in time is one of a traditional equilibrium whacked out of balance by the appearance of a competitor—the Georgian house type. Temporary balance was achieved by the incorporation of the competition. Then equilibrium was regained by a synthesis of the old and new, followed by the elimination of the old, and the relegation to rarity of the new, in their pure forms. The hall-and-parlor types generated from XY1 and XY2 base structures were abandoned and the Georgian house was not commonly built. The dominant types during the third phase of the traditional competence—from 1810 to about 1920—came to be the compromise types, especially the central-hall I house. This pattern, then, may be divided into three phases and six stages: phase I (balance), phase II (disequilibrium-expansion-synthesis), phase III (contraction–new balance). This dialectic process seems a credible theory for large-scale cultural change, general enough to be tested in other contexts and yet specific enough to account for what happened without secreting exceptions or making languid appeals to ineffability.

The pattern is not circular, for though it starts and ends in balance, those states are not identical: the pattern is helical. We might be able to view the pattern with more happiness if it did not include the contraction stage. Were change through time accumulative, leading continually to an enlargement of a culture's inventory, then change could not be seen as degenerative. But expansion is followed by contraction before balance is reachieved. Thus the functionalist can see change as leading to endless equivalence, and the historian can see change as leading to endless progress. Both notions are simplistic; it is plainly true that things neither stay the same nor necessarily improve. Although the pattern is not overturned by the facts it orders, it is a mechanical model rather than a sequential arrangement of facts. As a model it can be tested against ethnological information to bring it closer to the status of a principle and to guide comparative research. For example, in the late eighteenth century, south and east of Philadelphia, the architectural competence went from balance to disequilibrium to expansion and synthesis in a manner closely parallel to that of Mid-dle Virginia. The early house was built on a hall-and-parlor plan (balance). The Georgian type was introduced (disequilibrium), accepted (expansion), and meshed with the old type to create the central-hall I house (synthesis). However, the contraction and final balance stages were different from those in Virginia, for during contraction the early types were lost but the Georgian type did not become rare. It became dominant. And the third phase in the process of change was characterized not by a compromise between the old and the new, but by the new.[50] Thus we have an objective measure of Middle Virginia conservatism.

VII

Reason in Architecture

Old houses can be read to create statements of their designers' competence. Set into time's terrain, they illustrate the mechanics of the evolution of architectural abilities. But the builder did not plan in a vacuum; the process of design was constricted and driven by the context that held him. In the concrete artifact is written the tense conflict of what the designer could do and what he had to do. No matter how powerful and efficient his competence was, the designer could not do what his context would not allow.[1] His fancy was restricted by the conservatism of his clients and the realities of his environment. No matter what his context was, he could not do what he did not know how to do. Without considering context, we may be able to describe the competence, but we cannot use the competence to help us understand the decisions that define and refine a particular culture. Without considering context, we can explain how change takes place but not why a particular change took place. This chapter, then, will be devoted to an examination of the way Middle Virginia architectural reason worked in its context.

Social scientists call two different conceptualizations "context." Often no distinction is made between them. The particularistic context[2] is the observable environment of an expression of culture. When set into its particularistic context the expression is seen to be but one of a bundle of objects. The object being studied is made up of parts, and it is, in turn, one of the parts of a larger object, which, in turn, is part of a still larger object, which, in turn, is. . . . For observable interpersonal relations, the particularistic context consists of a hugely complicated communicative interchange. For an old house, the particularistic context would consist of the land concentrically ringing its walls:[3] the building provides the context for its parts, the farm or lot is the context for the building, the community is the context for the lot, the landscape is the context for the community, the political division is the context for the landscape, and so on and on until the universe gathers its own into order.

The particularistic context is the phenomenal setting, the behavioral surface. The other type of context cannot be seen; it is the abstracted context in mind. The abstracted context embraces portions of the particularistic context, ordering them into a concept, but it includes as well other unobservable conditions which are affective during design. The particularistic context surrounds the object in the real world; the abstracted context surrounds the competence. It serves to control and prod the competence so that the things generated out of it will fit into their particularistic contexts[4]—so that the house will protect its inhabitants from the weather and project the image that its maker desired.

In general, the abstracted context is the more profound concept; the particularistic context is a descriptive device, whereas the abstracted context is an explanatory device. The concept of abstracted context is especially useful when the analyst turns to the study of the autonomous, historical object, because of the particularistic context of the autonomous object may be only weakly germane to the scholar's problem. The particularistic context of a politician's diary might be rags in an old trunk, for example, and the particularistic context of a published myth might include some shallow data on the myth's original context, though more usually it consists only of texts of other, possibly unrelated, stories. The particularistic context of an old house is apt to be composed of things produced by the minds at variance with the builders, such as a tangle of weeds or a string of brick ramblers.

On the other hand, the particularistic context of the house could be quite instructive. The house, for example, might be the seat of a farm being worked in the way that the farm was worked when the house was new. This is often a very tempting assumption, but the analyst must resist a tendency to think that things have not changed. If one is to keep historic goals in focus, one must initially assume that the present context of an old artifact is irrelevant. Once the old thing has been analyzed in its own terms, the scholar can return to look at its modern setting for suggestions to aid in his argument.

Quick analogies are dangerous in artifactual analysis. It is odd that the artifact, like the folktale, is often studied more as being reflective of social realities than as expressive of a psychological reality. The reconstruction of the superficial particularistic context of a historical object is extremely difficult, yet it is regularly attempted. Some aspects of the deeper, stronger, abstracted context could be more easily described,[5] yet such is rarely attempted. Much clever thought, for example, has been devoted to how an ancient tool found isolated in a bog was actually used,[6] where less thought has been given to the more abstract but easier to grasp questions, answered by an analysis of the thing as shape and substance. It may never be known how a tool was used, but some interpretation can follow the observation that, whatever it was, it was a natural substance modified in the direction of an idea held in mind.

The abstracted context is a structure of potential source and consequence. It relates the object being composed in the designing mind to the maker's view of himself and to human, natural, and supernatural forces that exist beyond him. When the object is placed in its abstracted context, a prediction is made of the object's effect within the maker's design field—the field throughout which his act may have repercussions and by which his needs are defined. These needs and consequences are customarily termed functions. In the social anthropology of the recent past, the theory of function, built on an analogy between the living community and the living body,[7] has proved useful in the study of little communities. When the culture is complexly multifaceted,[8] or—and this is our problem—when the body is dead and decomposed and all that remains are some bones, a buckle, and a shred of leather, organic functionalism tends to be either simplistic or lethargically circular. This suggests a change from biological to mathematical metaphors[9] and the development of a multilinear functionalism that starts at the discrete object rather than at an unknown social organism and proceeds to weave distinct sets of dependent, variable relations into a web. This multilinear structure is discovered within the object, but it relates the object to things external to it, providing the analyst with some evidence of the object's existence as an agent for transferring its maker's energy through his design field. The structure of the abstracted context is internal, in mind, but it binds the object to such external variables as the materials available in nature or the expectations of the maker's group.

The relations that bind the object into its context endow the object with meaning. To explain the object the analyst needs to know something of its meaning, and to know its meaning he needs some understanding of its context. In the study of historic objects that lack observable contexts, this is obviously a problem. An analyst can guess much but know little about the particularistic context, so he turns to the reconstruction of the abstracted context. Some kinds of relations are closed to scrutiny;

they are forever lost and no amount of inventive speculation is going to resurrect them. Other structures within the abstracted context, however, might be discovered through an analysis of the objects available for study.

Without leaping willy-nilly into the unfathomable, the student of past architecture knows that the house functioned somehow within the structure that relates one person (the house's inhabitant) to the other members of his community (those who will see the house). The analyst also knows that the house functioned somehow within the structure that relates the person to nature, for the house was made of nature's substances and was located, literally, between people and the environment.

In attempting to isolate structures from the artifact, the analyst looks at objects, necessarily in some numbers, in order to discern patterns. Many possible patterns will appear, and the task becomes the separation of the "patterns" that are merely coincidences from those that might have been structures in the thought of the artifacts' makers. The structures might be isolated by means of a historical comparison. One might look, for example, at houses of different types and note the similarities that exist despite the differences that catch the eye. These similarities could be ordered into hypothetical structures which could be tested to see whether or not they hold. An easier means of locating structures is comparison in time. Sundry superficial elements changing at the same time and rate are likely to be indicators of a deep principle. Apparently unrelated aspects of houses—say, the height of a chimney and the color of a front door—might vary together in time. Noticing such surface changes can lead toward the recognition of structures in thought, much as the harpooner looks for disturbances on the water to find the whale beneath.

The structures that endure testing, that appear to be genuine dependent relations, are of two kinds. Some are those of the competence; they are the rules that order the object's shape. Other relations are unhindered by forms or levels or sets of rules. They cut across the architectural logic, unpredictably connecting apparently unconnected aspects of design, providing the whole system with a logic of interrelation that complements the logic of formal composition.[10] Important clues for reading the building as a sign seem to be held by these structures that are not essential to the house's shape. Basic forms carry meaning, but the house's meaning unfolds in strange and subtle ways which demand that close scrutiny of the house-as-artifact cannot stop at basic forms.

An interpretation of the house's meanings and functions, its possible extensions in context, is, at its most controlled, an essay in probabilities, and, at its least controlled, an act of pure courage. But hypothesis and a bit of scholastic overreaching are better than nothing.

THE HOUSE IN SOCIETY

Man, observed Le Corbusier, is architecture's content.[11] The original content of our houses has vanished. But knowing that the houses were the particularistic contexts for human beings allows us to offer small comments about what the houses did for them. To get at its social meanings, one must place the house in a mediating role within a system relating different kinds of human architectural content. By assessing the way in which the house performs its mediation, we will become able to characterize some of the relations in Middle Virginia society.

The house presents an index to the relation between its designer and its user. Although the designer and the user were often the same person, design and use may be conceptualized as an opposition—architecturally, the opposition of plan and use; anthropologically, that of culture and behavior; poetically, that of intellect and emotion. In the simplest formulation, these oppositions may be envisioned as idealized mental opposites, binary structures in abstracted context, which must be resolved in concrete terms, in real movements of human muscle that produce furrows or myths or houses. From the house's fabric may be read the nature of the resolution, whether the resolution favored one or the other of the contextual opposites (designer or user) or whether its locus was plumb central between them. Further, the resolution of one pair of oppositions is logically connected to the resolution of other oppositions, and this deeper bond yields an impression of a systematic structure of cultural meaning.

As projected by traditional humanism,[12] by the modern architect[13] and psychologist,[14] the ideal is for architectural form to be the material rendering of human need. Under the spell of Edward T. Hall's arguments,[15] the fieldworker comes to the house expecting it to be the end product of centuries of subtle metamorphoses which have molded it into a proxemic shell—a perfect projection of the volumetric needs of the building's human content.

It is not that simple. The house in our area is planned around a square volume; all things save that shape are variable, and the simplest house consists of only this unsplittable atom. In England this square house or room was generally sixteen feet on a side. The usual reason offered to explain these dimensions is that this was the amount of space comfortable for oxen,[16] but whether or not an ox byre or (as is more likely) some system of folk measurement lies at its origin, its persistence would seem to owe a debt to the comfort a carrier of Anglo-American culture feels within a square space about sixteen feet on a side. The minimal unit of housing consists repetitiously of that single bay cube (Fig. 10) in England,[17] on the frontier in Upper Canada,[18] along the eastern escarpment of the Appalachians,[19] and through the black countryside. Booker T. Washington began life "in a typical log cabin, about fourteen by sixteen feet square,"[20] and the great DuBois left us a description of the "box-like" house "with its one square room" that was strung across the Southern landscape, "now standing in the shadow of the Big House, now staring at the dusty road, . . . nearly always old and bare, . . . crowded. . . ."[21]

The square may not have seemed wholly alien to the forced immigrant from West Africa, even if he left behind a circular home.[22] Different house shapes seem to correlate with different kinds of societies; circular forms are more common among nomadic, polygynous people, and rectilinear houses are more common among sedentary, monogomous people.[23] Still, the circle and square may be lived in similarly, and they formally transform into each other. The square English house shape seems surely to be a descendent of the hut circle found prehistorically across Britain;[24] circular English hop kilns became square when conceptually transported to New York

State in the nineteenth century;[25] and the current introduction of rectangular forms into the areas of West Africa, where the round home is the norm, is leading simultaneously to the adoption of foreign housing ideas and the modification of circular forms in the direction of the square.[26]

Thus reinforced by its existence, at least potentially, in the cultural inventories of Afro- as well as Anglo-Virginians, the square became basic to New World domestic architecture. If that square were always measured by a sixteen-foot rod along each of its sides, we might be justified in defining it as the ideal existential volume for Middle Virginia people. Alternative explanations for the shape might be devised; it could be the optimum size for efficient heating with a single fireplace, and a depth of sixteen feet might be the ideal span for a single wooden beam. This last is the weakest idea. Sixteen to eighteen feet was often the maximum span in the English tradition of cruck building, in which timbers arch from the ground to the roof's peak in a single sweep (Fig. 66B), but crucked buildings of much greater depth were built.[27] More important, the technological limitations placed on a room's depth fail to provide any explanation for the room's width; in fact, the cruck-built bays tend to be closer to twelve feet wide.[28] And plenty of wood-technical traditions involve timbers running less or more than sixteen feet.

Around Gum Spring the square of some houses is sixteen feet, but the actual range is from twelve to nineteen feet on each side. The geometric idea, in short, was given precedence over the psyche's comfort. The squared volume was probably comfortably familiar, but it cannot be said that the designer was striving foremost to meet the needs of personal space; clearly his major directive was to adhere to an intellectual model that demanded a specific geometric image. If we return to antecedents, we find that the prehistoric circular homes of southwestern England averaged in the sixteen-foot neighborhood, but varied from ten to twenty-five feet in diameter;[29] ancient Teapot Hall in Lincolnshire was, like several of the houses in our area, nineteen feet square;[30] and, though many of the circular homes of Ghana seem to be about sixteen feet across, they range from at least ten to twenty-five feet.[31]

In rooms quite different in size the fireplace is identical in depth and breadth (see Fig. 36). The designer stuck to his model for hearths despite differences in the contexts in which they would have to perform. In winter the house's inhabitants had to shift into smaller rooms or huddle closely around the fireplace in a large room.

In resolving the opposition of intellect and emotion, the house is an expression of a cultural idea that valued the intellectual model over emotional need. It is not that the spaces provided by the house for human action were dysfunctional, but that the people were willing to endure chilly corners or rooms that may have felt a bit spacious or cramped in order to live in a house that was a perfect representation of an idea. Nonreflectively, perhaps, they would rather have a little house that looked like a big one, or a big one that looked like a little one, than to have a house that deviated from traditional plan to suit particular need. It is likely that any physical discomfort that resulted from adhering so tightly to type was not registered in the consciousness, and it is apparent that the designer

considered his task to be less that of building to suit behavioral need than that of giving substance to an idea. The mediation of behavior and idea has a measurable tolerance—the square can be four feet less or three feet more than sixteen feet on each side—but there was no compromise at all with the mind's geometry. The space was square. All the tolerance had to be absorbed by the folks within the rooms.

The designer's problem, as we have been lucidly shown by Christopher Alexander,[32] is fitting form to context. Alerted by recent communication theory to the complexities of creating that fit, many have founded models of the delicate contexting process on the assumption that such a fit is always the designer-communicator's goal. But the ethnographer of conversation soon finds that much talk is assertion despite context, that whole traditions of oral artistic performance are predicated on continuing the course of a presentation whether it prompts the proper audience response or not. If the human being acted in the way that the analyst knows he is theoretically capable of acting, all jokes would get laughs and all political speeches would get cheers.

To locate his form perfectly in context, the designer must strike an enormously complex balance among numerous possibilities. The possibilities, in fact, are so numerous that the design problem is theoretically too complicated to solve. It was solved, and successfully, because rather than thinking his act through as a series of problems,[33] the folk architect stuck by a traditional form that incorporated the results of millennia of experimentation. Acting with forms as givens, the folk designer's real problems were small ones with easy solutions. His greatest problems were solved when he accepted the traditional forms that were efficient summaries of problems already solved. His procedure was to keep on replicating forms—to stay within his traditional competence—until the form appeared wrong. So long as it did not appear wrong, he did not need to question it.

Once, while attempting to discover the patterns I knew were present in the proper audience behavior at country-and-western music performance, I repeatedly failed to develop a full description of correct etiquette—for correct behavior included so many features—until my attention was turned to the incorrect behavior manifested by drunks, children, college students new to the situation, and, especially, to the improprieties crystalized in the performance of hillbilly clowns. After the wrong was defined, the parameters of rightness emerged clearly.[34]

In like manner, it would seem that until the designer observes a failure in particularistic context, such as a big square room that is just too cold, he does not view his design as a composition of distinct structures and elements. Until something goes wrong, he does not resort to cogitating about abstracted context: the thing may not fit well, but it fits well enough. Because contextual problems are more often solved unconsciously through the making of form than consciously through the analysis of context, the expressed object solves problems that nobody knows it is solving. For this reason some have been tempted by facile but false superorganic explanations,[35] and Lévi-Strauss can speak of the myth as operating on its own in the minds of men.[36] Also, for this reason, when a form is disassembled all of the results of that fragmentation cannot be foreseen, and waves of latent functioning may spread from progress to decay.[37] By turning his back on tradition the architect can produce transcendent celebrations like Notre Dame du Haut, or he can produce for a college building an artistic looking ramp that is treacherously slippery in the Cambridge winter.

Imagine a continuum, defined against context, stretching from the superrational to madness, from perfect communication to introverted babbling. A culture's logic lies between these poles. There are some who strain to drive beyond the logic provided in their culture to ever more rational fits between form and context. Their efforts may lead to the improvement of their culture's logic, or they may lead to proof that the continuum, as always, is circular. Attempts to fit context perfectly may result in a madness identical to that created out of a competence too little conditioned by context. The folk architect's logic was culturally circumscribed and, therefore, normally in balance. He could build a fireplace that would draw and a room that was an acceptable image. Perhaps the corners were a bit cool, but if he started worrying about the corners, the middle of his design might cease to hold, and mental anarchy would reign. Of course, if the corners became too cold that was another matter: the composition would emerge in consciousness, and modest innovations would, of necessity, have to be tried.

The square is a constant, tying the houses of different times into a single tradition, but a second mediator of the structure of content underwent radical alteration in time. This is the relation between inhabitants and visitors— the opposition of internal and external humanity. With the buildings of the first architectural phase the visitor entered directly into the house's main room (X), where the family might be eating or chatting by the fire. About four steps would take him into the smaller room (Y), which served as the master bedroom. In the next phase, the visitor entered a hallway and had to walk half its length to reach the main room. To get to the bedroom, now situated on an upper floor, he would have to pass back through the hall, ascend a flight of stairs, and again traverse half the length of an upper hallway. Between the older and newer houses there was a near volumetric identity; basically, the small early house (type 5) and the small late house (the two-thirds subtype 14) had two rooms, and the large early house (type 6) and the large late house (types 14–15) had four rooms. But the arrangement of those volumes was dissimilar, and that dissimilarity signals a great change in the desire for privacy. In the new house the most public room was only as accessible as the most private room was in earlier buildings.

Another indicator of the increase in the need for privacy is found in a change in the location of the stairway. In the Georgian house, the stairway opened toward the front of the hallway, and that is how the stair is positioned in the early XY₃X I houses (Figs. 41, 43). In the nineteenth century, here as elsewhere in the South,[38] the stair was often reversed to lead up from the rear of the hall (Fig. 44), further removing the upper floor from the visitor. These changes may be taken as an example of the workings of the cultural unconscious. The hallway and the reversed stair may not have been consciously planned to achieve privacy, but they surely resulted in an increase in privacy. Their acceptance must be taken as a probably unconscious approval of that result and as an

indicator of a possibly conscious, probably unconscious, certainly genuine desire for privacy.

Slowly after this abrupt change, another occurred that served to diminish its impact. The first houses generated out of an XY₃X base structure were often located, as earlier houses had been, far off the road. From about the beginning of the nineteenth century houses came to be positioned closer and closer to the road, until by the end of the century they were built by the roadside. Although the early house had been planned so that one entered immediately into the center of the action of its inhabitants, it had been put at a great distance from the road, enabling its family to observe the arrival of strangers. The later house brought this transitional zone within its walls, but the house itself was located closer to the routes of public motion. This change might, then, be counted as a net functional balance, but it is more an approximate equivalence than an identity: the change for the person crossing the threshold was great, for he was standing in a dark, unheated hallway, not within the hearthside glow. The house types effected a greater distancing between the family and outsiders.

It had always been possible to follow a route through the house, but now that route was marked by the walls of the hallway (compare, in order, Figs. 31, 32, 41). An old action—that of passing through—which had formerly been one of the diverse uses of the main room, was now separated analytically and provided with its own specific form. The house-as-idea had been moved along Humphry Osmond's spectrum away from the sociopetal toward the sociofugal.[39] That means that the form was being used increasingly to move people through it rather

121

than into it, and people were a notch nearer being treated more like objects than human beings.

Although the house viewed against time reveals a steady escalation in the wish for privacy—in the separation of us and them—another characteristic of the house that lies within the same structure saw no mutations. The house's lower floor always follows with exactness one of a small set of recognizable architectural types. Upon entering the house for the first time, the local visitor would know its plan—predictable from its façade—and the uses to which each of its rooms was put. He could find his way through it effortlessly. The first floor conformed thoroughly to type; the upstairs, however, was often varied to suit idiosyncratic need (see rules III.A.1 and VI.A.2). The less private lower floor functioned as a sign of solidarity within the community; it was easily read and it said to the visitor that he shared with the people of the house a sense of immediate environment and a similar mode of thought.

In structuring its inhabitants in relation to other people, the house, through the predictability of its lower floor plan, was cohesive, but the path it dictated from the road to the house's center functioned as a separator.

THE HOUSE IN NATURE

"The central problem of anthropology," Lévi-Strauss wrote, is "the passage from nature to culture."[40] Man, contemplating his relationship with nature, soliloquizing in myth and totem about connective and disjunctive structures, is a regular player in the Lévi-Straussian theater. No expression of culture more obviously mediates between the natural and the cultural than the object of

material culture, for the artifact is the medium of transfer within the ecological system—that system which, as Robert Redfield noted, interrelates the coexistent "natural and artificial" realities.[41] And within the ecological system the most direct confrontation of culture and nature occurs in the heat of technological manipulation.

Technology is the means by which the natural literally becomes the cultural, by which the substances won from nature become useful to man.[42] The New World set a Herculean task for Old World technologies. With his back to the Atlantic winds, the new Virginian faced an endlessly dense, horrifying forest. He was not wholly unready. His anthropocentric Christian religion, from which animism had been banished,[43] gave him leave to strike into the natural woodlands, subduing them to his own design. His West African deities supported him similarly: Gu gave the Dahomeans iron, and Ogun gave it to the Yoruba—iron for piercing, cutting into the ground, stabbing enemies, and felling trees.[44] In West Africa his clearings had been surrounded by forests from which he regularly had to chop new grounds.[45] Although centuries

Fig. 51   AN ENGLISH FRAME. The interior of a barn in Checkenden, Oxfordshire, England (June 1972). It is contemporary with the buildings framed in the traditional Tidewater way (Fig. 52). Note the use of curved wood. This was due in part to the limited supply of timber, but English buildings of later date, when the timber supply was still shorter, display the same rigid, artificial lines seen in eighteenth-century American frames. Curved timbers also indicate an English willingness to deal with natural shapes.

of labor had largely eliminated the English and Irish forests,[46] at the time of settlement in America, farmers in Devonshire were still battling to clear portions of the wild waste, and English adventurers in Ulster were cutting through thick, dense timber.[47]

Arable land lay under the forests. If the trees were cut down, the turf would be exposed to the plow. If the trees were cut down, they could be altered from noisome encumbrances into building material. The first job of the new Virginian was to attack the trees. Come into "this Wildernesse of *Virginia*," the initial planters set to work in the woods immediately. May 1607: "Now falleth every man to worke, the Councell contriue the Fort, the rest cut downe trees to make place to pitch their Tents; some provide clapbord to relade the ships."[48] The next year the second supply of planters commenced its American sojourn similarly: "No sooner were we landed, but the President dispersed many as were able. . . . 30 of vs he conducted 5. myles from the fort to learn to make clapboard, cut downe trees, and ly in woods."[49] The clapboard and wainscot wrested from the wood were the first exports, and the same woodworking skills were used in building the houses which, in 1610, were described as being "as warme and defensiue against wind and weather, as if they were tiled and slated, being couered

Fig. 52 THE TIDEWATER FRAME. The plate and rafter framing and the large braces are all characteristic of eighteenth- and early nineteenth-century construction in the country west of the Chesapeake. The middle bent of house G is pictured; the rafters drawn above are those between the bents.

124

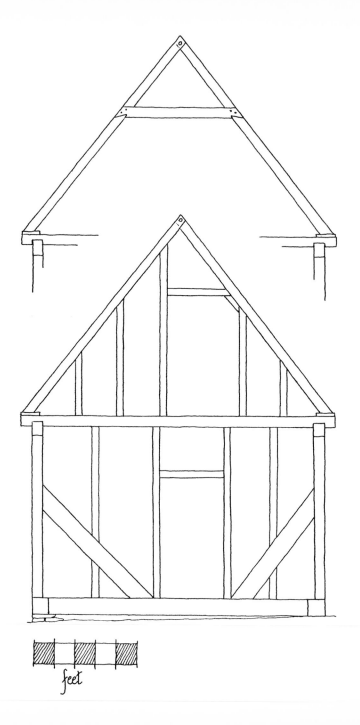

aboue with strong boards." [50] As the governor's report for 1611–12 noted, those houses were "of framed timber." [51]

It became *de rigueur* for the early commentators to compliment the colonists on their attempts at building in masonry, but the Virginia house was, through and through, a thing of wood. Hugh Jones wrote in 1724: "Here [Williamsburg], as in other parts, they build with brick, but most commonly with timber lined with cieling, and cased with feather-edged plank, painted with white lead and oil, covered with shingles of cedar, etc. tarred over at first. . . ." [52] Writing about sixty years later, Thomas Jefferson was annoyed by the prejudice of his fellow Virginians against masonry houses:

> The private buildings are very rarely constructed of stone or brick; much the greatest portion being of scantling and boards, plastered with lime. It is impossible to devise things more ugly, uncomfortable, and happily more perishable. There are two or three plans, on one of which, according to its size, most of the houses in the state are built. [53]

Only three of the old houses in our area were made of bricks (Fig. 32 is an example); the remainder were wooden. The Indian in Virginia planted into the earth pliable poles, unchanged from their natural dimensions, bent them into a barrel-vaulted shape, lashed them together, and covered the form with bark, boughs, or mats to make his home. [54] The newcomers to his land began with the same natural resource, but they served it more savagely, turning wood not into houses, but into lumber—and then into houses. In England, framing members had often followed the natural taper or curve of the tree as it grew (Figs. 51, 66). The sticks in the Middle Virginia frame, however, are sharply straight, and they were taken as far from the natural shape as the traditional technology would allow. The framing members were hewn square, then pitsawed into halves or thirds so that the posts at the corners and the large braces that were framed in between the posts and the sills (Fig. 52) were all, in section, rectangular to about a 2 : 1 or 3 : 1 ratio. The result was a delicate wall. Corner posts and interior timbers were laboriously hewn and adzed, large portions of their bulk being chopped away and wasted in order to maintain this effect (Fig. 53).

Old houses are often distinguished from newer ones on the basis of the thickness of their walls, but in Middle Virginia, the late nineteenth-century adoption of the balloon frame engendered no change in the house's appearance, for the walls of even the mid-eighteenth-century house were only about five inches thick. These walls were framed—in the early days framed after the manner traditional to the Tidewater (Fig. 54)—but one eighteenth-century house in our area, and one of much later date, were built out of horizontal logs (Figs. 35, 80). Log construction was unknown in England [55] and was not a major part of the domestic architectural traditions of the early Anglo-American colonies, [56] so it is to be expected that Middle Virginia would be a frame-using area.

In the middle of the nineteenth century the idea of log construction diffused eastward from the Appalachian domain. [57] It is, therefore, no surprise to find the Smith house, built around 1880 according to B. B. Harris who owns it, constructed in the Piedmont way: logs hewn on two faces, chinked with staubs and mud, and corner-timbered less well than houses found to the west in the Blue Ridge (Figs. 55c, 80). The construction of the earlier

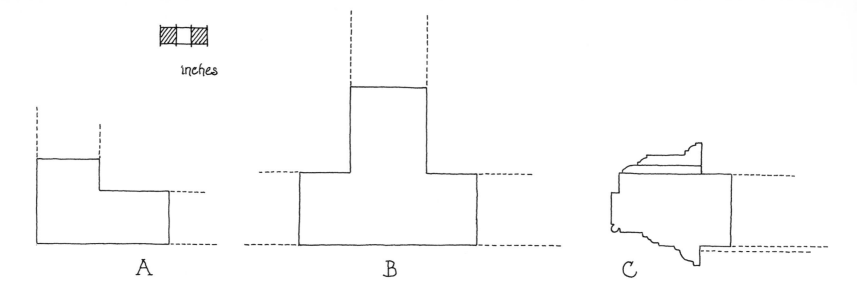

inches

A

B

C

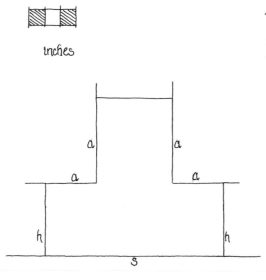

inches

Fig. 53 SECTIONS THROUGH VERTICAL FRAMING MEMBERS.
A. Corner post, house G. B. Post of the middle bent, house T. C.
Door frame, house V. B illustrates the technology clearly: the
front face is pitsawed, the side faces are hewn, the inside areas
are adzed—that is, a hewn beam was sawed in half, then adzed
away to produce a T-shaped post that kept the wall thin. C
illustrates the technical concept because here, as at house N,
the exterior molding and the door stop were formed out of a
single piece of lumber; wood was cut away, rather than being
built up. (The interior molding, at the top in the drawing, was
nailed on.) The old carpenters were remarkably good with their
tools.

Fig. 54 THE TIDEWATER FRAME. This photograph, taken in
July 1926, comes from the private collection of the architect
E. W. Donn. It shows the spinning house—Donn dated it 1700
to 1725—at King Carter's plantation at Weems, Virginia. The
typical plate and brace framing can be seen.

126

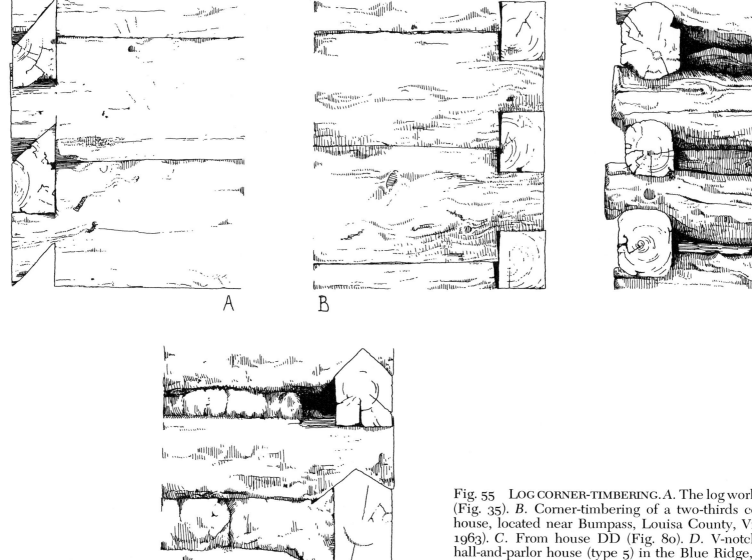

Fig. 55   LOG CORNER-TIMBERING. A. The log work of house M (Fig. 35). B. Corner-timbering of a two-thirds central-hall I house, located near Bumpass, Louisa County, Virginia (July 1963). C. From house DD (Fig. 80). D. V-notching from a hall-and-parlor house (type 5) in the Blue Ridge, located between Boonesville and Browns Cove, Albemarle County, Virginia (August 1964).

log house in our area, however, refuses to be explained away so neatly. Like another house—two-thirds of type 14—located east of our area near Bumpass (Fig. 55B), and like the garrison houses of New England[58] and a couple of inadequately explained houses in New Jersey[59]—but unlike the usual log houses built from Pennsylvania through the Upland South (Fig. 55D)—this house has no interstices between its logs (Fig. 55A). Now where the idea for this half-dovetailed construction came from I do not know, but it is technologically akin to the area's framed houses, for its walls are composed of square-hewn timbers, pitsawed in half to measure but 4¾ inches in width; the sawed faces were turned to the exterior and covered first with pitsawed clapboards and later with circular sawed vertical boards. The little eighteenth-century Parrish house, though log, presented the same light appearance as did the framed houses (Fig. 35).

Timbers with slim, planklike sections were used in framing great halls in northwestern England in the fourteenth century. It is not inconceivable that the practice survived late enough in the English West Country to have been known to the carpenters who emigrated in the seventeenth century, but the use of planklike framing members was not part of the normal building traditions of Britain at the time of American colonization.[60] Being accustomed to the heavy framing members of the Mid-Atlantic and Northern regions in the United States, I have often stopped in the field to contemplate the light timbers of the Chesapeake country. The plate of an old house in Pennsylvania, for example, might be a foot square, whereas the plate of the Lesser Dabney house (Figs. 46, 68, 69) measured 4 × 8 inches. It is certainly not that big

pieces of wood were not available or could not be handled. The summer beam supporting the first-floor joists of the Parrish mansion (Fig. 36) is a foot square (see also Fig. 53), but the wall framing members of that same house, like those of the Rigsby house (Fig. 41), are only 4 inches thick.

The frame composed of planks seems to have been a Tidewater innovation, and the delicate walls that resulted seem to have been part of a Tidewater aesthetic. Ruminating on the matter has carried me back across the Atlantic to places from which people came to Virginia, but not to Pennsylvania or New England. West Africa was a land of consummate woodworkers, and, according to Robert Farris Thompson, "relative delicacy" is a characteristic of the Yoruban aesthetic.[61] For example, canoes were dug out of logs around the Chesapeake Bay in the eighteenth and nineteenth centuries, in aboriginal America, Ireland, and West Africa.[62] In many parts of the world dugouts were made, but in Africa their walls were hewn to the thinnest dimensions.[63] In 1843 an American naval officer wrote concerning the "native canoe" of West Africa: "These little vessels are scooped out of a log, and are of even less size and capacity than the birch-canoes of our Indians, and so light that two men, using each a single hand, may easily carry them from place to place."[64]

Realizing that the slave was not, as had been suggested for so long, stripped of his culture, we are no longer surprised by the discovery of the endurance of African traditions in America, even material ones.[65] Folk traditions of African origin persisted, even within the most hostile contexts. The banjo, today the mainstay of bluegrass (the musical voice of rural white nativism), was brought, as Jefferson noted, "hither from Africa."[66] While visiting in Virginia in 1759, the good Reverend Burnaby observed the white folks performing "irregular and fantastical" dances they had learned "from the Negroes."[67] For centuries Afro-Americans have been sources of inspiration, as well as objects of scorn, for white America. Still, though it was mostly black energy that ripped those trees into lumber, the delicacy of the African woodworking tradition was, probably, at most a subordinate condition of the light-framing technology.

A more likely antecedent for the innovation might be located in English cruck building, as the great cruck blades were often hewn and then sawed lengthwise in half.[68] The principal rafters in the roof-framing tradition that succeeded crucked building, from Wiltshire west into Devon and Wales, are often sawed into planks like the cruck blades and like Tidewater corner posts. These observations, however, do not explain the technology of timber preparation in Virginia, especially because, unlike Englishmen in New England, Englishmen in Virginia did not simply continue an Old World practice. A list of possible sources for a practice is not an explanation of its existence.

The timber, it seems, was sawed after hewing, mainly to take it still further from its natural state. Hewn, then pitsawed, the framing member bore no reminder of its origin as a tree. Thin walls define a concept in the air with minimal obeisance to the natural substances of which they were composed. The main reason that wood was used was that it was present—too present. All those damned trees stood between man and his vision. The tree was chopped, drawn, hewn, sawed, chiseled, shaved,

pierced with nails, and hidden by paint. Nature was made to submit utterly to the ideas of men.

The house's skeleton was wood and so was its skin. Shingle roofs[69] and clapboard walls[70] are known in England, though they are limited in distribution. They were fading out of use in many areas at the time of colonization, to be replaced by tiles and thatch, plaster and slate—cladding that assisted in the conservation of the dwindling supply of wood. All the old wooden houses in our area were given an outside covering of boards: shingled tops, clapboarded sides. The interiors of early houses were often plastered (in England exteriors and floors had sometimes been plastered too), but the interiors, walls and ceilings alike, were also regularly covered with boards, as was often the case in the South.[71] Attic partitions—for example, in houses M and N—were occasionally sided with boards that overlapped like those of the exterior (a practice also apparently followed in the earliest New England houses[72]), but usually the boards, whether in early or late houses (G, U, and S are examples), were nailed to the studding horizontally and edge to edge (Fig. 56). Houses with plastered walls were often fitted with dadoes formed of horizontal boards (houses H and N are examples). Perhaps this internal and external redundancy of horizontal line had a quieting effect on the people of the houses—in some situations such a comment might seem preposterous, but, after all, these people existed within the great tradition that engulfs us as well. Whatever the cause, it is true that it would have been easier to apply the boards of the interior walls vertically in the way it was done in most of the United States. As was the case in the England of times long

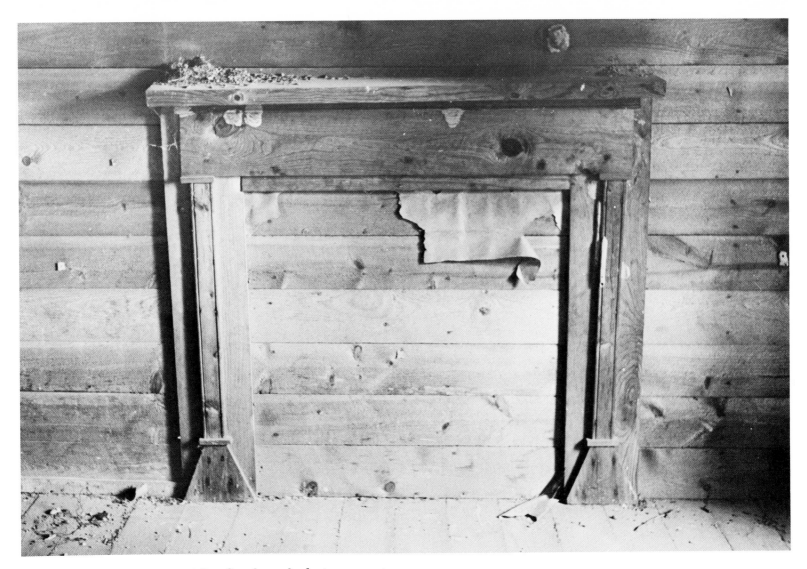

Fig. 56   BOARD INTERIOR. After fireplaces had given way to
stoves, houses were still fitted with mantels (see also Fig. 39A).
This is from house S (Fig. 42).

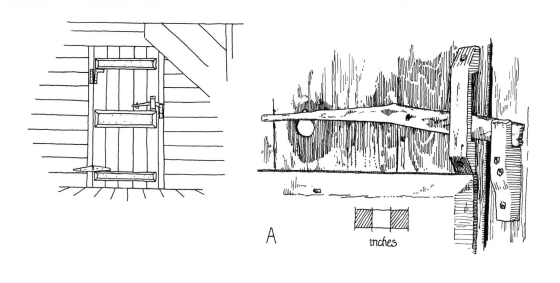

A

inches

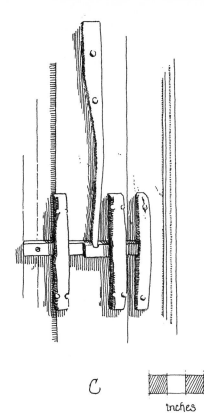

C

inches

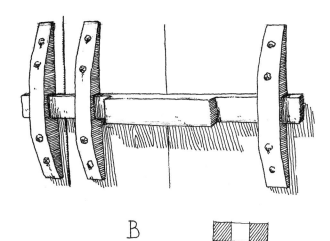

B

inches

Fig. 57   WOODEN LATCHES. *A*. Interior door, house G.
B. Front door, house M.
C. Upstairs interior door, house N.

past,[73] and in formative America[74] as well, even the latches on the doors were often carved out of wood (Fig. 57).

It is not the man of civilization, but the *Tempest*'s Caliban—"gentle," "monstrous," fit for a slave—who dwells in the forest, feeding on berries, pignuts, and marmoset meat.[75] When civilized man repairs to the forest he goes as fearfully as Young Goodman Brown, or he goes as militantly as an English or African peasant armed with honed iron. Looking only at the way wood was used, we can find no subtlety in the Middle Virginia mediation between nature and culture: the natural was violently altered to the cultural.[76] The romantic historian may impute to the old Virginians a love for nature[77] (a few of the Chesapeake Grandees of the eighteenth century may have been up on the latest French philosophies), but the average person has left his testimony in artifacts from which all hints of nature have been erased. For him, nature was both source and enemy.

A less sensational, albeit compatible, record is written in masonry. At the new house site a kiln was built where local clay was burned for bricks. Stone was available, and it was used to lay some foundations and build some chimneys up to the shoulders; stone chimneys were always topped out in brick (Figs. 29, 34, 44, 80). The simplest small house of all the historic phases, such as houses G, M, and DD, have stone foundations and chimneys, but brick was used in building finer houses (E, H, J, L, N, Q, R, T, V, for example). Twenty-two of the full XY₃X I houses (type 14) have external chimneys; all but two of these are brick (and one of those is covered with generations of whitewash). Half of the eight external

chimneys on the humbler two-thirds type 14 houses are stone (one of which is disguised as brick by red paint). Stone was clearly a sign of relatively low status, but there is nothing inherent in stone that should make it so. Many of the mansions in England were stone, and at least some of eastern Virginia's settlers left behind stone homes in southwestern England and the Welsh border country. Brick had been used in English construction through the Middle Ages, but it was during the sixteenth and seventeenth centuries that it became increasingly the dominant mode[78]—a fashion that was exaggerated during England's overseas expansion. Brickwork in Ireland stood out against the rocky backdrop as a symbol of the English planter's Georgian town.[79] Good resources for brick were among the attractions the New World held for the earliest settlers. In *A briefe and true report of the new found land of Virginia* (1586), Thomas Heriot wrote that the new planters would be "well supplied by bricke: for the making whereof in divers places of the Countrey there is clay both excellent good, and plentie...."[80]

Making a brick mass involved a central step in the technical procedure not present in stone masonry. Stones were collected, prepared, and made into foundations. In Ireland, Wales, Scotland, England, and Africa mud was comparably collected, prepared, and made into houses.[81] But a builder with bricks collects mud, prepares it, and makes it into bricks. Then he makes the bricks into a house. A burned brick outlasts a sun-dried mud wall, but this preference for brick over stone has, too, its cognitive dimension. The extra step in the kiln was logically the same as that taken in wood technology when logs were made lumber and then lumber was joined into a frame.

Burning the brick paralleled hewing and sawing the log; it marked man's unequivocal presence. This extra step was taken directly away from nature in the direction of artificiality. It generated repeatable, interchangeable units of uniform dimensions. Even when chiseled and pecked, the stone was a stone, but the brick was a man-made thing. The popularity of brickwork in the seventeenth, eighteenth, and nineteenth centures is an indication of the Anglo-American fondness for technological complication and conceptual simplification. It expressed a desire to control nature completely.

The more we peer, through artifacts, into the Middle Virginia mind, the more complicated its structuring appears. And yet the more logical that structuring appears. One of its oppositions was between the artificial idea (brick or timber, clapboard, shingle) and the natural substance (mud, trees). The resolution of that dichotomy came deeply out of the same mental drive that conquered the opposition of intellect (geometrical idea) and emotion (natural human need). These two oppositions, one a structure relating man to nature, the other a structure relating man to man, can be carried deeper into thought as a single opposition between the artificial and the natural. This culture inevitably resolves that opposition in favor of artificiality: geometry dominates need, the man-made dominates nature. These two structures are further bound tangentially by the opposition of geometry and nature—an opposition resolved wholly in the direction of geometry. The rules of the competence do not take into account the material of which the house will be built, except at one point, and at that point the problem of natural substances is explicitly excluded from the design-

ing process. This point is the rule (III.A.2) requiring that the size and shape of the room will not be influenced by the thickness of the walls defining it (Fig. 6). The house's internal shapes, then, will remain constant despite any change in the materials of which the house is composed. In many architectural traditions certain materials are invariably tied to certain house forms, but in Middle Virginia the abstract idea of house form is materialized without regard to the stuff of which it is constructed. The architect's decision to build of frame or log or brick will have no influence on the final shape of the dwelling; the substances won from nature must bow to geometric intentions. Because he is "preindustrial," the folk architect is often imagined as working through a problem by means of an organic dialectic of form and material, adapting one to suit the other in a free manner that suggests a high regard for natural substances.[82] The early Middle Virginia architect's technology was wholly preindustrial; it depended on muscle and sweat, but he still turned twisted logs into scantling of uniform dimensions, and he still exerted his mental geometry despite the natural substances with which he worked.

The oppositional structures examined so far do not exist in isolation as clean dichotomies. They are bound deeply to a multitude of other mental structures that serve to sharpen or soften the focus on our original oppositions. The relations between people, and between people and their natural environment, are structured together by a deep opposition of the internal and the external. In human relations, the internal-external opposition is that of the private and the public. In relations between man and nature, the opposition of internal and external is tied to that of the artificial and natural, for the internal is (private) artificial, man-handled land, as distinct from the external (public) raw wilderness. As a structure of cultural logic, then, our four discriminations are bound as two sets of two: man-man and man-nature internal to external structures; man-man and man-nature artificial to natural structures. These structures could also be read in the other direction with equal validity and suggestiveness: internal-external and artificial-natural man-to-man structures; internal-external and artificial-natural man-to-nature structures (Fig. 58). In each case, mediation favored the artificial and the internal in Middle Virginia. There are differences, however. The inferences drawn from old houses, as we shall see, indicate that artificiality and internalness were less aggressively mediated in man-to-man relations than in man-to-nature relations. People treated other people logically in the way they treated nature—but much less openly so. This is another indicator of the Middle Virginian's sin of *superbia* in natural contexts. It is evidence, too, that while he identified with his friends and neighbors, in his logic lay, coiled like a rattler, the potential for him to strike out against people as he had against trees.

One of the bonds, deep in thought, is seen clearly only when it is extended in time. The course of the mediation of the internal-external opposition in the nature-culture set was plainly established as soon as Captain John Smith's fellows started splitting trees into clapboard, but the parallel course of the mediation of the internal-external opposition in the man-to-man set was not obvious until the XY3X base structure enabled the builder to express his desire for privacy in wood. Earlier, the house

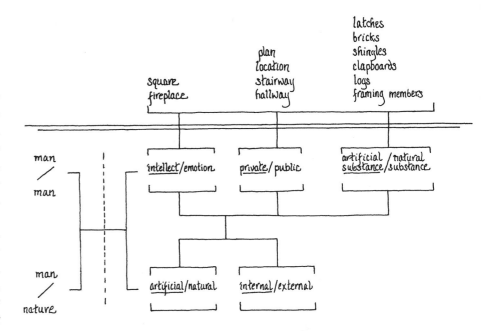

Fig. 58 PRELIMINARY DIAGRAM OF A SEGMENT OF THE MIDDLE VIRGINIA ARCHITECTURAL LOGIC. Above the double line are observable architectural phenomena that exhibit patterning. Below the lines are some of the oppositional structures in thinking. Those to the left of the dotted line are among the oppositions of the real world that are mediated by reference to the still more abstract categories to the right. The underlined term in each pair is that favored in Middle Virginia. Being totally interrelated, this structure can be rearranged into a large number of different binary sets. It is not, however, a sequence of binary oppositions; it is the simultaneous opposition of fourteen abstract possibilities. The realization of these possibilities is found in the architectural facts listed above the double line.

alone did not signal that desire, although its remote setting did. The feeling of separateness was always there, but it is brought into relief by comparison in time. Taking off from an insight dropped casually in the beautiful *Tristes Tropiques*[83]—an insight not incompatible with comments offered occasionally by historians of the frontier—New World man's separateness from nature and his separateness from other men are linked diachronically as well as synchronically. His first task was to distinguish himself from the wilderness. Once the colonist had tamed nature, then he could turn to the luxury of withdrawing farther from the company of other men. His prime distinction then shifted from cleared land versus the wilderness to private territory versus public space.

Moving to an examination of other relations manifested in houses, we find the mind unfolding continuously, variously, but within limits. Like the pointillist's canvas, which seems from one view chaotic but from another nicely patterned, the mind presents its logic to the critic.

The house's most obvious function is to provide a buffer between man and the weather so that he is free to attend to problems other than climatic ones. Ideal solutions to this problem have been found by students of the architecture paradoxically called primitive: the snow dome of the Arctic and the open home of the tropics are perfect shelters.[84] The mid-eighteenth-century Virginia house illustrates many of the principles known to be the proper response to the climate.[85] Writing in 1705, Robert Beverley, who identified himself as "an *Indian*" and by "Plainness" as a citizen of the New World, correctly[86] assessed Virginia's weather as "hot and moist" and noted that the Virginians had begun to build to suit their climatic context: "They always contrive to have large Rooms, that they may be cool in Summer. Of late they have made their Stories much higher than formerly and their Windows Large, and sasht with Cristal Glass. . . ."[87] Roofs of the old houses are pitched steeply to shed the rain, ceilings are high, and the building is "raised" between 3 and 6 feet off the ground (see Figs. 27, 38) to remove it from the steamy earth where mosquitoes play.[88] In following the medieval architectural norm of the British Isles, and designing his house to be but a single room in depth, the builder provided the dwelling with breezy cross ventilation[89] through windows and doors that were tall and wide.

This environmental savvy was surely among the affective conditions during the development of the architectural competence of the second phase, after the Georgian type had been introduced. If adopted, the double-pile Georgian plan would have blocked the flow of air through the building, but the Georgian central hallway assisted the air's movement. The hallway sucks air through the house as a microclimatic consequence of the fact that one side of the house would be hotter than the other.[90] Hugh Jones was aware of this back in 1724. After noting that a little movement in the air "is very grateful in violent hot weather," he stated that there is ". . . a passage generally through the middle of the house for an air-draught in summer. Thus their houses are . . . cool in summer; especially if there be windows enough to draw the air."[91]

The early Middle Virginia architect solved the problem of his humid, hot climate by building a raised house, one room deep, with a central hall, steep roof, and high ceilings. From the beginning of the nineteenth century on, the local architect proceeded to erect buildings less and less suited to the environment. Roofs became flatter, houses were no longer raised, ceilings fell, doors and windows became smaller, and appendages that in the eighteenth century were generally made to the house's ends, in order to maintain the airflow (Figs. 29, 31, 34, 35, 36, 41, 45), were placed on the backs of the houses (Fig. 19), thus preventing the circulation of air as effectively as the adoption of the two-room-deep Georgian plan would have.

Some of the early houses, located far off the main throughways, were so positioned that they did not align in a parallel manner with the road. Fourteen of the central-hall I houses were located at some remove from the road. Nine faced the road, but of those that did not, two faced east and one each faced north, south, and west (this last was named "Westview"). Among other early houses built so that they did not front the road were houses M, N, and V, all of which faced north.

The pattern of these situations is not clear. If a house faces the road (as most of them do), the variables in siting are too many for us to be able to reconstruct the builder's intentions, and we must assume that facing the road was an aesthetic desideratum. But when the house does not face the road, a possibility for speculation is opened. All of these houses were located on flat ground, save the Rigsby house, which faces downhill (Fig. 41), so it seems that topography is not the cause. It is possible that their locations were suggested by some aspect of the climate, such as prevailing winds. If that is so, then the fact that the later house invariably faces the road, no matter how subjected to wind or heat, is another instance of Faustian climatic contexting. The old house was always built for shade in a hardwood grove. This tradition continued into our century, though recently some people, much to their expressed chagrin, have cut away the trees, not realizing what function they filled until they were gone.

The overall effect of this failure of environmental suitability, seen in the later house itself and its invariable orientation to the road, was softened a bit by the factor of the front porch. The absence of a porch was another index to low status. Houses G, M, and DD, all of which have stone chimneys, never had porches; houses H, R, and V, all of which have brick chimneys, did have porches. The early fine house, however, might have had no porch (Figs. 38, 43), and if it did have one it was small (Figs. 31, 36, 41). The eighteenth-century porch was not dissimilar in size and shape to the porches built onto seventeenth-century English houses, still to be seen in the English West Country and in Ireland. The British porch is usually enclosed, whereas the porch in Virginia is open (a skeletal representation of the British prototype), but they functioned similarly as sheltered extensions of the entrance. The porch of the nineteenth century, however, was a living space between the indoors and the outdoors, a room that stretched the length of the façade (for all the world like a veranda in Yorubaland[92]), providing a place to escape from the inferno inside, to rock and watch the action on the road. Toward the beginning of the twentieth century the porch became less and less a usual appendage and people had to swelter inside or move their chairs into a shady patch in the yard.

The weather did not cool off during the nineteenth century. It is possible that later generations became more used to the heat and did not feel a need to plan for it, but the heat in August still comes on like a hangover and provides the major topic for phlegmatic conversations in the country stores. Possibly the people grew cooler. Be that as it may, we do have another proof of the principle that change in time is not necessarily productive of greater and greater technological efficiency.[93] Through time, the Middle Virginia house steadily became a less efficient modifier of the climate. This does not mean that the people went crazy, but that their primary problem became other than climatological or technological—"technomic," Lewis Binford would say[94]—and that the lessening of environmental suitability was a side effect of logical adjustment in another part of the design field.

The dwindling of the house's ability to defend its people against their climate is one of the faces of a larger change in time that starts near the end of the eighteenth century and does not seem to have stopped. Tearing a page from Robert Plant Armstrong's anthropological phenomenology,[95] we may name the more powerful opposition within which the house as climatic modifier was dependently, though not obviously, embedded as that of extensiveness versus intensiveness. The capacity of the house to fend off damp heat was subordinate to its existence as an expression of a logic that drifted constantly from the extensive toward the intensive. Our problem now is to determine whether the architectural phenomenon, as an expression of cultural logic, extends itself outward, or whether it is drawn back into itself.

The architectural characteristics that defined the house as being a good fit in a hot, wet context were all extensive: the house was lifted from the earth; the ceilings of its rooms ran high; the roof above reached sharply into the air; additions on its ends extended its length. These features made the summer sufferable. The devolution in environmental efficiency is an essay in the evolution of intensiveness. The early roof pitch was above 50 degrees; by the second quarter of the nineteenth century it had fallen to below 30 degrees. Not all the early houses were raised, but some were, and that option was lost in the 1800s. The ceiling of the fine early house was generally about 10 feet from the floor, but even a poor early house, like house G, had ceilings 8½ feet high (Figs. 29, 52), whereas the Smith house (Fig. 80), comparable in size and status but a century younger, has a ceiling a full 2 feet lower, barely 6½ feet high. The early house had high vertical windows. The first-floor windows of houses E, N, R, and T have nine-over-nine lights. The upper floor's windows are often lower; house N has nine-over-nine second-story sash, but the second-story windows of houses E and T are six-over-nine and those of house R are nine-over-six. The Watson house has nine-over-six windows on the first floor, and its second floor windows have six-over-six lights. Some early buildings, such as the Moore house (Fig. 31), had six-over-six windows, but by the middle of the nineteenth century only the six-over-six form was used. The nine-over-nine sash of the Brooking house were replaced at some point with six-over-six windows, the resultant space being blocked off (see Fig. 33). At the end of the century, windows generally had one or two lights in a sash of the size that once held six lights (Figs. 16, 48), but—as a tracer of the continuity of

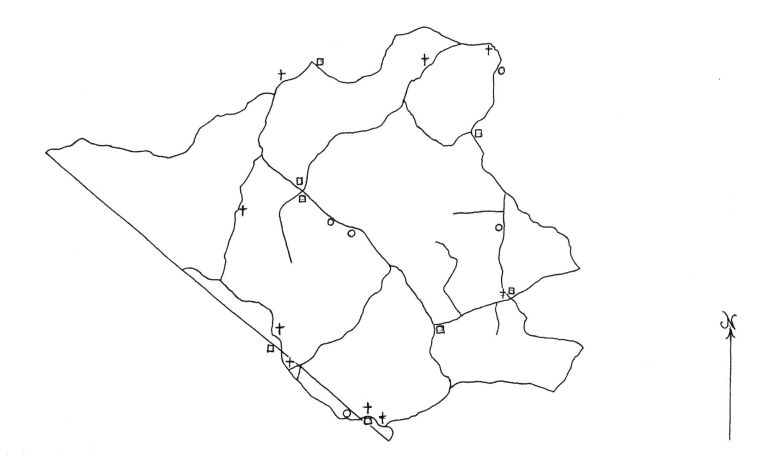

○   School

✝   Church

☐   Store

Miles

Fig. 59 DISTRIBUTION OF INSTITUTIONAL ARCHITECTURE.

139

the delicate aesthetic—the six-light sash was used in the building of many modest houses even into the twentieth century.

What this means is that through time windows became smaller, letting less air and light into the home. Doors, too, became narrower. Several of the end-of-the-eighteenth-century houses—E, R, and T, for example—had double doors. The front door of the Rigsby house is 3′ 8″ wide and that of the Rackett house is but an inch less (Figs. 41, 43). The Watson house, with only one room to a floor, has a single front door 3′2″ wide (Fig. 34), and even the front door of the little Parrish cabin is 3′1″ wide (Fig. 35). House S, though larger (four times the size of the Parrish house), was built in the last half of the nineteenth century, and its front door is 2′8½″ wide (Fig. 42). The front door of the contemporary Smith house is less than 6 feet high and less than 3 feet wide (Fig. 80). (Consider the reinforcing effect of entering and exiting from buildings through doorways that had, in less than a century, become more constricted by a full foot.) The dormer, extending out from the roof to bring light into the attic, was, with few exceptions, eliminated from the architectural vocabulary of the nineteenth century. And additions, instead of pushing out from the house's ends, were tucked around back. All of these indications of the shift away from extensiveness are tied to the house's role as shelter, but they do not exhaust the list of architectural indications of the transformation in thinking from the extensive to the intensive.

At its most coarse-grained, extensiveness is exhibited at the landscape level of the architectural particularistic context—in the settlement pattern. Old Virginia, our piece of it being no exception, is a land of scattered court houses and dispersed holdings.[96] Hamlets have developed around Gum Spring (listed at population, forty) and Inez, but like the Virginia of the eighteenth century there are "no towns of any consequence."[97] Stores, schools, post offices, and churches are located at crossroads, but not usually the same crossroads (Fig. 59). The dead are dispersed in numerous, independent family burying grounds. Lonely, its back to the woods, each farm is separated from the other. Even when the house was built directly on the road, there is rarely another facing it. Our image of medieval England includes compact and cooperative open-field villages.[98] Down the country's center, the farm people did cluster into agricultural villages, but when the settlement of America began farmers had been living for centuries on separated farms on the Dorset heath and in Devonshire in the west, Suffolk in the east, Cumberland and Yorkshire in the north, and in the hills of Ireland and Wales.[99] In Devonshire and Suffolk both, the practice of creating assarts in the forest as seats for farm homes had led to the same images that characterize the Middle Virginia landscape: the meandering proliferation of small roads and the lone farmhouse set away from the road at the end of a long lane. Behind many of the new Virginians lay open-field villages, but many others knew the dispersed plan and they lost no time in sowing it in the new soil.

When Captain Samuel Argall took over the government of Virginia in 1617,

> In *Iames* towne he found but fiue or six houses, the Church downe, the Palizado's broken, the Bridge in pieces, the Well of fresh water spoiled; the Store-house they vsed for the

Church; the market-place, and streets, and all other spare places planted with Tobacco: the Saluages as frequent in their houses as themselues . . . ; the Colonie dispersed all about, planting *Tobacco*.[100]

Although William Bradford read the auguries of dispersion when Plymouth Colony was still new,[101] it took much longer for the village to yield to the independent farmstead in New England.[102] From Virginia's beginning, however, the pattern was set. Neither danger nor disaster nor the many official complaints of "the Honourable company of Planters and well-willers to *Virginia, New-England and Sommer-Ilands*" could stay them; the massacre of 1622 found them off on scattered farms.[103] Laws were passed to encourage people to gather into towns, but the wild space had to be conquered, given no quarter, and claimed for man.

This act of dispersing habitations and services—an act that the city planner calls "scatterization"[104]—is extensive. Too, it mediates between culture and nature by altering virgin tracts to fertile farmland, chaotic forests to orderly yards. Productive of rapid artificiality, it also favors the internal over the external by creating a clearing out of the wilderness and by locating that clearing far from the public highways and far from the cleared territories of other people. At once the threatening land was brought to heel and zones were erected between greedy men. The movement toward intensiveness should have led from the scattered farms of the extensive eighteenth century to tight villages. Through the nineteenth century people moved closer to the road and closer to one another; scatterization was greatly diminished, but it did not give way to the village.

We cannot, of course, *know* what lay deep in the cultural logic, but if we have a desire to understand the Middle Virginian, we must consider alternative explanations of his behavior and, perhaps, settle on one of them as best.[105] The most efficient explanation for the facts at hand arises from the possibility that the extensive-intensive structure was related in thought to the artificial-natural and internal-external structures. Were a village created, then, the land would have to be surrendered back to the forest (given the fact of the slight rise in population) and privacy would be difficult to maintain. In fact, the forest has returned, reclaiming in pine much of the surface that was once farmed. Even so, fences still mark out man's domain, and even the brick ranchers are generally spaced broadly apart. In the settlement pattern of the nineteenth century there was a movement toward increased intensiveness balanced against the simultaneous movement toward privacy. The result—houses by the road, but separate—is the resolution of a new opposition relating two other oppositions. It is the three-point mediation between intensiveness, internalness, and artificiality: the new pattern is intensive (compacted), but only to the extent allowed by internalness (privacy) and artificiality (opposition to nature).

One of the major attributes of extensive thought is the analytical ability to fragment organic wholes, breaking into parts things that are conceptual units. Just as the settlement's functions—sacred and secular, mercantile and agrarian—were scattered over the land, the individual farm's functions were scattered into sundry buildings. In Britain, at the time of colonization, the farm's functions had often been gathered under the roof of a

141

single edifice or joined within a line or square of buildings.[106] A single architectural form sheltered the labor and life of men and women, children and parents, animals and humans. Intriguingly, in most of the rough areas where the settlement was most dispersed, such as parts of Devonshire and Wales, the farm's architecture was most unified. The longhouse, with people at one end and beasts at the other (Fig. 60), protected the cattle from two- and four-legged predators. Perhaps, too, it served as a compensatory fortress against the surrounding natural wilderness, which provided the habitat for wolves, ill-mannered wood spirits, and God knows what else.

There is some remembrance of the Old World's tight farm planning in the arrangement of buildings on early farmsteads in the northern[107] and Mid-Atlantic regions,[108] where vestiges of the old agricultural village also survive. In Virginia, though most of the people left either long-houses or communal villages behind, separate buildings were dribbled over the farm[109] as an architectural extension of human control over space and as an analytic separation of the lives of people and animals and the work of men and women. This early extensiveness could

Fig. 61   SUGGESTIONS OF EARLY FARM PLANNING, HOUSE Y. Seen from the stable.

Fig. 60   BRITISH LONGHOUSE. Upper Tor farmhouse, located near Poundsgate, Devonshire, England (June 1972). The door under the porch leads into a hallway from which one turns right into the house; to the left is the shippen for the cows, which also has an external entrance. The part of the building given over to the human beings follows the hall-and-parlor form. The plan of the house may be found in Barley's *The English Farmhouse and Cottage*, p. 110. I am indebted to its owners, the Richardsons, for allowing me to spend much time examining this exciting medieval house.

also be interpreted as a correct climatic fit, for it would have allowed for airflow between the farm's buildings. Again we might expect to find the farm layout being dragged through time away from climatic efficiency, from the extensively flung to the intensively ordered. Instead, the pattern reflected in surviving artifacts is exactly like that drawn at the larger level of particularistic context; being allied with artificiality and internalness, extensiveness continued to temper the intensive drive. Few very early outbuildings are left, but the old barns that remain are located far from the house (Fig. 61), whereas

Fig. 62 NINETEENTH CENTURY FARM PLANNING, HOUSE Z. The Ware farm.

Fig. 63 ALIGNED OUTBUILDINGS. These are the dependencies at house L.

the smokehouses are near it. Indications are that the old farm had two centers, the house and the barn, around which smaller dependencies were dropped. Beside the house are the outbuildings needed by the woman in order to get food on the table; beside the barn are the outbuildings needed by the man to keep the cattle fat. The nineteenth-century plan still shows this duality, but the farm would be best described as consisting of a house with a straggling row of outbuildings behind it. This row is arranged parallel to the house (Fig. 62) or perpendicularly to it. Later in the century the outbuildings were moved closer to each other and many were attached in strings (Fig. 63), but the plan never became geometri-

cally integrated; it remained topologically organized along male and female paths of labor.

Resolving a level lower in particularistic context, we find the same artificially analytic mind to be reflected in the house's posture over the land. The preindustrial architect is often a master of siting, creating a beautiful fit between his product and its environment.[110] But the Middle Virginia house was not modified to fit its site; the type was extended into space without regard for the particulars of topography. The land was level (and that helped), but even where it was not, an uneven foundation was provided on which the house could be built, as if the land had been graded to a geometrical plane. In many folk architectural traditions special buildings were devised to suit certain sorts of terrain. The early Pennsylvania Germans, for example, had types for hillsides and types for flat land. But the old Virginian did not, and even when he moved up into the Blue Ridge mountains he continued to build as if his land were level. West of the Blue Ridge crest, where Pennsylvanians settled, one finds banked barns, hillside houses, and outbuildings with semisubterranean cellars. The eastern slope, populated out of Middle Virginia, is built up with flatland architectural forms that refuse to admit they are perched on the side of a mountain.

Separated from the land on which it sits, separated from the farm's other buildings, from the community's other houses, the house itself could be separated. Its form could be broken down and broken apart by the rules for subtypification to produce partial representations of full house types. The fragmentary building, such as the two-thirds I house (Figs. 20, 43, 44) is a characteristic of American folk architecture. One- and two-story versions of the same plans were built in Britain and Ireland, but it is the subtraction in the horizontal plane, empowered by the subtypification rules, that is crucial. The diagnostic image is that of two-thirds or one-third of a tripartite concept given material existence. Partial versions of the medieval hall house were built in England.[111] Two-thirds versions of the English barn[112] and the Georgian house were built in England, but the house was largely confined to the town and neither became common.

In the United States such fragmentary buildings are characteristic features of the landscape. The central-chimney houses of New England,[113] the Yankee barns of New York,[114] the Georgian houses, central-hall I houses, and double-crib barns of Pennsylvania[115] were all three-sectioned types that were regularly materialized in two-thirds or one-third subtypes. The frequent employment of this fragmenting process is evidence of an analytic mindset in late-eighteenth-century America. And the process generated acceptable signs within the social hierarchy. Girded with the subtypification rules, the poorer man, from the end of the eighteenth century into the nineteenth century's last quarter, built not a different sort of house, but a house that was clearly a partial representation of the wealthier man's house. His house may not have been broad, but it was two stories high. With it, his lines of identity were openly established; he was aspiring to the same thing the rich man was. Sometimes he did assemble sufficient loot to add the missing third to his two-thirds I house and finish his life in an icon of modest success. The two-thirds I house was his statement of hope for upward mobility. Simultaneously, it stated his separation from people unable to build two-story houses—the poorest of the freeholders, living still in single-story dwellings, and, especially, those human beings thrust into rows of one-story squares off from the plantation's big house.

At the bottom level of the particularistic context we have been left very little data to consider. We cannot see how furniture was arranged in the rooms, but we can see that there was almost no built-in furniture—the only exception being a cupboard in a back room of house N (Fig. 36). Even the triangular area under both boxed and open stairways, often enclosed as a closet in American folk houses, was generally left open as dead space in this

Fig. 64   BOXED STAIRWAY. At house M.

area (Fig. 64). Beds and settles, benches and tables, cupboards and shelves were often built into the walls of houses in England, Ireland, and Scotland,[116] but here furniture was movable, extended into space rather than drawn back into the walls.

Our examination of the extensive-intensive opposition began with details out of the architectural lexicon that

146

were located in abstracted context between man and the weather. Other architectural features exhibit the same change toward intensiveness. One early two-thirds version of type 14 had its chimney built inside the gable wall, but all of the other early houses, of whatever type, have chimneys protruding from the ends (Figs. 27, 29, 32, 34, 35, 38, 41, 44, 75). The external chimney was a Mediterranean form that diffused early into Britain. The tradition was reinforced as external chimneys were added to extant houses from the sixteenth century on.[117] And it is a strong part of the folk architectural traditions of western Britain, in Shropshire and Herefordshire particularly (Fig. 78A). The external chimney has often been rationalized as a climatic fit. It would, indeed, have kept the warm back of the chimney outside of the house, thereby diminishing the amount of heat trapped inside the building. It would seem to suit a hot climate; nonetheless, in the nineteenth century the chimneys came to be built inside the house's walls (compare Figs. 36 and 37, and 41 and 42). The process was gradual but complete. The earliest full I house had an external chimney at each end; there are thirteen of these left. Nine I houses have an external chimney on one end and an internal one on the other (Fig. 75). In the newest I houses the chimney has retreated inside both end walls or all the

Fig. 65   TIDEWATER CHIMNEY. To the left is the chimney of house K. To the right is its English antecedent, built on a house in Tillingham, Essex (August 1973). See Fig. 78A for another English example of this chimney form.

147

way to its middle partitions. None of the one-story central-hall houses (type 12) had an external chimney on both ends, and only one had an external chimney on one end; all the houses of this type were built toward the end of the nineteenth century. At the same time, there was a change from fireplace to stove heat, but the inward shift began before the stove was imported.

Changes in the relationship between the top of the chimney and the top of the house follow the same course. The early chimney was designed so that the top of its flue stood out in the air away from the gable (Fig. 65). Before the chimney was gathered into the house the flue had been drawn tight to the wall. The early chimney was built up to a point high above the rooftop (Figs. 10, 31, 34, 41). This might have been a survival from a time when chimneys were rare on English houses and the builder wished to signal its presence, much as the early owner of a clock wanted it to tick and strike loudly. Or it could have remained from the time when houses were thatched. The thatch was heaped up over the ridge a foot and a half or more and, if thin shingles were nailed over the same rafters and lath, the chimney would be left standing high. But for about two centuries after chimneys had ceased to be a novelty and thatch had yielded to shingles, the chimney continued to extend upward over the ridge of the house. The towering chimney may have helped in fire prevention, but still, the nineteenth century brought the intensive change; the later chimney is stubby and short (Figs. 42, 44, 84B).

The plate assembly of the usual Tidewater frame differs greatly from that normally employed in Britain (Fig. 51),[118] although it is probably a conceptual relative of the techniques used in framing jetties[119] or the cross-ties of crucks in England (Fig. 66). The joists of the old house project as much as 10 inches over the plate to carry a plank, a second plate element, upon which the rafters foot (Fig. 67). This assemblage forms a cornice at the top of the wall. Interest was brought to the cornice through its encrustation with strips of molding (Fig. 68). The acceptance of log construction seems to diffuse together with the story-and-a-half house height. The old frame houses of the area do not have half-story attics (Fig. 69), but the early Parrish log house (Fig. 70A) and the later Smith log house (Fig. 80) do. The builder of the Parrish house was presented with the difficulty of framing the cornice, as the cornice required the extension of the joists, but in the log house the joists were generally framed into the wall at a point below the plate. In the Parrish house the joists rest two logs below the plate. In the Blue Ridge to the west, eastern Virginians, having adopted log construction from their Pennsylvania-bred neighbors, framed the cornice by placing the plate out onto the cantilevered ends of logs in the end walls (Fig. 70B). Our local builder fell upon the solution that had been used in frame construction (at house N, for example) when the stair interrupted the run of a joist. He dovetailed four short pieces into each top log. These thrust forward to carry the rafters (Fig. 70A). He went to a great deal of trouble to make that cornice to emulate one of the notable extensive features of the framed Tidewater house. During the next century house carpenters, whether working in log or frame, snapped the plate intensively back into the wall.

Just as the early chimney and plate broke out of the house, exposing themselves, early door hinges—all of

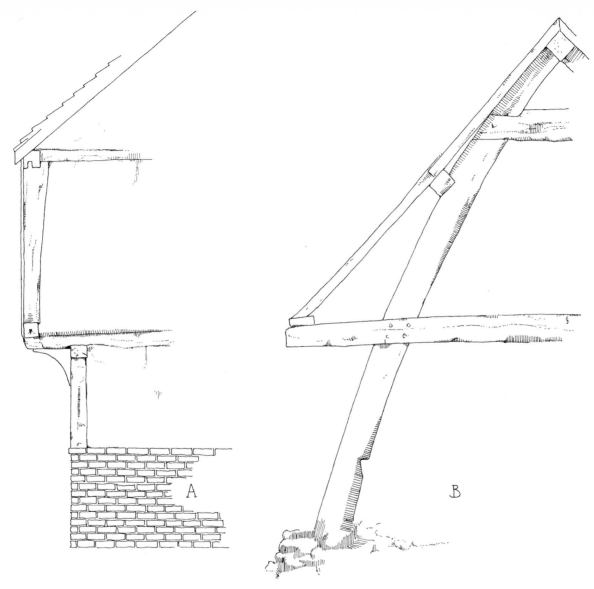

Fig. 66   ENGLISH FRAMING. *A.* Jetty on a box-framed house in Colchester, Essex (August 1973). *B.* Partial section through a cruck-framed Yorkshire house; after Innocent, *The Development of English Building Construction*, pp. 44–45.

149

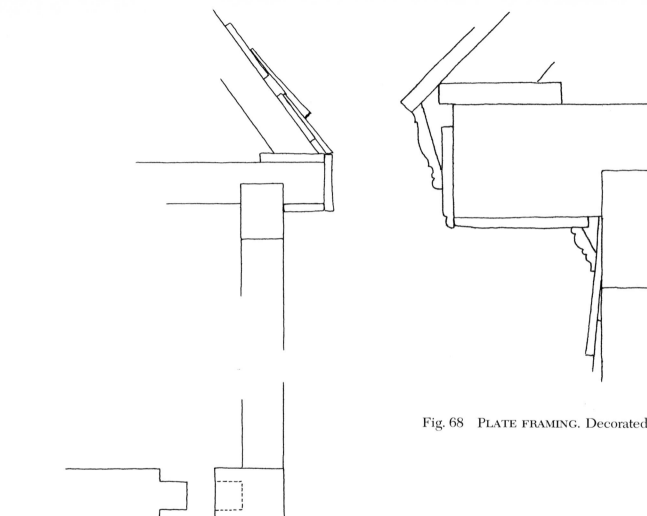

Fig. 68   PLATE FRAMING. Decorated cornice of house V.

Fig. 67   FRAMING DETAILS. Plate and sill of house G.

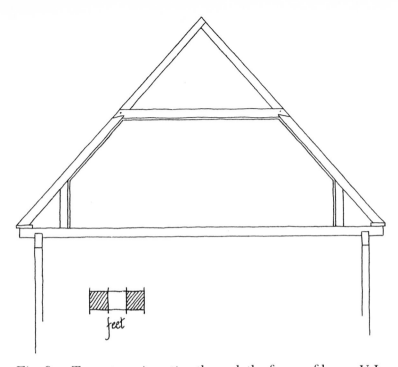

Fig. 69   THE LOFT. A section through the frame of house V. In general, nailing framing members together is viewed as a modern and degenerate practice, but nails were used in construction at an early date in Middle Virginia. In this eighteenth-century house the rafters are nailed together and the collars are nailed to the rafters. The nails used are all hand-wrought, rosehead nails.

which are the usual old American strap, H, or H-and-L varieties (Fig. 71)[120]—were exposed. In the nineteenth century the butt hinge was accepted, and hinges came to be clandestinely tucked out of sight. To say that the butt hinge was accepted because it was fashionable is to say little, because so many equally fashionable things were not accepted. It was convenient, in that the cast-iron butt hinge could be purchased, but many of the conveniences of nineteenth-century technological progress were ignored in Middle Virginia. This convenient fashion was probably accepted because it felt right to the local builder, and it probably felt right because the builder was unconsciously seeking for intensive images.

The extensive-intensive opposition seems to have been joined in thought to an opposition of complexity and simplicity. The loss of extensiveness (or gain in intensiveness) was paralleled across time by a loss of detailing (or gain in simplicity). The folk designer anticipated by nearly two centuries the Bauhaus master's call for architectonic honesty, for adherence to impersonal "type-forms" and the rejection of ornamental obfuscation.[121] However, in a critique of the modern artifact, a practicing industrial designer has noted that the lack of ornamental detail may signal a lack of patient care as much as the presence of clean, functional design.[122] The earliest builder had alternatives for chimney shape; the chimney would be external and its flue would be separated from the wall, but he could choose to express the fact that the chimney served two fireplaces, one above the other, by building a chimney with two sets of shoulders, or he could encase them both in a unitary shape. This option for elaboration was lost in time, and before the chimney

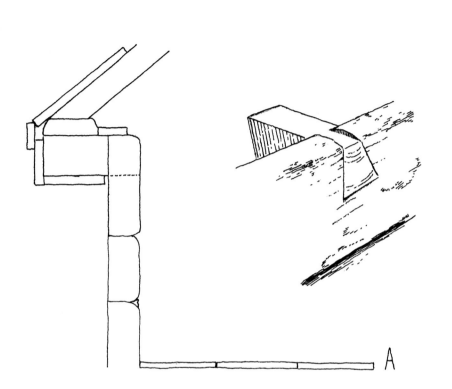

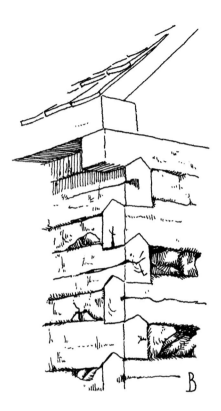

A

B

Fig. 70 FRAMING THE PLATE OF A LOG HOUSE. *A.* Plate of house M. To the left is a diagram; to the right is a view of the dovetailed piece from the inside. *B.* From a V-notched square cabin, located east of Woodville, Rappahannock County, Virginia (May 1963).

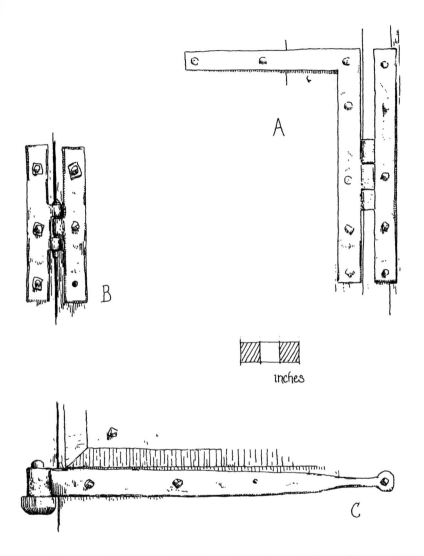

inches

Fig. 71   HINGES. *A.* HL hinge from the end door of house V. *B.* H hinge from the door in the partition of the loft of house M. *C.* Strap hinge from the back door of house M.

was gathered into the house only the simpler form was used. The chimneys on house Q provide a good example in that the original one has two sets of shoulders, and the shorter nineteenth-century replacement does not (Fig. 38).

During the analytic-extensive period of Middle Virginia thinking, constructional details were given individual identities. Early shingles in the Tidewater were often carved so that their ends were rounded.[123] Though I found no examples within our area—a shingle's chances of surviving a century and a half are slim—I did find them nearby in Hanover County, and it would not be far-fetched to assume they were once used here. If so, they were replaced by shingles with square ends (of which many examples are extant), which take the attention off the individual shingle and carry it to the homogenized horizontal row of shingles. Then, long after roofs had fallen to a flat pitch, shingles gave way to the use of sheet metal, thus unifying the roof's face into a single entity.

As one of the many indications that old houses in Middle Virginia have been altered physically much less than houses in many other areas, all of the area's old houses included at least patches of their original siding. Some of the early clapboarding was tapered, some was straight sided, but all of it had a bead along the lower edge (Figs. 72, 73), a common feature of eighteenth-century English and American building.[124] Internal boards, whether composing the wall's whole surface or a dado, were beaded (Fig. 74). There are beads, too, on the second-story floor joists of house G and on the joists of the kitchen of the Rackett house, as well as on the baseboards, chair rails, hook strips, and the door and

153

Fig. 72 BEADED SIDING. To the left are sections through local beaded siding. *A.* From house K. *B.* From house M. To the right is a photograph of contemporary beaded clapboarding from a house in Great Dunmow, Essex, England (September 1972).

Fig. 73 MOLDED OPENING. The window through the foundation of house R. Note the molding and the bead on the frame
and the siding.

window frames of all the early houses. Additionally, the earliest window and door openings of finer houses had a strip of molding planed into or applied onto the frame's outside edge (Figs. 53, 73). That molding was the first to go; the bead followed. By the late nineteenth century, clapboards, internal boards and trim, and the facing boards of openings were given no individual treatment. Once nailed on, they were lost in the overriding form.

During the change toward intensive simplicity, the Middle Virginia designer's choice of color became increasingly restricted. The boats of the Chesapeake Bay had been gaudily bedaubed in the eighteenth century[125] and the houses were comparably bright. As another marker of the segregation of man and nature, the house was always covered in some color that denied the wood of which it was built, picking it out from its setting. Old houses in New England were sometimes allowed to weather to silver, but in Middle Virginia only outbuildings were left unpainted. In the early days the small house, like some in Elizabethan England,[126] was painted barn red—or at least that was the first color on houses G and V. The large early house, such as N or R, was painted white. The late eighteenth- and early nineteenth-century American country house was usually white,[127] and though two old houses are still yellow with brown trim, those that have not lost their paint to poverty and the elements or have not been covered by asbestos shingles (as seventeen of the I houses have been) are now white.

The nearly invariable whiteness of the nineteenth- and early twentieth-century farmhouse not only marked a contraction of the traditional palette and the most abrupt possible separation from the natural tans, greens, and clay-reds that environed it, but also, like the two-story height, it was a democritizing sign: little homes of red and big ones of white spoke of strict class distinctions. It would be interesting to know whether the habitations of the slaves were whitewashed or left the color of wood. The early white house, however, was not bland. After white had covered its original red, the Lesser Dabney house had its cornice and one clapboard under it painted red; the corner boards were yellow, the shutters dark green, the front door red with yellow panels (Fig. 45). The trim of white houses was painted a dark color through the last century: house N has red trim; house P has black trim; house S had a blue-green cornice and corner boards, a green door frame, a blue door with white panels; house U has light green trim, a green door with white panels, and a brick-red back door with a blue frame. Green is the usual trim tint (except for porch ceilings, which are often powder blue), and, while this green was generally dark as a forest, an almost turquoise shade was used as well. Of all the white central-hall I houses, there are ten with green trim and one each with gray and brown trim. The balance are thoroughly white. Just as carpenters stopped planing a bead into the edges of frames, most house painters about fifty years ago stopped outlining openings in contrasting hues. In time the change was from several basic colors (white, red, yellow) to one color with multicolored trim (Fig. 45), to one color with one trim color (Fig. 79), and finally to blank white (Figs. 28, 38, 75)—blank as a tin roof, blank as an unbeaded clapboard, blank as a chimneyless gable.

We have wandered so far from his intention that it may be too distant to call his thought back to our aid, but

Robert Plant Armstrong convincingly isolated closure and enclosure as characteristics of what we have been calling intensiveness.[128] Even at its most extensive and detailed, the Middle Virginia ethic valued closure over openness. The extensive and disjunctive devices, whether painted over wood or carved out of wood or constructed in brick, served to frame the form, sundering it from its particularistic context[129] in the way that the prosody and melody of a ballad break it away from normal conversation. Inside the shape they exemplify the "golden rule of all ornament"[130] by accenting its totality and the boundaries of its formal components.

In both England[131] and Africa[132] there had been traditions of architectural decoration that broke out of formal bounds, racing into the wall's field, curling sculpturally across the façade of the dwelling. In northern Nigeria and in southeastern England one can see houses decorated with bold plaster representations of things drawn from the real world, such as plants and animals, and things drawn from the fantastical hidden world of the mind. But the detailing of Middle Virginia's homes was rigidly disciplined. The façade was framed horizontally by the cornice and foundation and vertically by the corner boards. Moldings created repetitious lines to mark sharply the edges of clapboards, door and window frames, and internal woodwork. The only elaboration tolerated was at openings—externally around the doorway, internally around the fireplaces. Even then that elaboration could consist only of straight, sober motifs. Dadoes were framed by caps at the top, baseboards below (Fig. 74).

As on the exterior, interior paint ran a thick outline

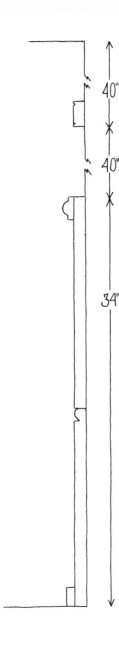

Fig. 74 INTERIOR WOODWORK. From the parlor of house H.

157

around shape, marking off the room's joints and openings. The walls were always lighter in color than the woodwork that bound them. At the Rigsby house (Fig. 41) the walls were originally a pale yellowy tan, the woodwork was a deep red-brown, and the doors were brown with yellow panels. Later the walls were painted pastel green with chocolate trim, and the room most recently painted is gray with sticky white enamel woodwork. The other old houses all seem to have had whitewashed walls originally. In house M the mantel and exterior doors were stained a muddy brown; the interior door was red. At house T the hallway's woodwork was burgundy colored; that of the main room and kitchen was black. The trim of the Greater Dabney house (Fig. 32) was originally a yellowish-brown, later painted deep blue, and most recently subjected to pink. One of the front rooms of house N had woodwork painted a rusty brown, the other had cream-colored woodwork later painted green, the hallway's trim was yellow, and upstairs it was pea green with black doors. The old pattern in paint persisted inside after most people had become wary of putting any color save white on the exterior. The Moore house's external yellow was long ago covered with white, but its recent internal paint job left it with light blue walls and rich brown woodwork. Most Middle Virginians seem now to favor ubiquitous hazy pastel walls and white trim. For over a century, however, dark colors and molded edges enclosed form, reinforcing it, holding it in control.

The nineteenth century witnessed the passing of the long file of ebullient, romantic revivals.[133] These "styles"—the plastic projections of a bourgeois identity crisis—tumbled along like a circus parade, heralded in the pages of innumerable handbooks for builders. They exerted only the most anemic influence in Middle Virginia, and such influence as they did have was bent under the control of a powerful principle in the Anglo-American folk aesthetic: decoration is subordinate to form.[134] Extensive and intensive expressions were deeply controlled in thought by the resolution of the tension between practical and aesthetic forces. As is illustrated by the absence of ornament except at formal points, the practical (the useful form) was given conceptual dominion over the aesthetic tendencies that are most obvious when expressed in nonutilitarian details. The Greek Revival flared up and burned out without leaving a wooden temple or so much as an eyebrow architrave window in the area. The Gothic and Italianate "styles"[135] (which were conflated into a rural Victorian idiom) brought sinuous detailing to many American farm houses, but the effect of the backwater Victorian in Middle Virginia was slight and wholly superficial (Fig. 75). On a few houses the boldly curved brackets of the Italianate manse are found, but they are reduced to nubs lined along the eaves to mark a seam in the form, perhaps as a fading compensation for the lost bold cornices of the previous era. Jigsawed gingerbread is uncommon and always subdued in comparison with the spirited extravagance found in the Midwest or even across the Blue Ridge in the Valley of Virginia. The only feature of the Gothic Revival that took was a central gable. This is found on twenty-five central-hall I houses (See Fig. 75), two I houses of the two-thirds subtype (See Fig. 28), two XX houses (one of two stories, the other of one), and nine central-hall houses of one story. It was supposed to soar, that peak, like the vaults of

Fig. 75 TYPE 14, HOUSE AA. This central-hall I house represents the usual extent of architectural Victorian gaiety in the
area.

Amiens or the gables of a Tudor yeoman's house (or the roof of a local house of a century before), but the extensive age had gone by and the gable spreads flatly in the center of the roof, in proportion more like a Georgian pediment than the perpendicularly hopeful, democratically medieval metaphor intended by Pugin and Ruskin.

THE HOUSE IN CONTROL

Our method has not been complicated. It begins with the recognition of a pattern of relationships at the phenomenal surface and leads through the search for explanations to the discovery of patterns in logic. I described these patterns in terms of the mediation of binary oppositions. This was due, of course, to the attractiveness of the discourse of Claude Lévi-Strauss. However, while the application of the method to unconscious cultural logic is primarily his gift, as an explanatory technique it is antique and widely employed. It has been used by old philosophers and modern scientists, by anthropologists, artists, and learned pedagogues.[136] If binary sets seem too simple or too pat to be the real structures of unconscious logic, their reality is not beyond good possibility, and they do provide us with a rigorous means for traveling toward a larger truth—that thought is structured and systematically so.

We could have entered this logic at any point, although I chose for us to enter by way of the square, basic to the local architectural idea, and to move from that to the opposition of intellect and emotion. From that point we proceeded, via a dialectic of the empirical and the abstract, to attend to binary structures until they could no longer account for surface patterns. When the surface

became confusing, our assumption was that reason still reigned, but that we, not the builder, had lost its premises. Forced to hunt for other relationships, we drove deeper and deeper into mind, finding ever more complex interrelations and ever more powerful structures which, when mediated, left the house an ever more logical (and historically useful) manifestation of thought. The concentration has been upon details, changeable things, expressions of relatively shallow and shifting ideas. But wherever we entered we would descend through sets of relations to the major opposition that held sway through the architectural competence, as well as through the selection of details, the arrangement of appendages, and the technological protocol. We would descend past the oppositions of the natural and the artificial, the internal and the external, the practical and the aesthetic, to that which ordered them: the opposition of chaos and control (Fig. 76).

It might seem like a reduction to the functionalist's balance to posit control, the terror of disorder, as the embracing structure of the Middle Virginia logic. Balance is requisite to human existence (at least as an idea to

Fig. 76 THE ARCHITECTURE OF DESIGN. Above the double line are listed the observable phenomena that exhibit patterning. Below the line is a diagram of the paradigmatic structure of the mind of the Middle Virginia architect—a guide to decision making. The underlined term in the opposition is that which was dominant at the earliest time. Arrows indicate the direction of change from about 1760 on.

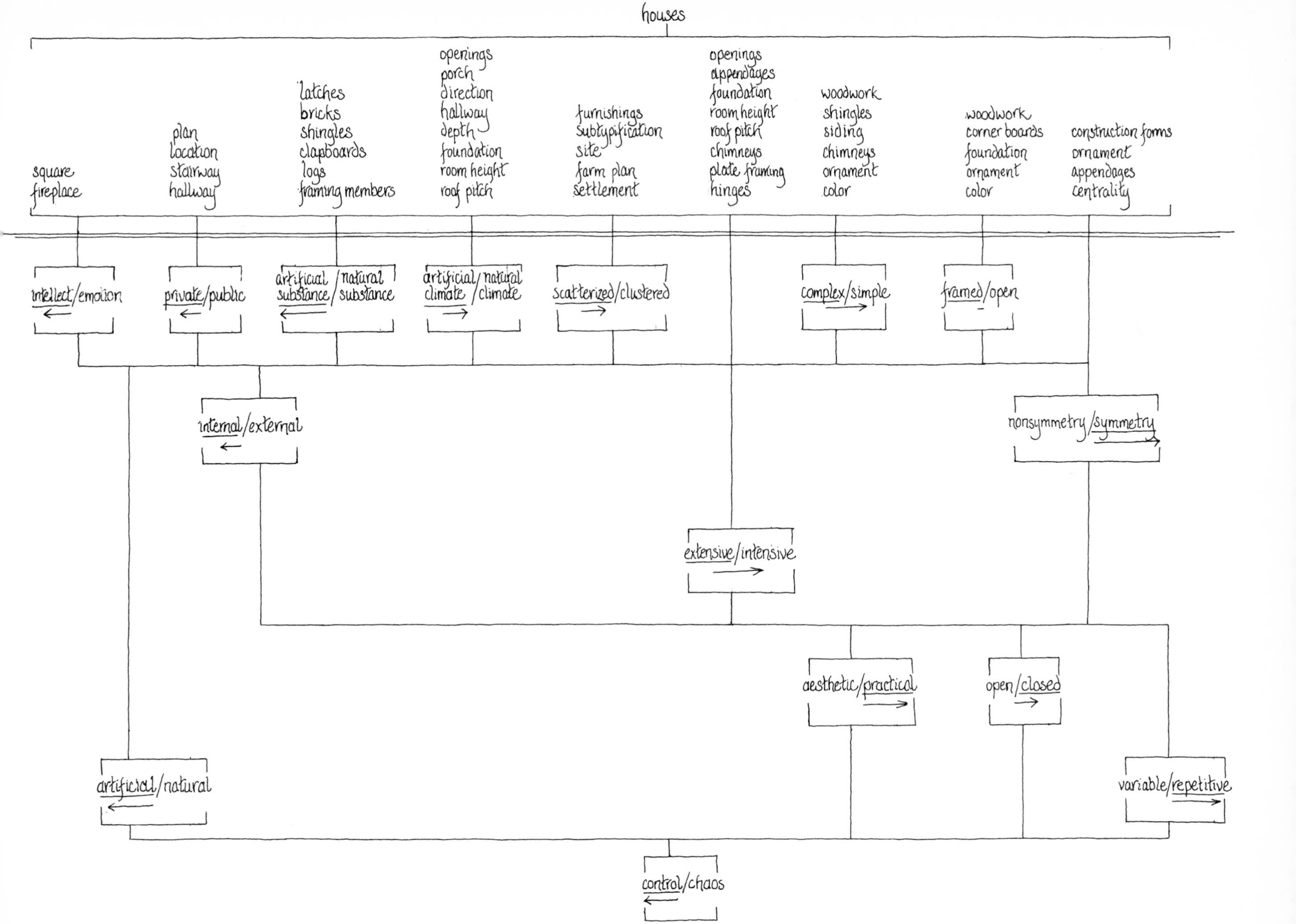

houses

square
fireplace

plan
location
stairway
hallway

latches
bricks
shingles
clapboards
logs
framing members

openings
porch
direction
hallway
depth
foundation
room height
roof pitch

furnishings
subtypification
site
farm plan
settlement

openings
appendages
foundation
room height
roof pitch
chimneys
plate framing
hinges

woodwork
shingles
siding
chimneys
ornament
color

woodwork
corner boards
foundation
ornament
color

construction forms
ornament
appendages
centrality

intellect/emotion ←

private/public ←

artificial substance ← / natural substance

artificial climate → / natural climate

scatterized/clustered →

complex/simple

framed/open —

internal/external ←

nonsymmetry/symmetry →

extensive/intensive →

aesthetic/practical →

open/closed →

artificial/natural ←

variable/repetitive →

control/chaos ←

reject), but it lies still deeper—probably a fundamental need of the animal. Balance will be, but it need not depend upon the mechanisms for control that grip the folk logic in Virginia, causing it to value the closed over the open, the practical over the aesthetic, the private over the public, the artifical over the natural. The ethnological treasury brims with proof of that assertion.[137]

The remnants we have to study are displays of control over two kinds of energy—over natural substances and spaces, over human will and ability. There is no data but old architecture. It is still probably fair to assume that control was exerted compatibly in areas of life that existed once but have vanished without a whisper.[138] How did the farmer-builder treat his wife and children? We cannot know. The most informed guess, though, paints an unpleasant scene. We do know how he treated nature and we do know how he treated his own energies: he held them both under fearful control.

As romantic signature, organically nonsymmetrical artwork held great appeal for those in the avant-garde of the first half of our century. But the "man in the street" is offended by the luxuriant curvaceousness of a Gaudí or a Guimard, by the furious uncontrol of a Pollock or a de Kooning. When the artifact is neither geometrically nor representationally repetitive, how the devil is the observer to know whether or not its maker was capable of expressing the idea he had in mind? Repetition is proof of control.[139] By repeating each stanza of his ballad to an identical melody, the Anglo-American singer proves the correctness of his rendition of the tune. The designer who reproduces a form with regularity and precision proves his control over mind and hand and material, his complete aloofness from the influences flowing naturally through existence. The Middle Virginia folk architect's competence was firmly constrained. The addition of minor, late rules to the competence could have given him the opportunity to produce a great variety of forms, such as house G (Fig. 29), but he elected to keep his repertoire small and to keep his output repetitious. The number of folk-house types in any area of the United States is surprisingly small. Even when competent to vary his practice, the folk architect chose to stick to one of the alternatives open to him. The Middle Virginia house carpenter knew six base structures, yet he designed three-quarters of his houses (118 out of 146) on one of them—the XY_3X structure. He could generate seven types out of that base structure, yet nearly two-thirds of the houses he built out of it (70 out of 118) were of one of those types—the central-hall I house with end chimneys (Figs. 41, 42, 75). His central-hall I house (types 14 and 15) could have a five-opening or a three-opening façade, but he used the five-opening configuration three times and the three-opening configuration seventy-nine times.

The folklorist's romantic heritage makes him think of folk actions as free and organically variable—as being lit by John Ruskin's "lamp of life"[140]—but the Anglo-American folk performer's practice was to ignore many of the chances for variation theoretically open to him, to perfect a form and then to repeat it over and over again, striving to make these repetitions identical. The audience wants to hear the tune played on the fiddle exactly as they have heard it before, and the architect's client demands that the builder keep his whimsy subdued. The measure of the Anglo-American folk performer's success is repetition, not innovation.

The folk designer's whole forms were repetitious, and, when they could be, the pieces of his artifact were identical. Horizontally aligned windows were the same shape and size and were composed of lights of the same shape and size. Rafters were framed as a series of identical couples. Identical fireplaces were built out of identical bricks. More powerfully, his competence directed him to structure his form repetitively. He was forced (by rules III.B.2, C.1b, D.1b, E.1, E.3.a1, and F.3; VIII.B.2b and B.4c) to locate doors, windows, and chimneys centrally so that the spaces on each side of the detail would be identical repetitions. His artifact, a repetitious structuring of repetitious elements, well expressed his intention for order. But he did have one worry.

In a bright essay, William Hansen has shown how superficial inconsistencies in the *Odyssey* are markers of consistencies deeper in the poet's logic.[141] Similarly, confusions in the pattern of door placement during the earliest architectural phase, requiring the existence of the competence's most confused rules (III.C.1b and C.1c.2), are evidence of a pattern in logic. Centrality pervades the competence, but given an XY base structure there was simply no way to have the door simultaneously central to the component in which it was located and to the whole façade. There was no way to have the door appear symmetrical from both the inside and the outside. Many things were tried but to no avail.

Then along came the XY3X base structure. The Geor-gian novelty was rapidly incorporated not because the local architects were willing to trudge thoughtlessly after urban leaders (none of the nineteenth-century modes that succeeded the Georgian style in the North even touched the Middle Virginian's gross architectural competence), but because it carried within it the solution to an old, bothersome problem. The door could now be located centrally to both its component and to the whole façade. The elaborate rules (III.B.2b, B.3b, and C.2a.1b) enabling two piercings per component continued in operation for a brief time, generating houses such as the Rigsby house (Fig. 41) with five-opening façades, but for most builders the simple early rule of one central opening per wall (III.B.2a) became all that was necessary. Many of the early rules (I.C.3 and D.2; III.F.1; VI, VI.B.1, B.2a and C; VII.A.1; VIII.A.2 and B.2a) drew the design toward symmetry, but now it could be brought into complete metrically symmetrical order.

In architectural histories the acceptance of the Georgian style is generally tallied as an abrupt complication in the stylistic sequence. Its perfect symmetry, however, crystalized an old wish and actually simplified the design process. Before observing that the asymmetrical form is an expression of "the desire for the organic . . . rather than the geometric," the sculptor Henry Moore commented that "a symmetrical mass being the same from both sides cannot have more than half the number of different points of view possessed by a non-symmetrical mass"[142]—that is, a symmetrical form may not be easier to make, but it is easier to think. It has twice the chance of being designed with precision as an organic form and half

Fig. 77 Type 15 house with end addition, House BB. This is a nineteenth-century central-hall I house with a two-story, one-room X addition on one end, creating a form similar to the early double-parlor house.

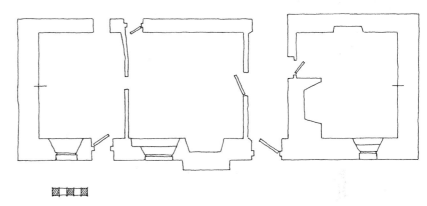

A

B

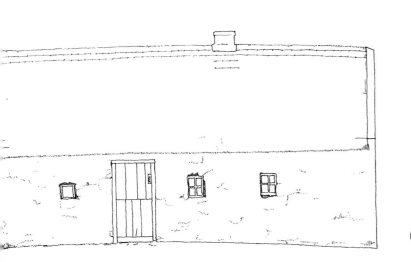

C

Fig. 78   THE NONSYMMETRICAL HOUSE OF ENGLAND AND IRELAND. *A.* A two-story double-parlor house, it has a basic hall-and-parlor plan, to which an additional room is linearly structured to the right. Its volumes are the same as those of the Greater Dabney house (Fig. 32), except that the extra room in the Virginia house was built as an ell, whereas in this English house it extends laterally into view. Located at Wooferton, Hereford (December 1972). *B.* The plan of a central-hall I house with a third room on the left end. Modern rear appendages were omitted from the plan. Located in Mortonhampstead, Devonshire, England (June 1972). As is the case with the house drawn in *A,* it can be seen that the double-parlor plan is not the result of additions; rather, the house was built in this form. This observation holds, too, for the Irish house that is illustrated. *C.* This house is situated southeast of Bellanaleck, County Fermanagh, Northern Ireland (August 1972). The front door opens into the "kitchen" (hall). To the right of the chimney is the "room" (parlor). The left window provides light for the third volume, a bedroom. The floor plan is drawn to scale (in feet), but the three drawings are not to the same scale: the Fermanagh house is smaller than the English ones.

165

its chance for errors in plan: it is twice as simple.

The abhorrence of disorder led through the replacement of the XY types with the XY₃X types to a change in the organization of appendages. Two of the early houses (J and Y) had ell additions on the rear, but the other early homes had appendages, usually shed kitchens, built around a chimney off the end—another of the practices known in New England[143] but persisting to a later date down South. These sheds were sometimes built on only one end (houses G, M, and R, for examples) though there was often, as at houses H, N, and V, an addition on each end, thus creating symmetrical extensions. Soon after the rigorously symmetrical façade had become dominant, additions were relegated to the back of the house. As one indication of the incompleteness of the I house's two-thirds subtype, five out of seventeen such houses have additions on the end (Fig. 43, 44), four of them being built in the visual gap on the hall end of the house, where a room would appear in a full expression of the house, even though it might have been more efficient to build the addition on the other end, where it could be served by the extant chimney (compare Figs. 43 and 44). Thus almost a third of the two-thirds I houses have end additions, but only four of the sixty-five full I houses have end additions (Fig. 77). The majority of the central-hall I houses do have appendages—seventeen have one-story ells, sixteen have two-story ells, six have sheds—but these were built on the back of the house.

This is the more remarkable because the appendages of folk houses in the British Isles are generally built on the end (Fig. 78). The folk houses of Ireland, with remarkably few exceptions, have a basic two-room XY sort of plan, with a third component built off one end, eliminating the possibility of a perfectly symmetrical façade. The appendages of English I houses are very commonly built off one end.[144] Houses of this "double parlor" kind were built early in the Tidewater,[145] but the norm—the general Anglo-American norm—came to be to construct the appendages on the rear. Putting them on the end, as in Ireland or England, would undermine the house's usefulness as a sign of order. Unconfused by lateral appendages (or by analytic and extensive detailing), the house's symmetry stood out clearly and simply, providing, like recent minimalist art,[146] an image of artificiality and control.

The nonsymmetrical rear addition did not soften the house's geometric impact, for the house was ordered according to one of the great principles of Western folk aesthetic: frontality. Like the New Mexican *bulto*, the house was designed to be seen from directly in front; it was conceptually three dimensional, but artistically two dimensional. The piercing of the ends and rear was variable (by rules III.E.3a and F.2), but that of the front was not. The Parrish mansion, for example, has the regular five-opening Georgian façade, but its four back openings are off balance (Fig. 36; see also Fig. 37). The Smith house has three openings on the front and rear, but those on the rear are asymmetrically arranged (Fig. 80).

Brickwork is another indicator of frontality. The front of the ancient Thoroughgood house in Princess Anne County was laid up in Flemish bond, but its sides and rear were laid in simpler, less fashionable English bond.[147] Similar practices were known in England[148] and are spread widely through the American countryside.

Fig. 79 SADDLEBAG HOUSE, HOUSE CC. This house consists of the arrangement of a partitioned Z house with an X house around a central chimney.

The Greater Dabney house has a fancy Flemish-bond façade, though its sides and back were laid up with six rows of stretchers between header rows (Fig. 32). The Lesser Dabney house has a full Flemish-bond foundation in front, but it has brick piers on the rear and ends, just as it has more elaborate window trim on the front than it has in back (Fig. 45). The Rigsby house's foundation has three stretcher rows between header rows, but the bond is irregular except in the front, and the ventilation through the foundation (into a cellar that was projected but never dug) is provided by framed, beaded and molded, and barred windows in the front (Figs. 41, 73), but by the patterned omission of bricks in the back.

The aesthetic of bound symmetry and the desire for privacy were, seemingly, the driving forces behind the development of a new house form in the later nineteenth century (types 11, 13). During the earliest architectural phase, when one little house was built onto another, they were generally lined up, but no attempt was made to unify them into a single composition (Figs. 33, 79). The power of symmetry, channeled by subtypification through the XY3X concept, overtook this idea, wrestling such additions under the control of the XX base structure and into independent type status. The XX types required the continuation of many of the rules of the first architectural phase (such as III.B.2b, B.3b, C.1b, and C.1c.2) that were no longer necessary in the design of central-hall I houses. After the middle of the nineteenth century two houses were built (types 11, 13; Figs. 19, 80) that incorporated the XX house's double-square, central-chimney concept in an XY3X structure, thus eliminating the need for the obsolescent rules (though some builders con-

tinued to use them up until the tradition's demise). The plan of these houses is exactly like that common in southeastern England[149] and early New England.[150] Houses that possibly shared this layout were built toward the beginning of Tidewater settlement,[151] but the two houses in our area (others were spotted nearby) seem not to be the products of survival, but a result of the adjustment of the old competence in accordance with changes in the culture's logic.

The change from the XX types 8 and 10 to types 11 and 13 was conditioned by the increased desire for privacy. Unlike the XX house, but like the central-hallway house, these houses provide an internal transitional zone—an entry located in front of the chimney. When the visitor crosses the threshold he is standing in this entry; he is in the house, but he is not in any of the house's rooms. The innovation of the central-chimney XY3X house seems to have been spurred, too, by the desire for enclosed symmetry. The XX form, although it could be symmetrical, was merely repetitious. It arranged no perimeters for the façade (a third X could be added, or a fourth), whereas the XY3X design was bound and complete as well as symmetrical.

The house's façade is also its people's façade;[152] it is the mask worn in unsuspected encounter. The mask is a face, bilaterally symmetrical, with its entrance at the lower center, glazed eyes. It is a projection of the human shape—the ultimate paradigm—but it is a negation of self. Blank, composed in total control, the mask divulges no personal information; completely predictable, its predictive utility is nil.[153] Like the mask of a Kwakiutl shaman, it opens to reveal not the human heart, but another

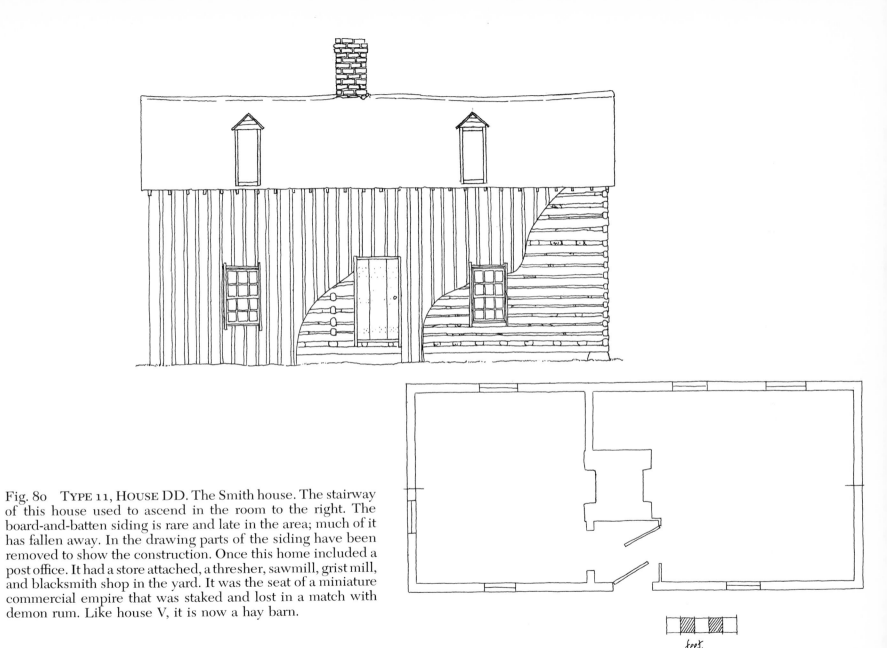

Fig. 80   TYPE 11, HOUSE DD. The Smith house. The stairway of this house used to ascend in the room to the right. The board-and-batten siding is rare and late in the area; much of it has fallen away. In the drawing parts of the siding have been removed to show the construction. Once this home included a post office. It had a store attached, a thresher, sawmill, grist mill, and blacksmith shop in the yard. It was the seat of a miniature commercial empire that was staked and lost in a match with demon rum. Like house V, it is now a hay barn.

feet

mask. Seeing the house's face, the visitor predicts what lies behind it. He enters and finds his prediction to be correct. Unlike early mansions, such as the Governor's Palace at Williamsburg,[154] and unlike the modern home, the interior and exterior are experientially united into an image of order (rule III.A.1). The façade carries no oddness and covers no arcane illogic. The house—its front and plan—is the denial of personality and the public presentation of an ethos.

Little is to be learned from old homes about flesh and feeling individuals, unless those buildings are exceptional in one direction (a porchless, unpainted, two-thirds I house with a rock chimney) or the other (bright, white, full Georgian house with chimneys laid up in Flemish bond). However, the house is one of the things with which the individual had to cope, and the house was the individual's expression of a collective persona. It is a statement of his wishes. As a member of a society the individual favored a symmetrical image that could be easily conceived and was, therefore, egalitarian. Most people were clever and wealthy enough to reproduce the cultural ideal perfectly. As an individual, however, he must have felt a need to repress his own potential behind a mask, for his humanistically perfectable house was a perfect image of enclosed, artificial control.[155]

During the later architectural stages, when the house was ordered by the statistically and conceptually dominant XY₃X structure, its design was simultaneously composed of odd- and even-numbered elements. The structure determined in the context is unitary, and it is bilaterally symmetrical. If a line is imagined down the middle of the house's façade (or its gable or its plan), that line separates identical halves. And yet this unitary, bilaterally symmetrical shape has three parts: a symmetrical, central one, different in size and configuration from the elements at each of its sides. These side elements are identical repetitions of each other. The whole design is similar to the unit of measurement used by the Middle Virginia builder; the unit is one yard, but it is also two cubits and three feet. The design is triple, yet double, yet single. It orders the house totally as pairs of elements. The central section is bilaterally symmetrical; the gable has a symmetrical chimney or window at its center; the central element of the façade has a door composed of symmetrical halves at its center, perhaps a symmetrical Gothic gable centered above; the plan has its central hall or chimney. Thus the building is mirrored in halves, and the design, though tripartite, is composed in two ways of only two ideas.

This bilaterally symmetrical, tripartite design was the perfect end to the builder's search for architectural order. Long before the Virginia farmer started turning the New World's wilderness into material culture, that design had been used in the structuring of artifacts of all sorts.[156] He knew it from furniture and gravestones, and it existed in his architectural competence, organically in house design and geometrically in barn design, prior to the Georgian introduction. The barn type characteristic of Western Europe and subsequently of colonial America[157]— the type used to provide stables or sheds for air-curing tobacco around Orchid and Gum Spring (Fig. 81)—has a central runway separating identical parts. The slowness of folk time is measured by the fact that the Middle Virginia architect already had the solution to his front-door dilemma in the barns he built, but he did not transfer it, waiting instead for the Georgian stimulus before perfecting his concept. From individual windows and doors to barns, houses, and churches (Fig. 82), his architecture was composed of a unit simultaneously divisible by two and three.

Bilaterally symmetrical, tripartite structures mark Western quests for control. The overriding structure of the ancient tale generally has three sections, and its central episodes unfold, like the architectural design, in units of three parts, one of which differs from two that are the same. The structure is sufficiently complicated to give the illusion of difficulty, but the façade is brought into symmetry—the hero does pass the test and marry the king's daughter, the raconteur does bring the tale to a close, and the audience knew it all along. Simple narratives shoved the child Jean-Paul in Sartre's *Words* through false fear into the feeling that progress led to the triumph of good.[158] The structure is optimistic in being within the mind's reach, in assuring the human being that he can successfully conquer the problems he faces and improve his lot.

The structure is complicated, it is optimistic, but it is closed; there is a limit to an individual's quest for improvement. The tale's hero leaves home and matures successfully through marvelous adventures, but the tale never ends interrogatively, as in Africa, nor does it end openly, like *Huckleberry Finn* with its hero splitting for the Indian Territory. The *märchen's* youth returns to the equilibrium of home, accepting the gift of wife, chattels, real estate, and position from the father figure he had left at the beginning and tricked in the middle. The structure

provides the folk performer with the ability to achieve a form complex enough to be interesting, but simple enough to unite its maker and its perceiver in a comfortable interchange based on a shared predictive ability. The structure dictates precise limits for the actions of the protagonist and for the actions of the teller. It is closed, circumscribing all aggressive tendencies, vanquishing any opportunity for wild, personal deviation.

The scholastic model used by Western thinkers to order wild reality is often structured similarly to the folktales and folk houses most appreciated by Western country people. The vertical, hierarchical model normally consists of three parts, the similarly structured higher and lower levels being dependent upon a variable central element. Thus the analyst isolates an object and then identifies a structural level below the object and a structural level above it. The object might be a house, and the analyst might call the lower level the architectural competence and the upper level the architectural context. When attempting social classification, the scholar will be apt to divide a society into three parts, the first and third of which are definitively dependent upon the middle one (lower, middle, upper; or conservative, normative, progressive; or folk, popular, academic). Or the scholar may simply divide society into two (low and high, working class and professional, mass and elite, poor and rich, the other half and our half). The horizontal model is structured similarly; it consist of two similar entities united by a third, different kind of entity. It consists, for example, of encoder (speaker), message, and decoder (listener), or it consists of a binary opposition that becomes a tripartite structure when mediated. The double-triple model or-

171

Fig. 81   THE WEST EUROPEAN TRIPARTITE BARN. To the left is an English example of the form, located at Kelmscott Manor, Kelmscott, Oxfordshire (June 1972). To the right is an example located in our area, and given the designation EE. It is a tobacco

barn. This same English barn form was used in Middle Virginia
for stables; an example located between houses K and T can be
found in *Pattern in the Material Folk Culture of the Eastern
United States*, Fig. 39A.

Fig. 82   CHURCH, FF. The South Anna Church. Its façade is an essay in tripartite bilateral symmetry. It is the opposite of the usual house in that its entry is at the gable end and it has two doors and one window instead of one door and two windows. That one window—puritanical Palladian—is also bilaterally symmetrical and tripartite.

174

ders data in a way familiar enough to be convincing to a Western thinker, balanced enough to seem complete, yet flexible enough to be usable.

Like the teller's *märchen* and the scholar's model, the dominant Anglo-American folk architectural design is closed; it is bilaterally symmetrical and tripartite. Like the tale, it is the attempt to contain fancy. Like the model, it is the attempt to control reality.

VIII

A Little History

Beyond the formal garden, across the drive where the coach waits, the great mansion soars, geometrically embracing its dependencies. Upstairs, the young master is practicing his Latin. Downstairs, the soft laugh of the cavalier melds with a tinkling spinet, and the aroma of rows of calfbound volumes drifts with the scent of waxed cabriole legs and polished silver. Brocaded gentility, liveried servility—leisurely elegance is our image of the old Virginia plantation. This image does not compare easily with that extracted through architectural analysis. This does not mean that the images are in conflict. The Carters and Blands, the Lees and Manns were real people, but there were not many of them. When I went into eastern Virginia to select a representative area I found many big plantation houses, but none of the grandiose mansion class. Had the survey circled deeper into Goochland, it would have included Tuckahoe, a seat of the Randolphs; then, too, it would have taken in hundreds of additional simpler homes (though Tuckahoe it-self is only a couple of pretentious I houses arranged into an H shape[1]).

Historians already know what the quantification of old houses proves—that the barons of the Chesapeake existed, but that there were few of them. Daniel Boorstin estimates the number of the ruling families of colonial Virginia at one hundred;[2] yet in 1750 the white population numbered about a quarter of a million.[3] Most of the people emigrated from England, Ireland, and Scotland as indentured servants who settled into seventeenth-century Virginia as yeomen on tracts of moderate dimensions.[4] By the end of the eighteenth century most white farmers owned slaves, but most owned very few slaves, and about as many owned none as owned many.[5] In Boorstin's description of old Virginia, he observes that the English gentleman was the model for the Virginia planter, that the Tidewater society might be divided into gentlemen, stewards, and peasants.[6] The connotations of this description leave us with too simple an understanding of that society, for the "peasants" were white as well as black, and the planter was usually a most modest "gentleman." Although the word sits uncomfortably in the American lexicon, the gentleman was as close to being a "peasant" (in the anthropological sense of being a participant in a conservative, insular, basically self-sufficent, agrarian community[7]) as he was to being an aristocrat. He established himself as the confident master of a country estate in the manner of an English gentleman. He controlled the labor of many farm laborers, though he did this by possessing slaves rather than renting to villagers or hiring seasonal workers. But his economy was limited, and the conflict between his aristocratic expectations and his peasant reality left his life more like that of the lonely farmer of Devonshire or Suffolk than like that of the manor's lord. His buildings were neither grander nor poorer than those of the contemporary British farmer.

The historian knows this, yet the hardscrabble Virginia farmer with his four slaves, his four-room English folk house, and his taste for ballads instead of books is obscured in the welter of ethnographies of opulence. I suppose that the survivalist explainer of this state would point out the surreptetitious elitist threads in the American fabric, and that the functionalist explainer would attribute it to the spirit of Reconstruction. The Southern historian, whose forefathers gambled and lost, wishes to make it appear that the game was worth entering, and the Northerner, whose ancestors took the pot, wants to make it appear that they bested worthy opponents. After skipping through the data the historian turns to describing the elegant lifestyle,[8] portrayed so tidily and convincingly at Williamsburg.[9] I hope the historian does not devote his descriptive energies to the rich and forget the vast majority because he considers them to be as a class "an historical nonentity."[10] As is the case today, the powerful had their intrigues and manias, but life among the people went on. The abundance of historical writing on the culture of wealth would seem mostly to be a consequence of the fact that the historian studies writing, and the wealthy left a lot of writing behind. From these writings we have come to know the Carters and the Randolphs, but when members of the majority break into print it is often a shock. Thomas Anburey, an English officer, left this account, written in 1779:

> at Colonel Randolph's, at Tuckahoe . . . three country peasants, who came upon business, entered the room where the Colonel and his company were sitting, took themselves chairs, drew near the fire, began spitting, pulling off their country boots all over mud, and then opened their business, which was simply about some continental flour to be ground at the Colonel's mill: When they were gone, some one observed what great liberties they took. . . .
>
> There were and still are, three degrees of ranks among the inhabitants, exclusive of negroes. . . .
>
> The first class consists of gentlemen of the best families and fortunes . . . for the most part they have had liberal educations. . . .
>
> The second class consists of such a strange mixture of characters, and of such various descriptions of occupations, being nearly half the inhabitants, that it is difficult to ascertain their exact criterion and leading feature. They are however, hospitable, generous, and friendly; but for want of a proper knowledge of the world, and a good education, as well as from their continual intercourse with their slaves,

over whom they are accustomed to tyrannize, with all their good qualities, they are rude, ferocious, and haughty, much attached to gaming and dissapation. . . .

The third class, which, in general composes the greatest part of mankind, are fewer in Virginia. . . .

The lower people possess that impertinent curiosity, so very disagreeable and troublesome to strangers . . . , they are averse to labor, much addicted to liquor, and when intoxicated, extremely savage and revengeful. . . .[11]

Those visitors to Tuckahoe come as no surprise to the serious student of old architecture. They are just the folks he had imagined walking the floors of the buildings he measures and photographs. They left no writing, but they did leave all these houses.

Even taking the care to choose a representative area, to conduct a methodical field survey, and to subject the data to rigorous analysis does not bring the scholar to a theoretical explanation of all of the people. Half of them were black. Several people described the slaves' houses to me, but, although a few quarters have survived in Virginia, I found none in the study area. Fortunately for history, the travelers who generally neglected to comment on the average planter did record descriptions—patchy and ugly descriptions—of the slaves' existence. If we rely on houses to provide us with information on antebellum Virginia, we are reduced to the study of the white half of the population. If we liberally grant 2 per cent of the total to the owners of places like Tuckahoe, Stratford, and Westover—places too rare to appear statistically within a representative sample—we are left with 48 per cent of the population. Women, unfortunately, expressed themselves in perishable artifacts, such as food and textiles; thus we are reduced to 24 per cent. But about

that rather sizable minority old houses have volumes to speak.[12] Once we have listened closely we can return to the written record to interpret it.

In his work of 1724, Hugh Jones set about to describe the "habits, life, customs, computations, etc. of the Virginians." "They have," he wrote, "good natural notions . . . ; but are generally diverted by business or inclination from profound study. . . .":

They are more inclinable to read men by business and conversation, than to dive into books, and are for the most part only desirous of learning what is absolutely necessary, in the shortest and best method. . . .

They are not very easily persuaded to the improvement of useful inventions (except a few, such as sawing mills) neither are they great encouragers of manufactures. . . .

So that though they are apt to learn, yet they are fond of, and will follow their own ways, humours, and notions, being not easily brought to new projects and schemes. . . .[13]

From that time to this, eastern Virginia has been a rural and conservative land. The rolling alliteration and the rhyming redundancy in T. S. Eliot's "Virginia"[14] demonstrate that the region entered his vision, two centuries after Jones, in much the same way. And Jones's evaluation complements the architectural statement, for the old houses manifest a mind both conservative and practical.

At the largest scale, conservatism is evidenced in the fundamental rejection of most of the national architectural modes and in the persistence across time of architectural forms with little change. It is reflected, too, in scratches on boards. The water-powered saw was known by the third century.[15] Although its early use in England was prohibited by law, the hydraulic saw was employed in Central Europe during the Middle Ages. By 1624 up-and-down saws were operating in Virginia, and in the seventeenth century they were grinding out boards throughout the colonies.[16] But the old boards in our area bear no marks of the up-and-down mill. Well into the nineteenth century the ancient pitsaw, called "stupid, slavish" by Hugh Jones,[17] powered only by men's muscles, continued to be the way to get boards out of logs. Like agriculturists of comparable estate in South Carolina and Scotland,[18] the human energy he controlled allowed the Middle Virginia farmer to indulge his technological conservatism.

The Old Dominion, it seems, was populated mostly out of western England. One would predict, then, that the west British crucked frame (Fig. 66) would have become the constructional norm in Virginia, just as the eastern English framing tradition was closely followed in New England. There are indications in old records and recent field discoveries that crucks were known in the seventeenth-century Tidewater.[19] The plate arrangement (Figs. 52, 67, 68) and planked, pitsawed timbers of the Virginia frame suggest possible relationships with crucked building, but the frame (Figs. 52, 54) was assembled out of straight scantling. The shape of the cruck blade, bent as the tree grew, was too natural to suit the Virginian's artificial intentions. He wanted all of the posts in his frame to be identical. The cruck's curves were abhorrent to his pragmatic aesthetic; he demanded precise, angular lines. He began with the same crooked oak that the English builder did, but it was necessary for him to invent a new means to frame his architectural idea.

In his doctoral dissertation, Thomas Jefferson Wertenbaker wrote that an increase in wealth in eighteenth-century Virginia produced "in the colony a love of elegance that was second only to that of the French nobility."[20] Nevertheless, one of the oppositions deep in old Virginia thought was so mediated that aesthetic tendencies were overwhelmed by utilitarian considerations. The more facts that are arranged, the more it seems that culture in Virginia was at least as "puritanical" as that of New England. The Puritan with back of black broadcloth has been replaced in recent scholarship by one attired in a variety of gay colors.[21] The figure cut by the elegant planter of the Chesapeake country was summed up in satirical verse by Eben. Cook, Gent., in 1708:

> . . . a numerous crew,
> In Shirts and Drawers of *Scotch-cloth* Blue.
> With neither Stockings, Hat, nor Shooe.
> These *Sot-weed* Planters Crowd the Shoar,
> In Hue as tawny as a Moor.[22]

Puritan stonecutters carved ornamentally curvaceous gravestones with coats of arms and portraits, as well as heads of death, cherubs,[23] and even depictions of God. Though nominal Anglicans, with no scruples about profaning the sacred through art, the old Virginians marked graves with austerely lettered slabs or silent chunks of rock. Nowhere in the American colonies does one find the rich molding and carving that grace the wooden house fronts of England, but the Yankee house carpenter often placed a decorative pediment over his doorway. In some instances this pediment swirls like the broken scroll atop the hood of a fine tall clock. The moldings of the Middle Virginia builder are curved in section, but the impression they leave is one of straight horizontal shadows; the lines are rigid. The finest doorway in our area

(Fig. 27) is the stiffest assemblage of straight lines. The Middle Virginia folk architect had an aesthetic.[24] His "grammar" of design guided him in building houses that were simultaneously workable and correct in appearance. The outline of the competence presented in chapter IV is precisely a statement of the fundamental architectural aesthetic of the Middle Virginia tradition; it enabled judgments by house builders and house users on the appearance and feel of houses.

It is probable, too, that the house carpenter took pleasure from construction, and he was surely capable of articulating judgments on technological qualities and surface finishes. But his aesthetic brooked no femininity, no gaiety, and it was dominated by formal efficiency. The house's appearance was correct, but nothing detracted obviously from its role as a tool. By the middle of the eighteenth century this practical aesthetic, old in the outposts of Atlantic Europe[25] (and the very opposite of that of the French nobility), had solidified in anticipation of the machined taste of the nineteenth century, which John Kouwenhoven has termed "the vernacular."[26] The American mind, which highly values the repetition of clean, usable shapes and efficient, solid plainness, is often considered to be the product of the industrial revolution. It was not until American industry had proved its success in the nineteenth century that intellectuals were compelled to confront—some in horror, some in rapture—the dominance of the mechanical vernacular. What seemed a novelty to the avant-grade thinker of the second quarter of the nineteenth century was, however, an old, old idea to the folk designer.

Old descriptions, bits of literature, reinforce the results of architectural analysis. Ebenezer Cook, Hugh Jones, and Thomas Anburey found the people of the Chesapeake country to be plainer by far than did historians of a later era, and the architecture itself provides the analyst with an inescapable impression of stiff simplicity. Still, a question of explanations lingers. After considering the folk buildings of Virginia we have been able to describe how change takes place, and we have been able to describe the nature of that change. Beginning about 1760 there was a change from organic to geometric symmetry, from extensive to intensive forms. There was an increase in the need for privacy and repetition, a sudden increase in the need for control (Fig. 84). But why this should be so has not yet been answered.

Two explanatory techniques are widely used in the contemporary study of culture. These techniques might be called the "correlative" and the "cognitive."[27] The correlative is the comparison of diverse phenomena and their arrangement into a pattern. An elaborate piece of recent correlative scholarship may be found in the cantometrics project directed by Alan Lomax. The computer was used to help define the singing styles of societies from around the world and to relate these styles to other cultural traits. Packed with humanistic suggestiveness, cantometrics demonstrated statistical compatibility between features of song and other manifestations of culture, such as economic and social type, varieties of sex role, and motion in dance.[28] Essays in the history of art often follow a similar course. Robert Plant Armstrong traced stylistic similarities through Yoruban sculpture, music, dance, literature, and manner of combat,[29] and Erwin Panofsky found thirteenth-century philosophy and architecture to be formally compatible.[30]

A correlative endeavor has trouble on each flank. When a correlative construct is examined with cause and effect in mind, it can easily dissolve into the chicken-and-egg conundrum. Or correlation can be overextended through coincidence to the establishment of pseudocorrelations,[31] and the analyst may be left with patterns lacking explanations and sets of influences that are not influential. As Panofsky remarked, "even a genuine parallelism does not make us really happy if we cannot imagine how it came about." [32] He was able to postulate a cause behind "mental habit," thus moving from correlation toward a cognitive explanation.

Cognitive explanations are models that explain correlations. A lack of data often prevents the scholar from moving past correlative constructs to cognitive structures, yet correlative constructs should be conceived as if they were the surface manifestations of an unknown mentality. Although things are often explained as if influences bobbed in the air waiting to alight on some object— to worm into it and alter its nature—influences are not influential unless they come into the mind of a human being. Correlative "explanations," then, are not explanations; they are an important first step in explanation. The task of the cognitive model is to explain the logic of a specific mind in small time and space. Once that is accomplished different cognitive models may be compared in order to come to a better understanding of the specific mind and to general principles of culture. The establish-ment of such principles is the ultimate goal of most of social science.

In a fascinating study, the anthropologist J. L. Fischer compared the art styles and social situations for a large group of societies from different parts of the world.[33] His assumption was that there should be correlations between artistic and social forms because both are manifestations of a culture's cognitive type. He was able to isolate artistic features that typified the opposite ends of a social spectrum, with hierarchical societies at one end and egalitarian societies at the other. Comparing our findings with his lends further credence to the principles toward which his hypotheses lead. It also exposes one face of the Middle Virginian's problem, for the culture manifested through houses seems to be trapped centrally between Fischer's social poles of hierarchy and egalitarianism. Like the art style of the egalitarian society, Middle Virginia architectural design is repetitive, but it is complexly repetitive, indicating a drift toward hierarchy. It is symmetrical, like the art usual in an egalitarian society, but it is strongly enclosed, like the art that Fischer found to be characteristic of the hierarchical society. The architectural design's central locus between the two ideal cognitive types would seem to accurately reflect the conflict in a society that is schizophrenically attracted at once—as American society is—to hierarchical social classification and to egalitarian activity. Middle Virginia architectural design would seem to be an exhibit of deep social tension. There are other indications that such social tension existed—remember those visitors to Tuckahoe.

My task was to find pattern—correlation, that is—in

actual buildings, and then to set up models—one of the architectural competence, one of the architectural abstracted context—to account for that pattern. I worked on the assumption that culture is not a collection of things, but a mental system, and that this mental system might be understood through an analysis of objects. One of the important correlations that appears as a pattern through the data from Middle Virginia is a link between apparently conflicting tendencies toward separateness and redundancy. This pattern is compatible with the observation that Middle Virginia folk architectural design seems to reflect a mind located between J. L. Fischer's social-artistic poles. The pattern is no accidental parallel, but instead is the logical manifestation of a culture that simultaneously places prime value on individualism (the separation of self) and repetition (the identical restatement of ideas), a culture based deeply on control and, more shallowly, on practicality, closure, intensiveness, internalness, and artificiality.

Individualism is found in the desire for privacy and in separation at every level of the architectural particularistic context, from movable furniture to dispersed settlement. The house, for example, is the shelter for one family. In England, even in the countryside, houses are often joined into duplexes or attached into strings. The XX house, with its two front doors, is, in England, generally a dwelling for two families (Fig. 83). I was told that when it served as slave quarters, the XX house in Virginia was the home for two families, but now it provides the residence for single nuclear families. Its two-door façade marks not the presence of two families, but the presence of a need for symmetrical, repetitious forms (rule I.D.2).

There are two houses in the study area that are aggregates, suggesting the possibility that they were the homes of two families—the families of brothers, perhaps, who worked a single farm. Similar oddly conjoined houses are found elsewhere in the eastern South as well as in England, where in some cases, at least, the house did shelter different branches of a family. However, the oral tradition of both of these Middle Virginia houses (Figs. 33, 34) is that only one family lived in them at a time. The 1850 census reported 876 dwellings and 878 families in Goochland, and 1,254 dwellings and 1,254 families in Louisa.[34] Today a few Afro-American houses shelter stem families, but the tradition persists of one family alone in one home.

In his consideration of the ways of cultural change, H. G. Barnett expressed the optimistic opinion prevalent in the West that "there is a positive correlation between individualism and innovative potential."[35] In the traditional architecture of Middle Virginia (as in most of the eastern United States), though the buildings are physically separate, they are closely similar. In the Anglo-American world of the eighteenth century the farther people moved apart, the more alike their architectural expressions became. Through time, the increase in individualism was accompanied by a contraction of the culture: the dominance of fewer house types, less variation within types once the fully symmetrical design had been achieved, and a diminishing of the inventory of detail and decoration. Houses once red, yellow, and white became white. Chimneys once internal or external with single or double shoulders became internal. Windows once had twelve, fifteen, or eighteen lights; they came to

Fig. 83 ENGLISH COTTAGES. These homes of rural workers are located in Upper Woodford, Wiltshire (June 1972). To the right is a form similar to the Middle Virginia type 9 (the two-story, end-chimney XX house), except this form comprises the homes for two families and amounts to two-thirds of a string of three connected houses.

have only twelve. This compares closely with the pattern James Deetz discovered in colonial New England ceramics. After the middle of the eighteenth century everyone ate off his plate instead of out of a communal trencher, but those plates were not personalized. They came in sets and were identical to each other.[36]

Broken plates, old houses, and the daily actions of human beings are not things that engage the attention of essayists in a rush to generalize about cultural styles. It is often argued that the rise of individualism and self-consciousness leads to a greater freedom to act. Such notions have to be formed in the vapor above ethnography, for in a society that values individualism it is possible for some people to assert themselves and become authorities, but most people withdraw and become authoritarian. In American society, at least, it seems hard to avoid the observation that the increase in individualistic possibilities has led to greater freedom for the few and an increase in fear and behavioral redundancy for most people.[37] The mistake is to contemplate individualism without recognizing that it can be structured interdependently with repetition.

The opposite error is the consideration of repetition alone. Repetitious behavior is not necessarily a sign of a community based on a oneness of will. Living in daily contact, people in villages, such as Chan Kom or Llareggub, can expose some idiosyncracies and develop an internal tolerance. Out of contact, people don masks that are identical in order to compensate for their lack of face-to-face knowing.

Once a correlation, such as that between individualism and repetitiousness, is seen to hold together in new situa-

tions and begins to help us to better understand problems claiming our interest, it is tempting to treat the relation stated by the correlation as the end product of study. The social scientist, in imitation of some image of the physical scientist, may stop his quest at endless tests of the correlation, leaving other possibilities to those he dismisses as "philosophers." Comparably, the historian is sometimes satisfied with a special brand of middle-range correlative "explanation," wherein existential man is set aside, while some of his expressions—his vote, for instance, or his poetry—are taken and ordered into a pattern of linear diachrony leading backward from the current status quo.

The theoretical problem of correlations remains: what caused the state of affairs that has been recognized? Immediately the pragmatic problem of correlative constructs arises; the supposed reality of correlations exerts so much force upon the scholar that when things get linked into a set of series, other things are considered only insofar as they can be related to the first, established set or series. Local architecture, then, often engages the architectural historian only to the extent that it can be correlated with the known stylistic sequence, and local history becomes important only as a "reflection" of national history. In nonhistorical comparative research the same procedure is followed when the analyst deems the local culture worthy of attention only to the extent that it can be related to an academic canon of oral literary genres, say, or kinship types. The trouble comes when the historian studies a community in order to find evidence of the impact of an embargo act, or the folklorist seeks in the same community for a legend tradition, because both will be successful. The scholar can describe the things he likes and can show why they are important to him, but too often he leaves no guide to their importance for the human beings he is ostensibly studying. The dangers of operating in such a manner suggest that the local chronology and the local repertoire should be built up first. Then research can expand to seek correlations with—and plausible causes for—the local patterns. Localized research should provide tough tests for old models. It should not be only the search for anecdotes and examples to insert in old patterns.

The past is not directly knowable. The historian cannot, therefore, be a scientist. Thus begins the defense of the historian who wishes to continue a scholarly practice that consists of writing elegant, convincing narratives founded on correlations.[38] However, the historian does have directly knowable objects in the form of the artifacts, and it is upon these artifacts that his study must be entirely grounded. These could be used to construct scientific descriptions and scientific tests.[39] The analogy with anthropology is exact, for culture is directly unknowable, but the awareness that it is unknowable does not prevent the ethnographer or ethnologist from proceeding scientifically. The historian can quantify and analyze his artifacts with the care that an astronomer gives to the stars or an archaeologist gives to chipped flint.

Once the artifact, whether document or house, has been analyzed, the student has a choice. He may stop; from the angle of scientific method, he cannot go farther. Or he may adopt the risky sort of explanation traditional to history and move from assembled facts to correlations to hypothetical causes, thus eschewing methodological purity for understanding. I prefer the latter course. Cor-relative guesswork should be held back, kept aside, until it becomes unavoidable. Then, after we have taken analysis as far as possible, we should follow even paths of inquiry known to lead into sloughs of circularity, if it seems that they may, by their very exploration, help us to comprehend our existence. Thus we will go beyond those influences, such as the weather, which we can be certain had effect within the abstracted context of the old builder, to discover some others that *may* have been influences.

The history of our locality, as it is written in folk houses, includes one revolution (Fig. 84). It is an explanation of that revolution that is wanting. During the early part of the third quarter of the eighteenth century, design became geometrically symmetrical. Extensiveness peaked and was overcome by intensiveness; an optimistic and aggressive, though enclosed, image was replaced by one of tight control. We know, of course, that dramatic events, such as the Civil War, occurred during the nineteenth century. The analysis of architecture suggests that these events served only to further and solidify the change that took place in the eighteenth century. There was no abrupt break in architectural design during the nineteenth century. But there was a violent break in the eighteenth. Our problem is to posit the conditions that might help us comprehend this change, this failure of cultural nerve.

In 1773 a whiggish and priggish young scholar, who had come down from Princeton to tutor the Carter children, wrote in a letter: "I believe the virginians have of late altered their manner very much. . . ." He attributed that change to economic matters, and the economy was

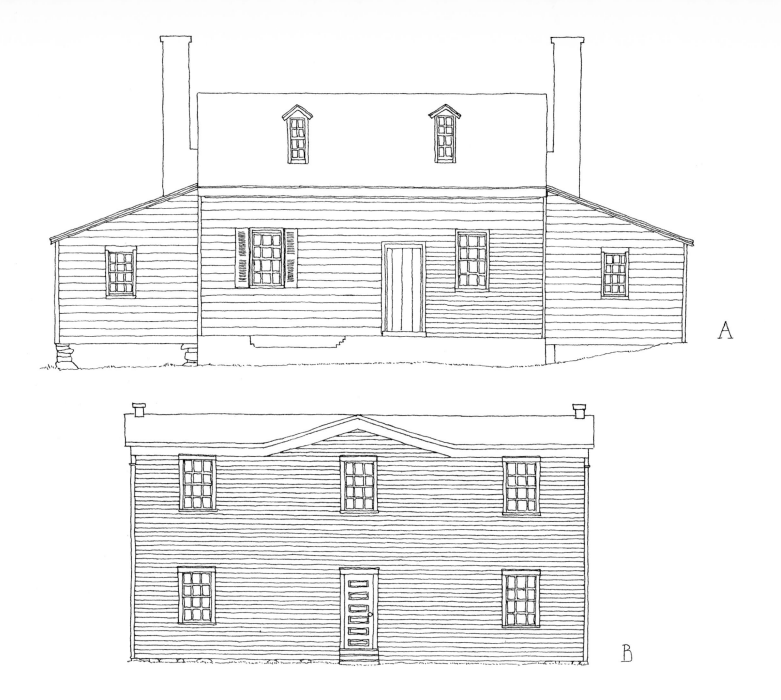

A

B

his journal's major interest, but he entered as well comments on politics. Half a year later he wrote: "The lower Class of People here are in a tumult on account of Reports from Boston, many of them expect to be press'd & compell'd to go and fight the Britains!" And three days later: "The general voice is *Boston*." Next month: "The reigning spirit in Virginia is liberty—And the universal topics politicks."[40] Since Bacon's Rebellion (a little feasibility study for revolution), politics had been a bother in Virginia. By the time architectural extensiveness yielded to intensiveness, problems between Mother England and her feisty American daughter were out in the open.

Fig. 84   DIAGRAM OF THE MIDDLE VIRGINIA HOUSING REVOLUTION. *A.* House H (type 5: Fig. 31). *B.* House S (type 14: Fig. 42). These houses correctly exemplify the local forms, both statistically and conceptually, before and after the housing revolution. Compare them for their presentation of symmetry and intensive and extensive features: height off the ground, height and shape of chimneys, height of ceilings and roofs. The great differences between these houses can be easily grasped when it is realized that the houses were drawn to the same scale and the one-story house actually extends higher into the air than the two-story house. The competence changed, and even previously built houses were changed. The extensive front porch of house H was removed and never replaced; its beaded clapboards have been largely replaced by plain boards; the shutters (effective environmental modifiers and, when painted, decorative features) remain on only one of the windows.

People's lives are touched more obviously by economics than by politics; in eighteenth-century Virginia that touch came least subtly through tobacco. Everyone's fortunes were ultimately connected to the price a hogshead could command,[41] and that price was forever fluctuating. During the middle of the century, when the sharp architectural change occurred, the tobacco market was skidding into hard times.[42] The wealthiest planters were also the government, so they made the usual shady deals that dulled the edge of the declining economy for themselves,[43] but the decline cut deeply into the hopes of most people. The richest farmers, too, could afford to own more manpower and undersell the modest planter, and throughout the eighteenth century the rift between poor and wealthy white farmers widened.[44]

Carl Bridenbaugh noted that a spirit of religious dissent in Virginia filled the social atmosphere with "neo-puritanical" strictness.[45] This could have been another of the conditions of pervasive culture change in our section of Middle Virginia, for the settlers were both Presbyterian and Anglican. The plain, severe Providence Presbyterian church, built about 1749, still stands, sheltering a tiny congregation west of Gum Spring, back from the Three Chopt Road, near the Rackett house. An indication of the local significance of religion is that the house of God is structured with its ridge and entrance aligned (Fig. 82), whereas all the houses of men and beasts are structured in the opposite manner (rule VIII.A.1)—a sign of radical separation. The Virginian was serious and fearful about his religion, and at the time that his architecture reveals such an abrupt change he was probably perplexed on one side by the lingering mood of the recent

Great Awakening, and on the other by rumors of the spirit of a Godless rationalism.

The greatest changes in the eighteenth century were social. In 1670 black people comprised 5 per cent of the colony's population; by 1730 they made up 26 per cent of the total; by 1770 they were about 50 per cent of the population.[46] Conspiracies had circled among black Virginians in the early eighteenth century;[47] a slave rebellion was a rumored possibility. Margaret Hunter Hall, a visitor from England in 1828, was displeased to find soldiers on perpetual parade in Richmond. Upon inquiring, she found that "the reason for having them is in case of an insurrection amongst slaves of which the Southern people live in constant dread. What a miserable existence it must be!"[48] Nothing so dramatic was necessary to cause the culture to curl in upon itself like a dying spider; it took no rebellion to send the culture into hiding behind a bland mask. In the middle of the eighteenth century the white Middle Virginian's political and religious traditions were unsteady. His own fortune was failing, yet the rich were getting richer. He was increasingly surrounded by black people who were involuntarily aiding his economic decline, who might revolt, whose very existence called his ethos into question. The world around him was losing its shape, falling apart. He had to hold it together, get it under control.

Stepping back for a longer look, we can catch a glimpse of the more distant past and future in the board walls and faded colors of the little eighteenth-century house. It was the expression of a culture under rigid control, a culture that would help a man walk straight and noble through the leaden hail at Gettysburg, to be splattered to scraps by Yankee shot without ever having really understood what it was all about.

The mind of the white farmer in eighteenth-century Virginia was characterized by many of the traits of modern mind that are normally explained as products of the nineteenth century's industrial revolution. More utilitarian than aesthetic, more analytic than organic, more individualistic than communitarian, emphasizing precise repetition, mechanical line, and geometric objectification, this mind, though rural and agrarian, was a cause of the industrial revolution, not a result of it.

Before taking another step backward, let us pause for a restatement. Architectural traditions are generally explained in terms of fashion or practicality. If a fashion were developed in an urban center and then accepted by everyone, the explanation for architectural change would be simple: people always follow fashions and architecture is no exception. If, on the other hand, fashions were never accepted, a different but equally simple explanation would be possible; these people, because of physical isolation or nativistic conservatism, adhere to the fashion of their own tradition without influence from urban centers. But the fact is, there is no area in the Anglo-American world where the architecture is either wholly fashionable or wholly traditional. Saying that a building is an expression of some fashion may indicate a relationship between the design of different localities, but it explains nothing. What needs an explanation is why that particular fashion was accepted.

The beginning of such an explanation is located when it is noted that normally the fashion of the urban center connotes an upper-class lifestyle, so that the decision to follow cosmopolitan fashion is an act of economic hopefulness. The historical reality of the acceptance of fashion, though, is still unexplained; the Georgian fashion was very influential in Middle Virginia, but the Greek Revival and Gothic Revival were not. The Georgian fashion must have offered something that the other "styles" did not, something needed by the people. That something can be seen in the Georgian elements which were accepted: the symmetrical façade and the central hallway. Fashion alone cannot have determined what would be acceptable; equally fashionable elements, such as the two-room depth, were not accepted. Thus, I have argued that the incorporation of the central hallway can be explained as a manifestation of the need for control and egalitarian imagery expressed through the vehicle of symmetry, as a statement of the wish for privacy, and as an accommodation to the weather. Also, the fashionableness of the central hall made it a useful sign within an upwardly mobile strategy. Fashion was an influence, but it is not a sufficient explanation.

The practical architectural explanation is deeply genuine, for the physical environment sets the outside limits for all architectural possibilities and provides the ultimate test of a tradition's sanity. But the practical explanation normally avoids the profound role of the environment and reduces man to a beast following the line of least resistance into his ecological niche. If there is a lot of wood around, he will build a wooden house. The lengths of the timbers will determine the house's shape. This sort of explanation always seems to work in given situations, and it always falls apart when the architecture of different areas sharing similar environments is compared. There were many trees in Middle Virginia; therefore the carpenter built of wood. But why did he build an angular shape instead of a rounded one as did the Indian in the same area, and why did he build of frame instead of log, like the Pennsylvania Germans, and why was his framed house different, in form and construction, from the houses of England and New England?

During its extensive period the house was a practical and ideal fit for a hot, humid climate. During its intensive period the house evolved into a form increasingly less well suited to the environment. The roof, for example, became flatter. Obviously some force other than practicality was acting upon the Virginia designer. Perhaps this force was fashion, for the flatter roof was fashionable in the earlier nineteenth century. But when, in the later nineteenth century, the steep roof became fashionable, the Middle Virginian's roof just kept getting flatter and flatter.

Fashion and practicality are real influences; they exert energy within the builder's abstracted context. Taken separately or together they are not sufficiently strong to explain all of what happened in any architectural tradition. Architectural fashion is used superficially as a means to deep ends. Things are fashionable insofar as that fashionableness answers the needs of the individual and insofar as that fashionableness fits the logic of his culture. The physical environment constrains, but it does not direct. It provides the stage upon which cultural options are sorted out, rejected, accepted, and ordered into a particular cultural logic. The cultural logic is not a free-will philosophy, however. Architectural thinking is bound to thinking about nonarchitectural matters, so that any theory explaining architecture in solely architectural terms may be somewhat correct, but it can never be enough. The social, economic, political, and religious conditions of life in Middle Virginia changed. People adapted to those changes, developing new modes of thought, and the things they did, the artifacts they made, manifested the changes that had taken place in their minds.

The great change in eighteenth-century Virginia is precisely parallel to a change that has taken place throughout the West during the past four hundred years. The characteristic house of New England, like that of Virginia, suddenly became more symmetrical during the eighteenth century.[49] In a rural Irish community where I studied intensely, domestic architecture changed rapidly from asymmetrical and open to symmetrical and closed at a time of political revolution and economic and religious troubles.[50] Through much of England the asymmetrically fronted, socially open house was replaced by one with a symmetrical façade and a floor plan that withdraws its inhabitants from outside contact. In many Midland and West Country (Fig. 85) areas this was accomplished, as it was in Virginia, by the inclusion of a central hallway.[51] In parts of northwestern England the old house was a balanced hall-and-parlor house quite like that of the southern United States (Fig. 31). It was replaced by a house in which the rear shed was symmetrically incorporated, as in New England, but instead of positioning a hallway or chimney stack in the center, the designer placed the stair there to block the entrance of a visitor (Fig. 86). There was no evolution of pain and blood in northwestern England to compare with that of America in 1776 or Ireland in 1916, when the comparable architectural changes occurred; still, the northwestern English housing tradition underwent the same functional alteration.[52] The change that has been described for Virginia, then, is too big for any set of localized immediate conditions to explain fully. In different areas the change has taken place at different times, it has been manifested through different forms, and it has been the result of different immediate conditions, but both basic cause and major effects have been the same.

Houses help us locate an important point in the evolution of the Western mind. It is the point at which the face-to-face community dies.[53] As the community begins to fail, aggressive tendencies are unleashed. Suddenly wealthy peasants in England built elaborate timber expressions of their new estate, like Paycocke's at Coggeshall; the less successful rushed into Ireland and then America to erect proud, extensive monuments to themselves in the woods. The trajectory of personal aggression carries through the accumulation of capital and prestige to the elimination of communal goals. Individualism becomes loneliness. The direct and known yields to the indirect and unknown, and a person's predictions become so weakened and complex that he despairs or struggles to achieve control. Unsure of his situation, he and his neighbors build identical houses with floor plans that suggest withdrawal and façades that suggest impersonal stability. Personal energies are removed from the immediate community and invested in abstract ideals, such as racial superiority, nationalism, or artificial, symmetrical order.

When we move back to take still more time into view, it

Fig. 85 WEST COUNTRY I HOUSE. Located near Woodland, east of Ashburton, Devonshire (June 1972), this house is closely similar to the central-hall I houses of Middle Virginia. Basically, the same form dominated the landscape of the Chesapeake Country and the west of England from the middle of the eighteenth century through the nineteenth.

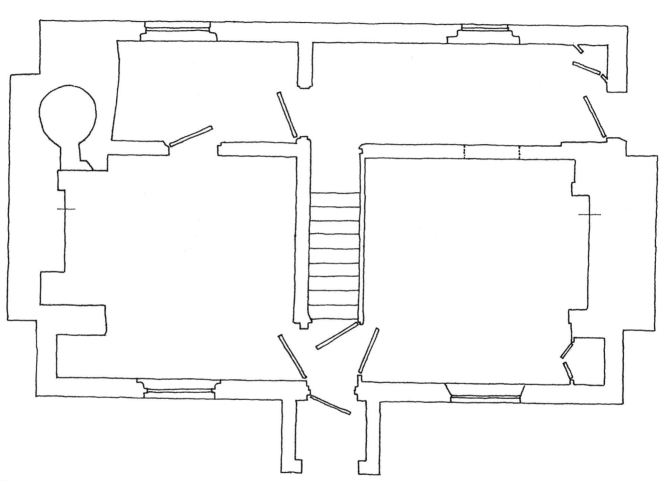

Fig. 86 PLAN OF A NORTHWESTERN ENGLISH HOUSE. This house was built in 1755 near Ford, Shropshire (October 1972). The porch is original. As one stands in an entry in front of the stairs, the kitchen is to the left, the parlor to the right. The arrangement of service rooms across the back shows that, though now covered under a symmetrical roof, they had their genesis in a shed appendage.

192

seems that what went on in eighteenth-century Middle Virginia was but a quickening in the movement of Western history. Coming into a wilderness and asserting there a culture based on artificial, repetitively individualistic control is one of the small events that furthered the momentum of Western time. Among the great events are these. At the European dawn a man directed that a ponderous wheel plow be dragged through thick clay by eight oxen; from then on man became increasingly separated from nature.[54] With the broad-scale enclosure of the countryside, communal obligations were replaced by individual land and labor; from then on man became increasingly separated from man.[55] In paint and print, silver and stone, the arrogant Quattrocento masters proclaimed their independence from public and social need;[56] the Reformation shattered the religious experience of Western man, beginning the end of faith; the scientists of the Puritan century offered their genius to technology in the name of progress;[57] from then onward art became increasingly separated from labor,[58] the spiritual and the material were progressively sundered, and knowing further parted from doing. In the middle of the eighteenth century factories commenced to draw farm folk from the fields, fathers from their homes; from then on work became increasingly separated from living in families,[59] and families broke down into smaller and smaller components as the social unit contracted from the community to the family to the individual. Into that overwhelming pattern the Middle Virginia folk mind fits with gallant reluctance, but awful inevitability. The pattern is the evolution of individualism and control over natural forces[60]—the evolution of alienation and boredom.

The old farmer of Middle Virginia is left standing alone at the end of a row. He watches, without motion, the dust spun from the auto's tires settle through his garden. He lifts his chin from the back of his hand, his hand from the hoe. He shoulders the hoe and crosses the yard, glancing to the left at the sleek mule in his pen, and drops himself into a chair on the porch, where, efficient and swift, the hands of his wife click snap beans into a pot. Staring down into the middle distance, he says to himself alone, "Many changes, many changes, many changes, many changes."

Notes

I: A Silent Land

1. Raus McDill Hanson, *Virginia Place Names* (Verona, Va.: McClure Press, 1969), 127.

2. *Heads of Families At the First Census of the United States, Taken in the Year 1790: Records of the State Enumerations: 1782 to 1795: Virginia* (Washington: Government Printing Office, 1908), 9.

3. J. B. D. DeBow, *Statistical View of the United States . . . a Compendium of the Seventh Census* [1850] (Washington: Beverley Tucker, 1854), 320, 322.

4. *Compendium of the Tenth Census (June 1, 1880)*, I (Washington: Government Printing Office, 1885), 376; *Twelfth Census of the United States, Taken in the Year 1900, William R. Merriam, Director: Population*, I (Washington: U.S. Census Office, 1901), 561.

5. *The Eighteenth Decennial Census of the United States: Census of Population: 1960*, I:48 (Washington: Government Printing Office, 1963), 48 ff.

6. See Tench Coxe. *Tabular Statements of the Several Branches of American Manufactures . . . of the Year 1810* (Philadelphia: A. Cornman, 1813), 88–114.

7. *Census for 1820* (Washington: Gales and Seaton, 1821), 23.

8. DeBow, *Statistical View of the United States*, 324–25.

9. *Compendium of the Tenth Census (June 1, 1880)*, I, 824–25; II (Washington: Government Printing Office, 1888), 1023.

10. Richard C. Wight, *The Story of Goochland* (Richmond, Va.: Richmond Press, 1935), 50, 51.

11. Jean Gottman, *Virginia at Mid-Century* (New York: Holt, 1955), 150, 152, 175–76.

12. Rosewell Page, *Hanover County: Its History and Legends* (n.p.: author, 1926), 39.

13. Robert Bolling Lancaster, *A Sketch of the Early History of Hanover County, Virginia* (Ashland: Hanover Chapter of the Association for the Preservation of Virginia Antiquities, 1957), 13.

II: A More Human History

1. Fustel de Coulanges considered history to be the most difficult of trades. In Marc Bloch, *French Rural Society: An*

Essay on its Basic Characteristics, trans. Janet Sondheimer (Berkeley: Univ. of California Press, 1970), xxiii.

2. Claude Lévi-Strauss, *The Scope of Anthropology*, trans. Sherry Ortner Paul and Robert A. Paul (London: Jonathan Cape, 1967), 21, 25.

3. Jean-Paul Sartre, *Search for a Method*, trans. Hazel E. Barnes (New York: Random House, 1963), 51–52, 80.

4. See Ferdinand de Saussure, "On the Nature of Language," in *Introduction to Structuralism*, ed. Michael Lane (New York: Basic Books, 1970), 47–56.

5. Claude Lévi-Strauss, *The Savage Mind* (Chicago: Univ. of Chicago Press, 1966), 256–62; Marvin Harris, *The Rise of Anthropological Theory: A History of Theories of Culture* (New York: Thomas Y. Crowell, 1971), 64.

6. Lynn White, Jr., "History: The Changing Past," in *Frontiers of Knowledge in the Study of Man*, ed. Lynn White, Jr. (New York: Harper, 1956), 71–72; Peter Laslett, *The World We have Lost: England Before the Industrial Age* (New York: Scribner's, 1965), 195; Richard M. Dorson, *American Folklore and the Historian* (Chicago: Univ. of Chicago Press, 1971), 142, 148–50.

7. J. M. Bocheński, *The Methods of Contemporary Thought*, trans. Peter Caws (New York: Harper, 1968), 120; Claude Lévi-Strauss, *Structural Anthropology*, trans. Claire Jacobson and Brooke Grundfest Schoepf (Garden City, N.Y.: Doubleday, 1967), 18.

8. See G. W. F. Hegel, *Reason in History: A General Introduction to the Philosophy of History*, trans. Robert S. Hartman (1837; rpt. New York: Bobbs-Merrill, 1953), 13; Marc Bloch, *The Historian's Craft*, trans. Peter Putnam (New York: Random House, 1953), 144; Lucien Goldmann, *The Human Sciences and Philosophy*, trans. Hayden V. White and Robert Anchor (London: Jonathan Cape, 1969), 30.

9. See W. K. C. Guthrie, *In the Beginning: Some Greek Views on the Origins of Life and the Early State of Man* (Ithaca, N.Y.: Cornell Univ. Press, 1965), chs. 4 and 5.

10. See Lucien Febvre, "Marc Bloch," in *Architects and Craftsmen in History: Festschrift Für Abbott Payson Usher*, ed. Joseph T. Lambie (Tübingen: J. C. B. Mohr, Paul Siebeck, 1956), 75–84.

11. William Lynwood Montell, *The Saga of Coe Ridge: A Study in Oral History* (Knoxville: Univ. of Tennessee Press, 1970); see especially the preface.

12. See Peter O. Wacker, *The Musconetcong Valley of New Jersey* (New Brunswick, N.J.: Rutgers Univ. Press, 1968); James T. Lemon, *The Best Poor Man's Country: A Geographical Study of Early Southeastern Pennsylvania* (Baltimore: Johns Hopkins Univ. Press, 1972).

13. See Bernard L. Fontana, J. Cameron Greenleaf, *et al.*, "Johnny Ward's Ranch: A Study in Historic Archaeology," *The Kiva*, 28:1–2 (Oct.–Dec., 1962), 1–115; Edwin Dethlefson and James Deetz, "Death's Heads, Cherubs, and Willow Trees: Experimental Archaeology in Colonial Cemeteries," *American Antiquity*, 31:4 (April 1966), 502–10.

14. See John Demos, *A Little Commonwealth: Family Life in Plymouth Colony* (New York: Oxford Univ. Press, 1970); Kenneth A. Lockridge, *A New England Town: The First Hundred Years* (New York: Norton, 1970); Philip J. Greven, Jr., *Four Generations: Population, Land, and Family in Colonial Andover, Massachusetts* (Ithaca, N.Y.: Cornell Univ. Press, 1970); Sumner Chilton Powell, *Puritan Village: The Formation of a New England Town* (Garden City, N.Y.: Doubleday, 1965).

15. Michael Polanyi, *The Study of Man* (Chicago: Univ. of Chicago Press, 1959), 84–85.

16. See Jan Vansina, *Oral Tradition: A Study in Historical Methodology*, trans. H. M. Wright (Chicago: Aldine, 1965); Richard M. Dorson, "The Debate over the Trustworthiness of Oral Traditional History," in *Folklore: Selected Essays* (Bloomington: Indiana Univ. Press, 1972); Richard M. Dorson, "Folklore and Traditional History," *Journal of the Folklore Institute*, VIII:2/3 (Aug.–Dec. 1971), 79–184.

17. Bloch, *The Historian's Craft*, 60–61.

18. See Hugh Dalziel Duncan, *Symbols in Society* (New

York: Oxford Univ. Press, 1972), 50–51.

19. See Lynn White, Jr., *Medieval Technology and Social Change* (New York: Oxford Univ. Press, 1964), v, 13, 39.

20. Bocheński, *Methods of Contemporary Thought*, 123; Kenneth Burke, *A Rhetoric of Motives* (Berkeley: Univ. of California Press, 1969), 111–12.

21. See Jean Piaget, *Insights and Illusions of Philosophy*, trans. Wolfe Mays (New York: World, 1971), 130–62, especially 135, 153, 158–59; Abraham Maslow, *The Psychology of Science: A Reconnaisance* (Chicago: Regnery, 1966), 19.

22. See André Malraux, *Museum Without Walls: The Voices of Silence* (Garden City, N.Y.: Doubleday, 1967), 80–81; Daniel Biebuyck, "Introduction," in *Tradition and Creativity in Tribal Art*, ed. Daniel Biebuyck (Berkeley: Univ. of California Press, 1969), 16–17; Robert Scholes and Robert Kellogg, *The Nature of Narrative* (New York: Oxford Univ. Press, 1968), 274–77.

23. See W. G. Hoskins, *Local History in England* (London: Longmans, 1965), 2, 106–38; Bernard L. Fontana, "Bottles, Buckets and Horseshoes: The Unrespectable in American Archaeology," *Keystone Folklore Quarterly*, XIII:3 (Fall 1968), 171–84; Alan Gowans, *On Parallels in Universal History Discoverable in Arts and Artifacts: An Outline Statement*, Univ. of Victoria Monograph Series, History in the Arts, 6 (Victoria, B.C.: Univ. of Victoria, 1972), 9–26, 95. An admirable new statement of the need for artifactual study in historical understanding is E. Estyn Evans, *The Personality of Ireland: Habitat, Heritage and History* (New York: Cambridge Univ. Press, 1973), ch. I in particular.

III: Prologue to Analysis

1. Noam Chomsky, *Syntactic Structures*, Janua Linguarum, 4 (The Hague: Mouton, 1957), 13, 50–51.

2. Claude Lévi-Strauss, "Interview," trans. Peter B. Kussell, *Diacritics*, I:1 (Fall 1971), 44.

3. See George A. Miller, *The Psychology of Communication: Seven Essays* (Baltimore: Penguin, 1969), 66.

4. Henry Glassie, "The Variation of Concepts in Tradition: Barn Building in Otsego County, New York," in *Man and Cultural Heritage*, ed. H. J. Walker and W. G. Haag, Geoscience and Man, 5 (Baton Rouge: Louisiana State Univ. Press, in press).

5. See Robert K. Merton, *On Theoretical Sociology: Five Essays, Old and New* (New York: Free Press, 1967), 147–49.

6. Robert Brown, *Explanation in Social Science* (Chicago: Aldine, 1963), 171.

7. See Thomas S. Kuhn, *The Structure of Scientific Revolutions*, International Encyclopedia of Unified Science, II:2 (Chicago: Univ. of Chicago Press, 1970), ch. IV.

8. *Annals of the Association of American Geographers*, XXVI (1936), 179–93.

9. For some suggestions on technique, see the last section in the bibliography.

10. Fred Kniffen, "Folk Housing: Key to Diffusion," *Annals of the Association of American Geographers*, 55:4 (Dec. 1965), 550.

11. See Kathleen Booth Williams, *Marriages of Louisa County: 1766–1815* (n.p. [probably Alexandria]: author, 1959).

12. A couple of months before I began this book I wrote an article, "Structure and Function, Folklore and the Artifact," *Semiotica*, VII:4 (1973), 313–51, containing amplifications of some of the theoretical points involved here, as well as some (somewhat premature) statements of the method used in parts of this book.

13. Noam Chomsky, *Language and Mind* (New York: Harcourt, Brace, and World, 1968), 4, 61–62.

14. Frank Lloyd Wright attributed the qualities he saw in "folk-buildings" to a natural, human "grammar of architectural forms." See "The Sovereignty of the Individual" in *Frank Lloyd Wright: Writings and Buildings*, ed. Edgar Kaufmann and Ben Raeburn (Cleveland: World, 1969), 85, 89, 93.

15. Of the many references that could be offered at this

point, the most relevant and important is James Deetz, *Invitation to Archaeology* (Garden City, N.Y.: Natural History Press, 1967), 83–96.

16. See Lévi-Strauss, *Structural Anthropology*, 29–31, 68, 82.

17. See *Language and Mind*, 64, 66, 77.

IV: The Architectural Competence

1. See Franz Boas, *Primitive Art* (1927; rpt. New York: Dover, 1965), 11. See also Clovis Heimsath, *Pioneer Texas Buildings: A Geometry Lesson* (Austin: Univ. of Texas Press, 1968), 4–19; Rudolf Arnheim, *Art and Visual Perception: A Psychology of the Creative Eye* (Berkeley: Univ. of California Press, 1971), 53.

2. My intention is to refer to Lévi-Strauss' concept of *bricolage*; see *The Savage Mind*, 14–22.

3. Opinions vary wildly as to how much of a person's competence is innate in the human mind, how much is learned in behavioral context. See Chomsky's antibehaviorist position in his *Aspects of the Theory of Syntax* (Cambridge: M.I.T. Press, 1965), 47–59, for an interesting discussion of the problem. I am most satisfied by Jean Piaget's formulation in *Structuralism*, trans. Chaninah Maschler (New York: Basic Books, 1970), 12–13, 60–96, 141–42.

4. Chomsky, *Language and Mind*, 16.

5. See Claude Brémond, "Morphology of the French Folktale," *Semiotica*, II:3 (1970), 247–76; A. Julien Greimas, "The Interpretation of Myth: Theory and Practice," in *Structural Analysis of Oral Tradition*, ed. Pierre Maranda and Elli Köngäs Maranda, Univ. of Pennsylvania Publications in Folklore and Folklife, 3 (Philadelphia: Univ. of Pennsylvania Press, 1971), 81–121; Robert A. Georges, "Structure in Folktales: A Generative-Transformational Approach," *The Conch*, II:2 (Sept. 1970), 4–17.

6. See Alan Dundes, "Introduction to the Second Edition," V. Propp, *Morphology of the Folktale*, American Folklore Society, Bibliographical and Special Series, 9; Indiana Univ. Research Center in Anthropology, Folklore, and Linguistics, 10 (Austin: Univ. of Texas Press, 1968), xii.

7. See Bocheński, *Methods of Contemporary Thought*, 40–42.

8. Jean Piaget, *Structuralism*, 8–13.

9. See Michael Polanyi, *The Tacit Dimension* (Garden City, N.Y.: Doubleday, 1967), 16–17.

10. See Roland Barthes, *Elements of Semiology*, trans. Annette Lavers and Colin Smith (Boston: Beacon Press, 1970), 12.

11. Roman Jakobson and Morris Halle, *Fundamentals of Language*, Janua Linguarum, 1 (The Hague: Mouton, 1956), 14, 37–38, 60–61.

12. See Jerry A. Fodor, "How to Learn to Talk: Some Simple Ways," in *The Genesis of Language: A Psycholinguistic Approach*, ed. Frank Smith and George A. Miller (Cambridge: M.I.T. Press, 1968), 114.

13. See Robert A. Hall, Jr., "Why a Structural Semantics is Impossible," *Language Sciences*, 21 (Aug. 1972), 1–6.

14. This procedure, general in modern social scientific analysis, was clearly formulated by Descartes in his *Discourse on Method* in the second discourse.

15. As set out, the competence program is not the most perfect or parsimonious outline possible. It was planned to be a clear statement of a *cultural* competence and to be of optimum use for my historical purposes. The statement meets only the requirement of observational adequacy as held in linguistics. Even if this account makes no contribution to the theory of human mentality that linguists are working toward (I do not claim that it does), I feel sure that the ultimate adequate explanation of thinking will need to come out of the comparison of generative models for nonlinguistic as well as linguistic phenomena. See Chomsky, *Aspects of the Theory of Syntax*, 41–47.

16. Quoted in *Faulkner in the University: Class Conferences at the University of Virginia, 1957–1958*, ed. Frederick L. Gwynn and Joseph L. Blotner (New York: Vintage Books,

1965), 103. Faulkner extends the same metaphor in anticipation of the theory of *bricolage* in Cash's monologue in the penultimate chapter of *As I Lay Dying* (1930).

17. LeCorbusier, *The Modulor: A Harmonious Measure to The Human Scale Universally Applicable to Architecture and Mechanics*, trans. Peter de Francia and Anna Bostock (Cambridge: M.I.T. Press, 1968), ch. 7.

18. J. Marshall Jenkins, "Ground-Rules of Welsh Houses: A Primary Analysis," *Folk Life*, 5 (1967), 65–91.

19. See Arthur J. Lawton, "The Pre-Metric Foot and its Use in Pennsylvania German Architecture," *Pennsylvania Folklife*, XIX:1 (Autumn 1969), 37–45.

20. I worked this problem out using scale models rather than formulas, so these measures are conceptually, rather than mathematically, exact. This rationalization leaves its product in keeping with the practice of carpenters (I have worked as a carpenter); at the same time, it prevents us from being led into theoretical chaos by the reality of the behavioral uniqueness of every performance. Again, an analogy with language could help: the same word, even spoken by the same person with the same semantic intent, may be pronounced in slightly different ways.

21. See Hunter Dupree, "The Pace of Measurement from Rome to America," *Smithsonian Journal of History*, 3 (1968), 19–40.

22. See A. Hunter Dupree, "The English Systems for Measuring Fields," *Agricultural History*, XLV:2 (April 1971), 124.

23. A syntagm is a sequential structure, an abstraction that retains the order of sensate reality. See Barthes, *Elements of Semiology*, 63

24. See William A. Baker, *Colonial Vessels: Some Seventeenth-Century Sailing Craft* (Barre, Vt.: Barre Publishing Co., 1962), 21–22.

25. See Alexandre Koyré, *From the Closed World to the Infinite Universe* (Baltimore: Johns Hopkins Univ. Press, 1968), 101.

26. It would be incorrect to say that the terms being used here were borrowed, but it would be dishonest not to point out that their employment was influenced by Christian Norberg-Schulz's profound volume, *Intentions in Architecture* (Cambridge: M.I.T. Press, 1968), 131–40.

27. Ronald R. Butters, "Competence, Performance, and Variable Rules," *Language Sciences*, 20 (April 1972), 29–32.

28. See Deetz, *Invitation to Archaeology*, 45–52.

29. The full structural description of each house type can be found in Figs. 11, 13, 15, 17, 21.

30. Lévi-Strauss, *Structural Anthropology*, 31.

31. First delivered at the American Folklore Society meeting in 1970, Jacobs' paper has been published as "Areal Spread of Indian Oral Genre Features in the Northwest States," *Journal of the Folklore Institute*, IX:1 (June 1972), 10–17.

32. Deetz, *Invitation to Archaeology*, 83–95.

33. Chomsky, *Syntactic Structures*, 18.

34. Norberg-Schulz, *Intentions in Architecture*, 211.

35. Robert A. Georges and Alan Dundes, "Toward a Structural Definitition of the Riddle," *Journal of American Folklore*, 76:300 (April–June 1963), 113.

36. Greimas, "Interpretation of Myth," 83, 92.

37. Noam Chomsky, *Cartesian Linguistics: A Chapter in the History of Rationalist Thought* (New York: Harper, 1966), 17; *Syntactic Structures*, 15; *Language and Mind*, 61. His later position is set out in *Aspects of the Theory of Syntax*, 77, 135–47.

38. See Dell Hymes, "Directions in (Ethno-) Linguistic Theory," in *Transcultural Studies in Cognition*, ed. A. Kimball Romney and Roy Goodwin D'Andrade, *American Anthropologist*, 66:3, part 2 (1964), 22–23; Dell Hymes, "Sociolinguistics and the Ethnography of Speaking," in *Social Anthropology and Language*, ed. Edwin Ardener, ASA Monograph, 10 (London: Tavistock, 1971), 55–59.

39. A nice discussion of how a thing exists simultaneously as object and sign, and how things can be accordingly studied, may be found in Roland Barthes, *Mythologies*, trans. Annette Lavers (New York: Hill and Wang, 1972), 111–31.

V: Counting Houses

1. Claude Lévi-Strauss, *The Raw and the Cooked: An Introduction to a Science of Mythology: I*, trans. John and Doreen Weightman (New York: Harper, 1970), 15.
2. This idea is expanded in "Structure and Function, Folklore and the Artifact," 314–15, 322–24.
3. See Chomsky's *Cartesian Linguistics*, for example, or the closing chapter of Lévi-Strauss' *Totemism*, trans. Rodney Needham (Boston: Beacon Press, 1963).
4. See Octavio Paz, *Claude Lévi-Strauss: An Introduction*, trans. J. S. Bernstein and Maxine Bernstein (London: Jonathan Cape, 1970), 98–99.
5. Lévi-Strauss, *The Savage Mind*, 232–37, 256–63; *The Scope of Anthropology*, 25, 46–50; *Structural Anthropology*, 13 (from whence comes the quote); and G. Charbonnier, *Conversations with Claude Lévi-Strauss*, trans. John and Doreen Weightman (London: Jonathan Cape, 1969), 32–42.
6. Lévi-Strauss, *Scope of Anthropology*, 21.
7. See Bob Scholte, "Lévi-Strauss' Penelopean Effort: The Analysis of Myths," *Semiotica*, I:1 (1969), 111.
8. Piaget, *Structuralism*, 111–28.
9. See Hugo Nutini, "Lévi-Strauss' Conception of Science," in *Échanges et Communications: Melanges Offerts à Claude Lévi-Strauss*, ed. Jean Pouillon and Pierre Maranda, I (The Hague: Mouton, 1970), 545–48.
10. Lévi-Strauss, *The Raw and the Cooked*, 1–9.
11. See Ray L. Birdwhistell, *Kinesics and Context: Essays on Body Motion Communication* (Philadelphia: Univ. of Pennsylvania Press, 1970), 157.
12. Chomsky, *Syntactic Structures*, 16; Lévi-Strauss, *Structural Anthropology*, 326. See also Laslett, *The World We Have Lost*, 235.
13. Kniffen, "Folk Housing: Key to Diffusion," 553–57.
14. Francis Benjamin Johnston and Thomas Tileston Waterman, *The Early Architecture of North Carolina* (Chapel Hill: Univ. of North Carolina Press, 1947), 28.
15. Ernest Pickering, *The Homes of America* (New York:

Bramhall House, 1951), 204–10; Richard N. Campen, *Architecture of the Western Reserve: 1800–1900* (Cleveland: Press of Case Western Reserve Univ., 1971), 221.
16. Talbot Hamlin, *Greek Revival Architecture in America* (1944; rpt. New York: Dover, 1964), 258.
17. Peirce F. Lewis, "The Geography of Old Houses," *Earth and Mineral Sciences*, 39:5 (Feb. 1970), 35.
18. Thomas Tileston Waterman and John A. Barrows, *Domestic Colonial Architecture of Tidewater Virginia* (New York: Scribner's, 1932), xiv.
19. Hugh Morrison, *Early American Architecture from the First Colonial Settlements to the National Period* (New York: Oxford Univ. Press, 1952), 473.
20. See Frank Lawrence Owsley, *Plain Folk of the Old South* (1949; rpt. Chicago: Quadrangle Books, 1965); Blanche Henry Clark, *The Tennessee Yeoman, 1840–1860* (Nashville: Vanderbilt Univ. Press, 1942); Herbert Weaver, *Mississippi Farmers: 1850–1860* (Nashville: Vanderbilt Univ. Press, 1945).

VI: The Mechanics of Structural Innovation

1. See Robert L. Carneiro, "The Culture Process," in *Essays in the Science of Culture in Honor of Leslie A. White*, ed. Gertrude E. Dole and Robert L. Carneiro (New York: Thomas Y. Crowell, 1960), 145–47.
2. Albert B. Lord, *The Singer of Tales* (New York: Atheneum, 1965), 22–29.
3. Bruce A. Rosenberg, *The Art of the American Folk Preacher* (New York: Oxford Univ. Press, 1970), 24–26.
4. Paul Klee, *On Modern Art* (London: Faber, 1966), 45–51.
5. Henry Glassie, "Eighteenth-Century Cultural Process in Delaware Valley Folk Building," *Winterthur Portfolio*, 7 (1972), 45–46.
6. When I refer to specific rules, my intention is to enable the reader to return to chapter IV where the rule is explicitly

stated. Then one may turn to the diagrams in Figs. 11, 13, 15, 17, and 21, where one can see how often the rule was applied as well as the base structures and types with which it was used. There, too, one can find the other rules with which it was structured in actual performance.

7. See H. G. Barnett, *Innovation: The Basis of Cultural Change* (New York: McGraw-Hill, 1953), 188, 193–94.

8. George Kubler, *The Shape of Time: Remarks on the History of Things* (New Haven: Yale Univ. Press, 1962), 39–53.

9. See C. H. Waddington, "Theories of Evolution," in *A Century of Darwin*, ed. S. A. Barnett (Cambridge: Harvard Univ. Press, 1958), 1–18.

10. See Anthony N. B. Garvan, *Architecture and Town Planning in Colonial Connecticut* (New Haven: Yale Univ. Press, 1951), 104, 119; Walter Muir Whitehall, Wendell D. and Jane N. Garrett, *The Arts in Early America* (Chapel Hill: Univ. of North Carolina Press for Institute of Early American History and Culture at Williamsburg, Va., 1965), 63.

11. J. Frederick Kelly, *Early Domestic Architecture of Connecticut* (1924; rpt. New York: Dover, 1963), 6–20.

12. The worst offender among these is Richard Pillsbury and Andrew Kardos, *A Field Guide to the Folk Architecture of the Northeastern United States*, Geography Publications at Dartmouth, 8 (Hanover, N.H.: Dept. of Geography, Dartmouth, n.d., c.1970).

13. See Sartre, *Search for a Method*, 170; Lévi-Strauss, *Totemism*, 103; John R. Searle, *Speech Acts: An Essay in the Philosophy of Language* (Cambridge: Cambridge Univ. Press, 1969), 16–19.

14. See Piaget, *Structuralism*, 20, 139–41; Barnett, *Innovation*, 9–10, 19–20, 49, 54, 81, 147, 202, 209; Norberg-Schulz, *Intentions in Architecture*, 70–71, 78–79; Karl R. Popper, *The Poverty of Historicism* (New York: Harper, 1964), 9–11, 147.

15. Henry C. Mercer, *The Dating of Old Houses* (New Hope, Pa.: Bucks County Historical Society, undated modern reprint of a paper read in 1923 and published in the *Bucks County Historical Society Papers*, V), 3–10; Lee H. Nelson, *Nail Chronology as an Aid to Dating Old Buildings*, AASLH Technical Leaflet, 48 (Nashville: American Assoc. for State and Local History, 1968); Bernard L. Fontana, "The Tale of a Nail: On the Ethnological Interpretation of Historic Artifacts," *The Florida Anthropologist*, XVIII:3, part 2 (Sept. 1965), 85–96.

16. Coxe, *Tabular Statement of the Several Branches of American Manufactures*, 94–95.

17. Bloch, *The Historian's Craft*, 183–84.

18. See Ivor Noël Hume, *Historical Archaeology* (New York: Knopf, 1969), 128.

19. See Warren E. Roberts, "The Waggoner Log House Near Paragon, Indiana," in *Forms Upon the Frontier: Folklife and Folk Arts in the United States*, ed. Austin and Alta Fife and Henry Glassie, Monograph Series, XVI:2 (Logan: Utah State Univ. Press, 1969), 30.

20. Alfred Von Martin, *The Sociology of the Renaissance* (New York: Harper, 1963), 1.

21. R. W. Brunskill, *An Illustrated Handbook of Vernacular Architecture* (New York: Universe Books, 1970), 100–1; M. W. Barley, *The English Farmhouse and Cottage* (London: Routledge and Kegan Paul, 1961), 63, 70–71, 95–97, 104, 123, 133, 201.

22. Brunskill, *Illustrated Handbook of Vernacular Architecture*, 102–3; Raymond B. Wood-Jones, *Traditional Domestic Architecture in the Banbury Region* (Manchester: Manchester Univ. Press, 1963), 31–42, 55–72, 84–112; Christopher Stell, "Pennine Houses: An Introduction," *Folk Life*, 3 (1965), 12, 14, 17; Sir Cyril Fox and Lord Raglan, *Monmouthshire Houses*, II (Cardiff: National Museum of Wales, 1953), 18–32; III (1954), 53–55.

23. See Nigel Harvey, *A History of Farm Buildings in England and Wales* (Newton Abbot: David and Charles, 1970), 34–35.

24. See Iorwerth C. Peate, *The Welsh House: A Study in Folk Culture* (London: The Honourable Society of Cymmrodorion, 1940), 59–97; S. R. Jones and J. T. Smith, "The Houses of Breconshire," *Brycheiniog*, IX (1963), 5–34; X

(1964), 115–46; XI (1965), 50–89; XII (1966/67), 23–56.

25. See W. G. Hoskins, *Old Devon* (Newton Abbot: David and Charles, 1966), 21–22, 24.

26. Barley, *English Farmhouse and Cottage*, 116–17, 178, 201; P. Eden, "Smaller Post-medieval Houses in Eastern England," in *East Anglian Studies*, ed. Lionel M. Munby (Cambridge: W. Heffer and Sons, 1968), 89.

27. Henry Glassie, *Pattern in the Material Folk Culture of the Eastern United States*, Univ. of Pennsylvania Monographs in Folklore and Folklife, I (Philadelphia: Univ. of Pennsylvania Press, 1969), 64, 66–68, 78, 80–81, 124–25, 150–53; Kelly, *Early Domestic Architecture of Connecticut*, 7–8; Norman M. Isham and Albert F. Brown, *Early Connecticut Houses: An Historical and Architectural Study* (1900; rpt. New York: Dover, 1965), 18–70; Henry Chandlee Forman, *Tidewater Maryland Architecture and Gardens* (New York: Bonanza, 1956), 55–59; Henry Chandlee Forman, *Virginia Architecture in the Seventeenth Century* (Williamsburg: Virginia 350th Anniversary Celebration Corp., 1957), 39–40.

28. Åke Campbell, "Irish Fields and Houses: A Study of Rural Culture," *Béaloideas*, V:I (1935), 57–74; E. Estyn Evans, "Donegal Survivals," *Antiquity*, XIII:50 (June, 1939), 209–20; E. Estyn Evans, "The Ulster Farmhouse," *Ulster Folklife*, I (1955), 27–31; Caoimhín Ó Danachair, "The Combined Byre-and-Dwelling in Ireland," *Folk Life*, II (1964), 58–75; F. H. A. Aalen, "The House Types of Gola Island, Co. Donegal," *Folk Life*, 8 (1970), 32–44; Peate, *The Welsh House*, 98–128; Sir Cyril Fox, "Some South Pembrokeshire Cottages," *Antiquity*, XVI:64 (Dec. 1942), 307–19; Fox and Raglan, *Monmouthshire Houses*, II, 43–44, 46–48; Fox and Raglan, *Monmouthshire Houses*, III, 38, 40; Sidney Oldall Addy, *The Evolution of the English House*, Social England Series (London: Swan Sonnenschein, 1898), 48 ff.; Basil Oliver, *The Cottages of England: A Review of Their Types and Features from the 16th to the 18th Centuries* (London: Batsford, 1929), 23–24; W. J. Turner, *Exmoor Village* (London: Harrap, 1947), 26–29, house charts, plates V, 5–8; Brunskill, *Illus-*

trated Handbook of Vernacular Architecture, 101 (h, 1).

29. Henry Glassie, "The Types of the Southern Mountain Cabin," in *The Study of American Folklore*, ed. Jan Harold Brunvand (New York: Norton, 1968), 353, 355–61.

30. See Howard Wight Marshall, "The 'Thousand Acres' Log House, Monroe County, Indiana," *Pioneer America*, III:1 (Jan. 1971), 48–56; Donald A. Hutslar, "The Log Architecture of Ohio," *Ohio History*, 80:3/4 (Summer–Autumn 1971), 242, fig. B.

31. See Robert Redfield, *The Little Community* (Chicago: Univ. of Chicago Press, 1960), 43–44, 144–46; Edit Fél and Tamás Hofer, *Proper Peasants: Traditional Life in a Hungarian Village*, Viking Fund Publications in Anthropology, 46 (New York: *Current Anthropology*, Wenner-Gren Foundation for Anthropological Research, 1969), 17, 22–23, 28; Edward P. Dozier, *Hano: A Tewa Indian Community in Arizona*, Case Studies in Cultural Anthropology (New York: Holt, Rinehart and Winston, 1966), 29–31; Barnett, *Innovation*, 307, 332–33; Alan P. Merriam, *The Anthropology of Music* (Evanston, Ill.: Northwestern Univ. Press, 1964), 134–44; Petr Bogatyrev, *The Functions of Folk Costume in Moravian Slovakia*, trans. Richard G. Crum, Approaches to Semiotics, 5 (The Hague: Mouton, 1971), 46–51, 56–60, 84–88; Monni Adams, "Designs in Sumba Textiles, Local Meanings and Foreign Influences," *Textile Museum Journal*, III:2 (Dec. 1971), 33; Henry Glassie, " 'Take That Night Train to Selma': An Excursion to the Outskirts of Scholarship," in *Folksongs and Their Makers*, ed. Henry Glassie, Edward D. Ives, and John F. Szwed (Bowling Green Univ. Popular Press, 1970), 30–52; Edward D. Ives, *Lawrence Doyle: The Farmer-Poet of Prince Edward Island: A Study in Local Songmaking*, Univ. of Maine Studies, 92 (Orono: Univ. of Maine Press, 1971), 243–49.

32. Brunskill, *Illustrated Handbook of Vernacular Architecture*, 104–5; Lewis Mumford, *Sticks and Stones: A Study of American Architecture and Civilization* (1924; rpt. New York: Dover, 1955), 39–47.

33. See Jakobson and Halle, *Fundamentals of Language*,

62; Oscar Lewis, *Life in a Mexican Village: Tepoztlán Restudied* (Urbana: Univ. of Illinois Press, 1963), 446; Marc Bloch, *Feudal Society*, I, trans. L. A. Manyon (Chicago: Univ. of Chicago Press, 1968), 43–47.

34. Barley, *English Farmhouse and Cottage*, 24.

35. See Elizabeth Melling and Anne M. Oakley, *Kentish Sources: V: Some Kentish Houses* (Maidstone: Kent County Council, 1965), 44, 64–66.

36. Kelly, *Early Domestic Architecture of Connecticut*, 8–17; Abbott Lowell Cummings, *Architecture in Early New England*, Old Sturbridge Village Booklet Series (Sturbridge, Mass.: Old Sturbridge Village, 1964), 3–17.

37. See Jones and Smith, "The Houses of Breconshire," IX (1963), 34–62; X (1964), 86–87, 100–14, 150–54; XI (1965), 32–33, 41–49, 89–120; XII (1966/67), 56–62.

38. See Paul S. Dulaney, *The Architecture of Historic Richmond* (Charlottesville: Univ. Press of Virginia, 1968), 45–51, 54, 58–71, 74, 105–7, 109–10, 112–13, 132, 136, 139–40, 142, 145–47, 149, 153.

39. Glassie, "Eighteenth-Century Cultural Process in Delaware Valley Folk Building," 35–38.

40. Peter O. Wacker, "New Jersey's Cultural Landscape Before 1800," *Proceedings of the Second Annual Symposium of the New Jersey Historical Commission, 1970* (Newark: New Jersey Historical Commission, 1971), 51–53.

41. Kniffen, "Folk Housing: Key to Diffusion," 555; Glassie, *Pattern in the Material Folk Culture of the Eastern United States*, 66–69, 75, 78, 96, 99, 101, 107, 129, 156; Frances J. Niederer, *The Town of Fincastle, Virginia* (Charlottesville: Univ. Press of Virginia, 1966), 37–39; Rexford Newcomb, *Old Kentucky Architecture* (New York: William Helburn, 1940), plates 5, 6; David Sutherland, "Folk Housing in the Woodburn Quadrangle," *Pioneer America*, IV:2 (July 1972), 18–24; *History of Homes and Gardens of Tennessee*, ed. Roberta Seawell Brandau (Nashville: Parthenon Press for Garden Study Club of Nashville, 1936), 197; Wilbur D. Peat, *Indiana Houses of the Nineteenth Century* (Indianapolis:

Indiana Historical Society, 1962), plates 4–6, 23, 33, 58, 59, 97, 98.

42. See Glassie, *Pattern in the Material Folk Culture of the Eastern United States*, 69 (Fig. 20D).

43. See Lewis A. Coffin, Jr., and Arthur C. Holden, *Brick Architecture of the Colonial Period in Maryland and Virginia* (New York: Architectural Book Pub. Co., 1919), 5–8. The clear drawings in John Fitzhugh Millar's *The Architects of the American Colonies; or, Vitruvius Americanus* (Barre, Vt.: Barre Publishers, 1968) show that the academic eighteenth-century American architect could not do much, when asked to design a house, except repeat the hip-roofed, paired-chimney, five-opening Georgian form. He was much less creative than the country builder. See the Virginia mansions in Millar's book, pp. 40–53, 60–68, 72.

44. See Carl Julien and Chlothilde R. Martin, *Sea Islands to Sand Hills* (Columbia: Univ. of South Carolina Press, 1954), 45.

45. Glassie, *Pattern in the Material Folk Culture of the Eastern United States*, 89, 94–98, 101.

46. Richard V. Francaviglia, "Mormon Central-Hall Houses in the American West," *Annals of the Association of American Geographers*, 61:1 (March 1971), 65–71.

47. Barnett, *Innovation*, 3, 16, 181–82, 186–87, 236–37, 250–51, 416, 433.

48. See Robert D. King, *Historical Linguistics and Generative Grammar* (Englewood Cliffs, N.J.: Prentice-Hall, 1969), 39, 84–86.

49. Lewis Mumford, *From the Ground Up* (New York: Harcourt, 1956), 72, 78.

50. See Glassie, "Eighteenth-Century Cultural Process in Delaware Valley Folk Building," 35–40, 43–48.

VII: Reason in Architecture

1. See Dell Hymes, "Introduction: Toward Ethnographies

of Communication," in *The Ethnography of Communication*, *American Anthropologist*, ed. John J. Gumperz and Dell Hymes, 66:6, part 2 (Dec. 1964), 5–7, 10–11, 21–22.

2. See Talcott Parsons, "The Social System: A General Theory of Action," in *Toward A Unified Theory of Human Behavior*, ed. Roy R. Grinker (New York: Basic Books, 1957), 62.

3. See Christian Norberg-Schulz, *Existence, Space and Architecture* (New York: Praeger, 1971), 27; Bruce G. Trigger, "The Determinants of Settlement Patterns," in *Settlement Archaeology*, ed. K. C. Chang (Palo Alto: National Press Books, 1968), 55.

4. See Christopher Alexander, *Notes on the Synthesis of Form* (Cambridge: Harvard Univ. Press, 1971), 19–27.

5. See Eóin MacWhite, "On the Interpretation of Archaeological Evidence in Historical and Sociological Terms," in *Man's Imprint from the Past: Readings in the Methods of Archaeology*, ed. James Deetz (Boston: Little, Brown, 1971), 223.

6. See Axel Steensberg, "Tools and Man," in *Man and his Habitat: Essays Presented to Emyr Estyn Evans*, ed. R. H. Buchanan, Emrys Jones, and Desmond McCourt (London: Routledge and Kegan Paul, 1971), 63–66.

7. A. R. Radcliffe-Brown, "On the Concept of Function in Social Science," *American Anthropologist*, 37 (July–Sept. 1935), 394–402.

8. See Merton, *On Theoretical Sociology*, 79–82.

9. *Ibid.*, 75.

10. In folktale scholarship, structures that affect, but do not generate, basic shape are termed "paradigmatic," in contradistinction to "syntagmatic" structures—those used in formal composition.

11. Le Corbusier, *The Modulor*, 76.

12. See Geoffrey Scott, *The Architecture of Humanism: A Study in the History of Taste* (1924; rpt. Garden City, N.Y.: Doubleday, 1956), 161–77.

13. Le Corbusier, *When the Cathedrals Were White*, trans. Francis E. Hyslop, Jr. (New York: McGraw-Hill, 1964), 205–7; Norberg-Schulz, *Existence, Space and Architecture*, 37.

14. Robert Sommer, *Personal Space: The Behavioral Basis of Design* (Englewood Cliffs, N.J.: Prentice-Hall, 1969), 5.

15. Edward T. Hall, *The Hidden Dimension* (Garden City, N.Y.: Doubleday, 1969); also ch. 10 of Hall's *The Silent Language* (Greenwich, Conn.: Fawcett, 1964).

16. Addy, *Evolution of the English House*, 17, 32–34, 66–69; Reginald Turnor, *The Smaller English House: 1500–1939* (London: Batsford, 1952), 12; Henry Chandlee Forman, *The Architecture of the Old South: The Medieval Style: 1585–1850* (Cambridge: Harvard Univ. Press, 1948), 15, 121; Garvan, *Architecture and Town Planning in Colonial Connecticut*, 82.

17. See Wood-Jones, *Traditional Domestic Architecture in the Banbury Region*, ch. VIII; Harry Batsford and Charles Fry, *The English Cottage* (London: Batsford, 1950), 16, 87–88.

18. Marion Macrae, *The Ancestral Roof, Domestic Architecture of Upper Canada* (Toronto: Clarke, Irwin, 1963), 228; John I. Rempel, *Building with Wood and Other Aspects of Nineteenth-Century Building in Ontario* (Toronto: Univ. of Toronto Press, 1967), 13.

19. Glassie, "The Types of the Southern Mountain Cabin," 349–54.

20. Booker T. Washington, *Up From Slavery* (1901; rpt. New York: Avon, 1965), 29.

21. W. E. Burghardt DuBois, *The Souls of Black Folk* (1903; rpt. Greenwich, Conn.: Fawcett, 1967), 91, 92, 106–7.

22. For the circular West African house, see: Labelle Prussin, *Architecture in Northern Ghana: A Study of Forms and Functions* (Berkeley: Univ. of California Press, 1969), 21–65; Barry Floyd, *Eastern Nigeria: A Geographical Review* (London: Macmillan, 1969), 55; Paul and Laura Bohannan, *Tiv Economy*, Northwestern Univ. African Studies, 20 (Evanston, Ill.: Northwestern Univ. Press, 1968), 14–15; Kwamina B. Dickson, *A Historical Geography of Ghana* (Cambridge: Cambridge Univ. Press, 1971), 61, 282–87.

23. John W. M. Whiting and Barbara Ayres, "Inferences from

the Shape of Dwellings," in *Settlement Archaeology*, 117–33.

24. See Grahame Clark, *Prehistoric England* (London: Batsford, 1962), 57–59, 67, 70; V. Gordon Childe, *The Dawn of European Civilization* (New York: Knopf, 1958), 333; Wallace Thorneycroft, "Observations on Hut Circles Near the Eastern Border of Perthshire, North of Blairgowrie," *Proceedings of the Society of Antiquaries of Scotland*, LXVII:7 (1932–33), 187–208; Arthur Raistrick, *The Pennine Dales* (London: Eyre and Spottiswoode, 1969), 61–63.

25. See Glassie, *Pattern in the Material Folk Culture of the Eastern United States*, 161–65.

26. Inspect the plan on p. 53 of Ian Archer, "Nabdam Compounds, Northern Ghana," in *Shelter in Africa*, ed. Paul Oliver (New York: Praeger, 1971). There you will find alien rectangular houses, traditional round houses, and squared houses closer in size and shape to the old round houses than to the new rectangular ones.

27. See F. W. B. Charles and Walter Horn, "The Cruck-Built Barn of Leigh Court, Worcestershire, England," *Journal of the Society of Architectural Historians*, XXXII:1 (March 1973), 5–29. The Leigh Court barn is 33 feet wide.

28. Raistrick, *Pennine Dales*, 53–54.

29. Aileen Fox, *South West England* (London: Thames and Hudson, 1964), 89.

30. C. F. Innocent, *The Development of English Building Construction*. Cambridge Technical Series. (Cambridge: Cambridge Univ. Press, 1916), 27.

31. See Prussin, *Architecture in Northern Ghana*, 33, 45.

32. *Notes on the Synthesis of Form*.

33. In Herbert A. Simon's terms, the folk architect is a "satisficer" rather than an "optimizer"; see Simon's *The Sciences of the Artificial* (Cambridge: M.I.T. Press, 1969), 62–66.

34. See Erving Goffman, *Interaction Ritual: Essays on Face-to-Face Behaviour* (Hammondsworth: Penguin, 1967), 80.

35. See Edward Sapir, "Do We Need a 'Superorganic'?," *American Anthropologist*, 19 (July–Sept. 1917), 441–47.

36. Lévi-Strauss, *The Raw and the Cooked*, 11–12, 245.

37. See Harry Swain and Cotton Mather, *St. Croix Border Country* (Prescott, Wis.: Trimbelle Press for the Pierce County Geographical Society, 1968), 13, 15–16.

38. See Ava D. Rodgers, *The Housing of Oglethorpe County, Georgia: 1790–1860* (Tallahassee: Florida State Univ. Press, 1971), xi, 35.

39. Humphry Osmond, "Some Psychiatric Aspects of Design," in *Who Designs America?*, ed. Laurence B. Holland, Princeton Studies in American Civilization, 6 (Garden City, N.Y.: Doubleday, 1966), 314.

40. Lévi-Strauss, *Totemism*, 99. His later softened opinion is briefly stated in *The Savage Mind*, 247n.

41. Redfield, *The Little Community*, 26.

42. See David Pye, *The Nature of Design* (New York: Reinhold, 1967), 46–53; Robert F. G. Spier, *From the Hand of Man: Primitive and Preindustrial Technologies* (Boston: Houghton Mifflin, 1970), 2.

43. Lynn White, Jr., "The Historical Roots of Our Ecologic Crisis," in *Man and the Environment*, ed. Wes Jackson (Dubuque: Wm. C. Brown Co., 1971), 22–30.

44. Melville J. Herskovits and Frances S. Herskovits, *An Outline of Dahomean Religious Belief*, Memoirs of the American Anthropological Association 41 (Menasha, Wis.: American Anthropological Association, 1933), 14–15; G. J. Afolabi Ojo, *Yoruba Culture: A Geographical Analysis* (London: Univ. of Ife and Univ. of London, 1966), 169–70.

45. P. Amaury Talbot, *Tribes of the Niger Delta: Their Religions and Customs* (1932; rpt. New York: Barnes and Noble, 1967), 279–80; Floyd, *Eastern Nigeria*, 55–56, 174–78; Ojo, *Yoruba Culture*, 56–59, 74, 140.

46. W. G. Hoskins, *English Landscapes* (London: British Broadcasting Corp., 1973), ch. 2; Evans, *Personality of Ireland*, 36.

47. W. G. Hoskins and H. P. R. Finberg, *Devonshire Studies* (London: Jonathan Cape, 1952), 325–30; Eileen McCracken, "The Woodlands of Ulster in the Early Seventeenth Century," *Ulster Journal of Archaeology*, 10 (1947), 15–25.

48. *The Proceedings of the English Colony in Virginia*, in

Travels and Works of Captain John Smith, I, ed. Edwin Arber and A. G. Bradley (Edinburgh: John Grant, 1910), 91.

49. *Ibid.*, 126; see also 154.

50. *The Generall Historie of Virginia, New England, and the Summer Isles*, in *Travels and Works of Captain John Smith*, II, ed. Arber and Bradley, 502.

51. *Ibid.*, 511.

52. Hugh Jones, *The Present State of Virginia From Whence Is Inferred a Short View of Maryland and North Carolina*, ed. Richard L. Morton (Chapel Hill: Univ. of North Carolina Press for the Virginia Historical Society, 1956), 71; see also 74, 76.

53. Thomas Jefferson, *Notes on the State of Virginia* (Boston: Wells and Lilly, 1829, advertisement dated 1787), 159; see also 160–62.

54. David I. Bushnell, Jr., *Native Villages and Village Sites East of the Mississippi*, Bureau of American Ethnology Bulletin, 69 (Washington: Government Printing Office, 1919), 30–37; Lewis H. Morgan, *Houses and House-Life of the American Aborigines* (1881; rpt. Chicago: Univ. of Chicago Press, 1965), 119–24.

55. Innocent, *Development of English Building Construction*, 109.

56. See Harold R. Shurtleff, *The Log Cabin Myth: A Study of the Early Dwellings of the English Colonists in North America* (1939; rpt. Gloucester, Mass.: Peter Smith, 1967).

57. See Fred Kniffen and Henry Glassie, "Building in Wood in the Eastern United States: A Time-Place Perspective," *The Geographical Review*, LVI:1 (Jan. 1966), 54–57, 63.

58. Stuart Bartlett, "Garrison Houses Along the New England Frontier," *Pencil Points*, XIV:6 (June 1933), 253–68; Henry C. Mercer, "The Origin of Log Houses in the United States," *Collection of Papers Read Before the Bucks County Historical Society*, V (1924), 574–76, figs. 2–12; J. Frederick Kelly, "A Seventeenth-Century Connecticut Log House," *Old-Time New England*, XXI:2 (Oct. 1940), 28–41.

59. Jewett A. Grosvenor, "An Architectural Monograph on the Wooden Architecture of the Lower Delaware Valley," *The White Pine Series of Architectural Monographs*, VI:3 (June 1920), 4, 6; Peter O. Wacker and Roger T. Trindell, "The Log House in New Jersey: Origins and Diffusion," *Keystone Folklore Quarterly*, XIII:4 (Winter 1968), 255–56.

60. Letter from R. W. Brunskill to Henry Glassie, March 17, 1972.

61. Robert Farris Thompson, *Black Gods and Kings: Yoruba Art at UCLA*, Occasional Papers of the Museum and Laboratories of Ethnic Arts and Technology, 2 (Los Angeles: Univ. of California, 1971), ch. 3, p. 2.

62. Henry Glassie, "The Nature of the New World Artifact: The Instance of the Dugout Canoe," in *Festschrift für Robert Wildhaber*, ed. Walter Escher, Theo Gantner, and Hans Trümpy (Basel: Schweizerische Gesellschaft für Volkskunde, 1973), 153–70.

63. James Hornell, *Water Transport* (Cambridge: Cambridge Univ. Press, 1946), 189–95.

64. Horatio Bridge, *The Journal of an African Cruiser*, ed. Nathaniel Hawthorne (1845; rpt. London: Dawsons of Pall Mall, 1968), 43; see also 54, 76, 123, 133.

65. See Robert Farris Thompson, "African Influence on the Art of the United States," in *Black Studies in the University: A Symposium*, ed. Armistead L. Robinson, Craig C. Foster, and Donald H. Ogilvie (New Haven: Yale Univ. Press, 1969), 122–70; Judith Wragg Chase, *Afro-American Art and Craft* (New York: Van Nostrand, 1971), 58–59.

66. Jefferson, *Notes on the State of Virginia*, 147.

67. Andrew Burnaby, *Travels through the Middle Settlements in North-America in the Years 1759 and 1760. With Observations Upon the State of the Colonies* (1775; rpt. Ithaca, N.Y.: Cornell Univ. Press, 1960), 26.

68. See F. W. B. Charles, *Medieval Cruck-Building and Its Derivatives: A Study of Timber-Framed Construction Based on Buildings in Worcestershire*, Society for Medieval Archaeology Monograph Series, 2 (London: Society for Medieval Archaeology, 1967), ch. III.

69. H. L. Edlin, *Woodland Crafts in Britain* (London: Batsford, 1949), 94; Margaret Wood, *The English Mediaeval House* (London: Phoenix House, 1965), 293.

70. Martin S. Briggs, *The English Farmhouse* (London: Batsford, 1953), 81–82; Batsford and Fry, *The English Cottage*, 82–83.

71. See T. J. Woofter, *Black Yeomanry* (New York: Holt, 1930), 215; James A. Nonemaker, "History in Houses: The Redman-Thornton House in Atlanta, Georgia," *Antiques*, LXXXI:3 (March 1962), 292–95; Rodgers, *Housing of Oglethorpe County*, 13, 22, 23, 25, 28, 36, 41, 45, 54, 56, 62; James Agee and Walker Evans, *Let Us Now Praise Famous Men* (1941; rpt. New York: Ballantine Books, 1966), 147, 171.

72. Richard M. Candee, "A Documentary History of Plymouth Colony Architecture, 1620–1700," *Old-Time New England*, LIX:4 (Spring 1969), 110; LX:2 (Oct.–Dec. 1969), 49.

73. Innocent, *Development of English Building Construction*, 234–37.

74. Henry C. Mercer, "Notes on Wrought-Iron Door Latches," *Old-Time New England* (Jan. 1923), 139–40; Kenneth Duprey, *Old Houses on Nantucket* (New York: Architectural Book Publishing Co., 1959), 23, 55, 101; Ned Goode, "An Album of Chester County Farmhouses," *Pennsylvania Folklife*, 13:1 (Autumn 1962), 24; Henry Glassie, "The Double-Crib Barn in South Central Pennsylvania," *Pioneer America*, I:1 (Jan. 1969), 15; I:2 (July 1969), 42.

75. My thinking about the *Tempest* as a nature-culture "myth" for seventeenth-century Englishmen was prompted by Leo Marx's interesting book, *The Machine in the Garden: Technology and the Pastoral Ideal in America* (New York: Oxford Univ. Press, 1967). Caliban, Ike McCaslin, and Mustapha Mond provide a full spectrum of human resolutions of the opposition of nature and culture from English and American literature.

76. See Demos, *A Little Commonwealth*, 29.

77. See Morris Talpalar, *The Sociology of Colonial Virginia* (New York: Philosophical Library, 1968), 278–79.

78. Innocent, *Development of English Building Construction*, 148–51; Barley, *English Farmhouse and Cottage*, 188–91; Gwyn I. Meirion-Jones, "The Domestic Buildings of Odiham, Hampshire," *Folk Life*, 9 (1971), 111–12.

79. Caoimhín Ó Danachair, "Materials and Methods in Irish Traditional Building," *Journal of the Royal Society of Antiquaries of Ireland*, LXXXVII:1 (1957), 68.

80. In Richard Hakluyt, *The Principal Navigations, Voyages, Traffiques, and Discoveries of the English Nation*, VIII (Glasgow: James MacLehose, 1904), 373.

81. E. Estyn Evans, *Irish Heritage: The Landscape, The People and Their Work* (Dundalk: W. Tempest, Dundalgan Press, 1963), 61; Patrick Duffy and Pádraig Mac Gréine, "The Making of an Irish Mud Wall House," *Béaloideas*, IV:1 (1933), 91–92; E. Estyn Evans, "A Cardiganshire Mud-walled Farmhouse," *Folk Life* 7 (1969), 92–100; Alexander Fenton, "Clay Building and Clay Thatch in Scotland," *Ulster Folklife*, 15/16 (1970), 28–40; Innocent, *Development of English Building Construction*, 134–38, 145; Brunskill, *Illustrated Handbook of Vernacular Architecture*, 48–49; R. W. Brunskill, "The Clay Houses of Cumberland," *Transactions of the Ancient Monuments Society*, 10 (1962), 57–80; Clough Williams-Ellis and John and Elizabeth Eastwick-Field, *Building in Cob, Pisé, and Stabilized Earth* (London: Country Life Ltd., 1950), 14–15, 82–102, 136–60; Prussin, *Architecture in Northern Ghana*, 28–31, 42–44, 57–58, 73–74, 86–88, 99–103.

82. See Christopher Williams, "Craftsmen of Necessity," *Natural History*, LXXXI:9 (Nov. 1972), 48–52, 57–59.

83. Claude Lévi-Strauss, *Tristes Tropiques*, trans. John Russell (New York: Atheneum, 1970), 90, 98–99.

84. See James Marston Fitch and Daniel P. Branch, "Primitive Architecture and Climate," *Scientific American* 203:6 (Dec. 1960), 134–44; James Marston Fitch, "New Uses for the Artistic Patrimony," *Journal of the Society of Architectural Historians*, XXX:1 (March 1971), 8–14.

85. See Amos Rapoport, *House Form and Culture*, Foundations of Geography Series (Englewood Cliffs, N.J.: Prentice-Hall, 1969), 93–95.

86. See Foy N. Hibbard, "Climate of Virginia," *Climate and Man: Yearbook of Agriculture*, House Document, 27, 77th Congress, 1st Session (Washington: U.S.D.A., 1941), 1159–69.

87. Robert Beverley, *The History and Present State of Virginia*, ed. Louis B. Wright (1705; rpt. Chapel Hill: Univ. of North Carolina Press for the Institute of Early American History and Culture at Williamsburg, Va., 1947), 289, 9, 296.

88. See William O. Scroggs, "Rural Life in the Lower Mississippi Valley, About 1803," *Proceedings of the Mississippi Valley Historical Association*, VIII (1914–15), 270–71.

89. See Thomas Tileston Waterman, *The Dwellings of Colonial America* (Chapel Hill: Univ. of North Carolina Press, 1950), 21.

90. This was explained in conversation once by James Marston Fitch, than whom no better authority could possibly be cited.

91. Jones, *Present State of Virginia*, 71.

92. See Ojo, *Yoruba Culture*, 147.

93. See Lewis R. Binford, "Archaeology as Anthropology," in *Man's Imprint from the Past*, ed. Deetz, 254.

94. *Ibid.*, 251–53.

95. Robert Plant Armstrong, *The Affecting Presence: An Essay in Humanistic Anthropology* (Urbana: Univ. of Illinois Press, 1971), 69–79.

96. See John W. Reps, *Town Planning in Frontier America* (Princeton: Princeton Univ. Press, 1969), 111–15.

97. Jefferson, *Notes on the State of Virginia*, 111.

98. W. G. Hoskins, *The Making of the English Landscape* (Baltimore: Penguin, 1971), 45–66, 180–84; W. E. Tate, *The Enclosure Movement* (New York: Walker and Co., 1967), 39–43, 57, 64, 72.

99. Christopher Taylor, *Dorset* (London: Hodder and Stoughton, 1970), chs. 2–4; Hoskins and Finberg, *Devonshire Studies*, 265–88, 290, 310–15, 320; D. P. Dymond, "The Suffolk Landscape," in *East Anglian Studies*, ed. Munby, 27–30, 34; Norman Scarfe, *The Suffolk Landscape* (London: Hodder and Stoughton, 1972), 141–47, 177–87; Ronald E. Frankenberg, *Communities in Britain: Social Life in Town and Country* (Baltimore: Penguin, 1966), 66–85; E. Estyn Evans, *Irish Folk Ways* (New York: Devin-Adair, 1957), 20–34; Conrad Arensberg, *The Irish Countryman* (1937; rpt. Garden City,

N.Y.: Natural History Press, 1968), 36–38, 48–55; R. H. Buchanan, "Rural Settlement in Ireland," in *Irish Geographical Studies in Honour of E. Estyn Evans*, ed. Nicholas Stephens and Robin E. Glasscock (Belfast: Department of Geography, Queen's University, 1970), 146–61; Kevin Danaher, *The Pleasant Land of Ireland* (Cork: Mercier, 1970), 14–19; R. Alun Roberts, *Welsh Home-Spun: Studies of Rural Wales* (Newton: Welsh Outlook Press, 1930), 7–17; Alwyn D. Rees, *Life in a Welsh Countryside* (Cardiff: Univ. of Wales, 1950), 18–20; Iowerth C. Peate, *Tradition and Folk Life: A Welsh View* (London: Faber, 1972), 71–73; E. G. Bowen, "The Dispersed Habitat of Wales," in *Man and His Habitat*, ed. Buchanan, Jones, and McCourt, 186–201.

100. *The Generall Historie of Virginia, New England, and the Summer Isles, Travels and Works of Captain John Smith*, II, ed. Arber and Bradley, 535.

101. John Demos, "Notes on Life in Plymouth Colony," *The William and Mary Quarterly*, XXII:2 (April 1965), 264–68.

102. See Powell, *Puritan Village*, 4–29, 92–101; Lockridge, *A New England Town: The First Hundred Years*, 82–87. Although unsophisticated with regard to Old World antecedents and theoretically too simple, Glenn T. Trewartha's "Types of Rural Settlement in Colonial America" provides an overview of settlement pattern. See *Readings in Cultural Geography*, ed. Philip L. Wagner and Marvin W. Mikesell (Chicago: Univ. of Chicago Press, 1967), 517–38.

103. *Generall Historie of Virginia, New England, and the Summer Isles, Travels and Works of Captain John Smith*, II, ed. Arber and Bradley, 584, 587, 614.

104. Victor Gruen, *The Heart of Our Cities: The Urban Crisis: Diagnosis and Cure* (New York: Simon and Schuster, 1964), ch. 5. Scatterization is a modern problem, but it is an old American reality that became a problem only when there came to be so many Americans.

105. See Kenneth Burke, *A Grammar of Motives* (Berkeley: Univ. of California Press, 1969), 55–58; Chomsky, *Aspects of the Theory of Syntax*, 37–47, 193–94.

106. M. E. Seebohm, *The Evolution of the English Farm* (Cambridge: Harvard Univ. Press, 1927), 100, 282; Harvey, *History of Farm Buildings in England and Wales*, 50, 53–59, 71–83; P. Smith, "The Long-House and the Laithe-House: A Study of the House-and-Byre Homestead in Wales and the West Riding," in *Culture and Environment: Essays in Honour of Sir Cyril Fox*, ed. I. Ll. Foster and L. Alcock (London: Routledge and Kegan Paul, 1963), 415–37. See also references in ch. VI, footnotes 23–25.

107. Wilbur Zelinsky, "The New England Connecting Barn," *The Geographical Review*, XLVIII:4 (Oct. 1958), 540–53; Russell V. Keune and James Replogle, "Two Maine Farmhouses," *Journal of the Society of Architectural Historians*, XX:1 (March 1961), 38–39; Henry Glassie, "The Wedderspoon Farm," *New York Folklore Quarterly*, XXII:3 (Sept. 1966), 165–87.

108. Glassie, "Eighteenth-Century Cultural Process in Delaware Valley Folk Building," 49–57.

109. See Wilbur Zelinsky, "Where the South Begins: the Northern Limit of the Cis-Appalachian South in Terms of Settlement Landscape," *Social Forces*, 30:2 (Dec. 1951), 173.

110. See Rapoport, *House Form and Culture*, 77–78.

111. R. T. Mason, "Four Single-Bay Halls," *Sussex Archaeological Collections*, 96 (1958), 9–16.

112. J. E. C. Peters, *The Development of Farm Buildings in Western Lowland Staffordshire up to 1880* (Manchester: Manchester Univ. Press, 1969), ch. IV, types 4a, 5e.

113. Alfred Easton Poor, *Colonial Architecture of Cape Cod, Nantucket and Martha's Vineyard* (1932; rpt. New York: Dover, 1970), plate 118; Ernest Allen Connally, "The Cape Cod House: An Introductory Study," *Journal of the Society of Architectural Historians*, XIX:2 (May 1960), 47–56.

114. Glassie, "The Variation of Concepts Within Tradition: Barn Building in Otsego County, New York," in press.

115. Glassie, "Eighteenth-Century Cultural Process in Delaware Valley Folk Building," 36–39; Glassie, "The Double Crib Barn," *Pioneer America*, I:2 (July 1969), 44–45; II:2 (July 1970), 28–30.

116. Eric Mercer, *Furniture: 700–1700* (New York: Meredith Press, 1969), 56–62, 72–75; Alan Gailey, "Kitchen Furniture," *Ulster Folklife*, 12 (1966), 18–34; F. H. A. Aalen, "Furnishings of Traditional Houses in the Wicklow Hills," *Ulster Folklife*, 13 (1967), 61–68; I. F. Grant, *Highland Folk Ways* (London: Routledge and Kegan Paul, 1961), 168–70; James Walton, "The Built-in Bed Tradition in North Yorkshire," *Gwerin* III:3 (1961), 114–25; Caoimhín Ó Danachair, "The Bed Out-Shot in Ireland," *Folk-Liv*, XIX–XX (1955–56), 26–29; Desmond McCourt, "The Outshot House-Type and its Distribution in County Londonderry," *Ulster Folklife*, 2 (1956), 27–34.

117. Sigurd Erixon, "West European Connections and Culture Relations," *Folk-Liv*, 2 (1938), 165–66; Innocent, *Development of English Building Construction*, 269; Barley, *English Farmhouse and Cottage*, 98, 112, 145, 156, 201, 221; Joscelyne Finberg, *Exploring Villages* (London: Routledge and Kegan Paul, 1958), 135.

118. See Charles, *Medieval Cruck-Building and Its Derivatives*, 43–64; Cecil Alec Hewett, *The Development of Carpentry, 1200–1700* (Newton Abbot: David and Charles, 1969), 188–94.

119. Cecil A. Hewett, "Jettying and Floor-Framing in Medieval Essex," *Medieval Archaeology*, X (1966), 106.

120. Albert H. Sonn, *Early American Wrought Iron*, II (New York: Scribner's, 1928), 10, 12–13; Herbert Schiffer, *Early Pennsylvania Hardware* (Whitford, Pa.: Whitford Press, 1966), 40–43.

121. Walter Gropius, *The New Architecture and the Bauhaus*, trans. P. Morton Shand (Cambridge: M.I.T. Press, 1965), 19–44.

122. Richard S. Latham, "The Artifact as Cultural Cipher," in *Who Designs America?*, ed. Holland, 266–67. See also the excellent comments in Allan Janik and Stephen Toulmin, *Wittgenstein's Vienna* (New York: Simon and Schuster, 1973), 252–255.

123. Marcus Whiffen, *The Eighteenth-Century Houses of Williamsburg* (Williamsburg, Va.: Colonial Williamsburg, 1960), 69.

124. *Ibid.*, 67–68; Kelly, *Early Domestic Architecture of*

Connecticut, 82–83; Antoinette Forrester Downing, *Early Homes of Rhode Island* (Richmond, Va.: Garrett and Massie, 1937), 123; Henry Glassie, "A Central Chimney Continental Log House," *Pennsylvania Folklife*, XVIII: 2 (Winter 1968–69), 34–36.

125. Arthur Pierce Middleton, *Tobacco Coast: A Maritime History of the Chesapeake Bay in the Colonial Era* (Newport News, Va.: Mariner's Museum, 1953), 223–24; M. V. Brewington, *Chesapeake Bay Log Canoes and Bugeyes* (Cambridge, Mass.: Cornell Maritime Press, 1963), 19.

126. Charles, *Medieval Cruck-Building and Its Derivatives*, 59.

127. See Richard M. Candee, *Housepaints in Colonial America* (New York: Chromatic Pub. Co., 1967), 2–3, 11–12.

128. Armstrong, *The Affecting Presence*, 120.

129. See Meyer Schapiro, "On Some Problems in the Semiotics of Visual Art: Field and Vehicle in Image-Signs," *Semiotica*, I:3 (1969), 223–29; Arnheim, *Art and Visual Perception*, 5.

130. See Herbert Read, *Art and Industry: The Principles of Industrial Design* (Bloomington: Indiana Univ. Press, 1961), 90.

131. Oliver, *Cottages of England*, 44–47; Sydney R. Jones, *English Village Homes and Country Buildings* (London: Batsford, 1947), 96–97; Brunskill, *Illustrated Handbook of Vernacular Architecture*, 64–65.

132. Friedrich Schwerdtfeger, "Housing in Zaria," in *Shelter in Africa*, ed. Oliver, 69.

133. See Marcus Whiffen, *American Architecture Since 1780: A Guide to the Styles* (Cambridge: M.I.T. Press, 1969).

134. See Henry Glassie, "Folk Art," in *Folklore and Folklife: An Introduction*, ed. Richard M. Dorson (Chicago: Univ. of Chicago Press, 1972), 268–79.

135. See John Maass, *The Gingerbread Age: A View of Victorian America* (New York: Branhall House, 1957), ch. 3.

136. See Burke, *A Grammar of Motives*, 402–44; Gregory Bateson, *Steps to an Ecology of Mind* (New York: Ballantine, 1972), 94–106; Redfield, *The Little Community*, ch. IX; Paul Klee, *Pedagogical Sketchbook*, trans. Sibyl Moholy-Nagy (New York: Praeger, 1965), 30–33. I delight in finding the author of the *Tristra-paedia* conceptualizing health as the mediation of the opposition of radical heat and radical moisture in Laurence Sterne's great *The Life and Opinions of Tristram Shandy* (1759–67), vol. V, ch. 33.

137. Thrill-seeking in sport, in art, in life, is not necessarily an escapist moment, a developmental phase, or an antisocial posture; it can be a cultural possibility. See Herbert J. Gans, *The Urban Villagers: Group and Class in the Life of Italian-Americans* (New York: Free Press, 1965), ch. 11 in general, 28–31 in particular; R. Lincoln Keiser, *The Vice Lords: Warriors of the Streets* (New York: Holt, 1969). It is not only an urban possibility. Along the Irish border, where I spent much time and where young men make bombs and young women go alone to the city to experience a different life, where old men drink "to feel different" and old women go to town on market day to pick fights, there is no escaping the reality that culture is not necessarily predicated on the search for security and peace.

138. See Lévi-Strauss, *Structural Anthropology*, 21–22; Bernard L. Fontana, William J. Robinson, Charles W. Cormack, and Ernest E. Leavitt, Jr., *Papago Indian Pottery* (Seattle: Univ. of Washington Press for the American Ethnological Society, 1962), 133–34; and the excellent opening and closing comments in James Deetz, *The Dynamics of Stylistic Change in Arikara Ceramics*, Illinois Studies in Anthropology, 4 (Urbana: Univ. of Illinois Press, 1965).

139. See Lévi-Strauss, *The Raw and the Cooked*, 340; Herbert Read, *Icon and Idea: The Function of Art in the Development of Human Consciousness* (New York: Schocken, 1965), 48.

140. The argument in ch. V of John Ruskin's *The Seven Lamps of Architecture* (Sunnyside, Orpington: George Allen, 1880) is an architecture-specific example of the nineteenth-century romantic philosophy that lies at the source of much of folkloristic thinking.

141. Wm. F. Hansen, *The Conference Sequence: Patterned Narration and Narrative Inconsistency in the Odyssey*. Univ. of California Publications: Classical Studies, 8 (Berkeley: Univ. of California Press, 1972), 11, 16, 39, 45–47, 58–59.

142. Henry Moore, "On Sculpture and Primitive Art," in *Modern Artists on Art: Ten Unabridged Essays*, ed. Robert L. Herbert (Englewood Cliffs, N.J.: Prentice-Hall, 1964), 139. See also Arnheim, *Art and Visual Perception*, 44–58.

143. Candee, "A Documentary History of Plymouth Colony Architecture, 1620–1700," *Old-Time New England*, LIX:4 (Spring 1969), 105, 110.

144. See Barley, *English Farmhouse and Cottage*, 70–71, 216–17; Eden, "Smaller Post-medieval Houses in Eastern England," 77, 79–83.

145. See Henry Chandlee Forman, *Early Manor and Plantation Houses of Maryland* (Easton, Md.: author, 1934), 148; Thomas Tileston Waterman, *The Mansions of Virginia* (Chapel Hill: Univ. of North Carolina Press, 1946), 19–21.

146. See Mel Bochner, "Serial Art, Systems, Solipsism," in *Minimal Art: A Critical Anthology*, ed. Gregory Battcock (New York: Dutton, 1968), 93.

147. Waterman and Barrows, *Domestic Colonial Architecture of Tidewater Virginia*, 2–7.

148. Innocent, *Development of English Building Construction*, 151.

149. *An Inventory of Historical Monuments in the County of Cambridge: Volume One: West Cambridge* (London: Royal Commission on Historical Monuments, 1968), xlv–lii; Harry Forrester, *The Timber-Framed Houses of Essex* (Chelmsford: The Tindal Press, 1965), 14–16; Cecil A. Hewett, "Some East Anglian Prototypes for Early Timber Houses in America," *Post-Medieval Archaeology*, 3 (1969), 107–8, 111; Cecil A. Hewett, "Seventeenth-century Carpentry in Essex," *Post-Medieval Archaeology* 5 (1971), 83–84.

150. See Kelly, *Early Domestic Architecture of Connecticut*, 7–8.

151. Whiffen, *Eighteenth-Century Houses of Williamsburg*, 116–17; William T. Buchanan, Jr., and Edward F. Heite, "The Hallowes Site: A Seventeenth-Century Yeoman's Cottage in Virginia," *Historical Archaeology*, V (1971), 41.

152. See Hall, *The Hidden Dimension*, 104.

153. See Erving Goffman, *Behavior in Public Places: Notes on the Social Oganization of Gatherings* (New York: Free Press, 1969), 35.

154. See Ivor Noël Hume, *Here Lies Virginia: An Archaeologist's View of Colonial Life and History* (New York: Knopf, 1963), 99–114.

155. The opposite situation is excellently described by Ruth L. Bunzel, *The Pueblo Potter: A Study of Creative Imagination in Primitive Art* (1929; rpt. New York: Dover, 1972), 23, 27–29, 52–68, 88. The painting on the pottery is asymmetrical and highly variable; sometimes, then, the potter is unable to materialize her articulated ideal, and the art remains a vehicle for personal expressiveness.

156. See Glassie, "Folk Art," 269, 272–79.

157. See Glassie, "The Variation of Concepts Within Tradition: Barn Building in Otsego County, New York," in press.

158. Jean-Paul Sartre, *The Words*, trans. Bernard Frechtman (Greenwich, Conn.: Fawcett Publications, 1968).

VIII: A Little History

1. See Robert A. Lancaster, Jr., *Historic Virginia Homes and Churches* (Philadelphia: Lippincott, 1915), 168–73.

2. Daniel J. Boorstin, *The Americans: The Colonial Experience* (New York: Random House, 1958), 103.

3. John Fiske, *Old Virginia and Her Neighbors*, II (Boston: Houghton Mifflin, 1899), 191.

4. Philip Alexander Bruce, *Economic History of Virginia in the Seventeenth Century*, I (1895; rpt. New York: Peter Smith, 1935), 502–32; Thomas J. Wertenbaker, *The Planters of Colonial Virginia* (Princeton: Princeton Univ. Press, 1922), 45–83; Carl Bridenbaugh, *Myths and Realities: Societies of the Colonial South* (Baton Rouge: Louisiana State Univ. Press, 1952), 5, 7.

5. Wertenbaker, *Planters of Colonial Virginia*, 150–55.

6. Boorstin, *The Americans: The Colonial Experience*, 103.

7. See Robert Redfield, *Peasant Society and Culture*

(Chicago: Univ. of Chicago Press, 1960), 18–22; Eric R. Wolf, *Peasants*, Foundations of Modern Anthropology Series (Englewood Cliffs, N.J.: Prentice-Hall, 1966), 1–17; Philip K. Boch, *Peasants in the Modern World* (Albuquerque: Univ. of New Mexico Press, 1969), 1–5; Milton B. Newton, Jr., "The Darlings Creek Peasant Settlements of St. Helena Parish, Louisiana," in *The Not So Solid South: Anthropological Studies in a Regional Subculture*, ed. J. Kenneth Morland, S. A. S. Proceedings 4 (Athens: Univ. of Georgia Press for the Southern Anthropological Society, 1971), 38–48.

8. See Thomas J. Wertenbaker, *The Golden Age of Colonial Culture* (Ithaca, N.Y.: Cornell Univ. Press, 1959), ch. 6; Louis B. Wright, *The First Gentlemen of Virginia: Intellectual Qualities of the Early Colonial Ruling Class* (San Marino, Cal.: Huntington Library, 1940).

9. See John L. Cotter, "Colonial Williamsburg," *Technology and Culture*, 11:3 (July 1970), 417–27.

10. This is exactly the rationale offered in Talpalar's *The Sociology of Colonial Virginia*, 204. His strange book is not the work of a normative historian, but the idea is not his alone. The historian Herbert Butterfield published a good and likable critique of his discipline in 1939. As I read *The Whig Interpretation of History* (New York: Norton, 1965) I found myself cheering him, except when he wrote (p. 95) that the historian must study everyone in his own terms except the bore. Surely people that the historian finds boring have a great place in the chronicle.

11. Thomas Anburey, *Travels Through the Interior Parts of America*, II (Boston: Houghton Mifflin, 1923), 215–17.

12. It is not possible to state what percentage of the original houses remain to represent these men. Exact statistics are available in chapters I and V, but to put the case approximately: between 1790 and 1960 the combined population of Louisa and Goochland grew by about one-fifth, and roughly 40 per cent of the standing houses were built in the eighteenth and nineteenth centuries. It seems that the sample is large enough.

13. Jones, *Present State of Virginia*, 80–81.

14. T. S. Eliot, *The Waste Land and Other Poems* (New York: Harcourt, 1958), 77–78.

15. Marc Bloch, *Land and Work in Mediaeval Europe*, trans. J. E. Anderson (New York: Harper, 1969), 142.

16. James Marston Fitch, *American Building: The Forces that Shape It* (Boston: Houghton Mifflin, 1948), 8; Henry C. Mercer, *Ancient Carpenter's Tools* (1929; rpt. Doylestown, Pa.: Bucks County Historical Society, 1960), 16–31; Whiffen, *Eighteenth-Century Houses of Williamsburg*, 3–5; Edlin, *Woodland Crafts in Britain*, 16–17, 140.

17. Jones, *Present State of Virginia*, 142.

18. Guion Griffis Johnson, *A Social History of the Sea Islands* (Chapel Hill: Univ. of North Carolina Press, 1930), 48; Alexander Fenton, "Material Culture as an Aid to Local History Studies in Scotland," *Journal of the Folklore Institute*, II:3 (1965), 334.

19. Forman, *Virginia Architecture in the Seventeenth Century*, 31–32, mentions the commonly cited comment by Captain John Smith and supposes the cruck-built house to have once been common in Virginia. An early house in Maryland has been discovered that has its roof framed by cruck trusses standing on the ceiling joists of the first floor (letter from J. Richard Rivoire, June 25, 1973).

20. Thomas J. Wertenbaker, *Patrician and Plebeian in Virginia: or the Origin and Development of the Social Classes of the Old Dominion* (Charlottesville, Va.: Michie Co., 1910), 110–11.

21. Demos, *A Little Commonwealth*, 53–54.

22. Ebenezer Cook, *The Sot-Weed Factor: Or, a Voyage to Maryland. A Satyr* (London, 1708), in *Early Maryland Poetry*, ed. Bernard C. Steiner, Maryland Historical Society Fund Publication, 36 (Baltimore: Maryland Historical Society, 1900), 12 [2]. The poet became the main figure in John Barth's excellent novel, *The Sot-Weed Factor* (New York: Bantam, 1969), and the poet's disenchantment with the Chesapeake reality became one of Barth's themes. Barth worked the bit of poetry quoted into his prose at the point when Eben first encounters the truth of life in the colony (part II, ch. 17); he

quotes part of it later (part II, ch. 32); and he uses "scotch cloth" recurrently as a sign of moderate estate, a reminder of the unexpected harshness of the New World situation.

23. See Allan I. Ludwig, *Graven Images: New England Stonecarving and its Symbols, 1650–1815* (Middletown, Conn.: Wesleyan Univ. Press, 1966), 43–44; James Deetz and Edwin S. Dethlefsen, "Death's Head, Cherub, Urn and Willow," *Natural History*, LXXVI:3 (March 1967), 28–37.

24. The opposite opinion is expressed in ch. 13 of Alan Merriam's *The Anthropology of Music* (Evanston, Ill.: Northwestern Univ. Press, 1964). His idea is quite clearly stated; while I would prefer to call what he terms an "aesthetic" a "verbalized" or "critical aesthetic," I could grant his point. But then, we would need a new word to cover the unstated aesthetic that is unconsciously held and articulated in actions rather than words. It does not seem to me that a person needs to verbalize an aesthetic to have one, any more than a person needs to be able to diagram sentences in order to speak. See the Introduction of Boas' *Primitive Art*; my "Folk Art" paper; and Michael Owen Jones, "The Useful and the Useless in Folk Art," *Journal of Popular Culture*, VI:4 (Spring 1973), 794–818. On the other hand we may refer to Merriam's position in order to point out that the word "aesthetic" gets overused in discussions of things like folksongs and tribal masks. The word is used to legitimize arts other than those of the Western elites, but it often obscures intentions and functions.

25. See A. T. Lucas, "Ireland," in *European Folk Art in Europe and the Americas*, ed. H. J. Hansen (New York: McGraw-Hill, 1967), 77–80.

26. See John A. Kouwenhoven, *The Arts in Modern American Civilization* (1949; rpt. New York: Norton, 1967).

27. The correlative and cognitive modes of explanation are conceptionally allied with the kinds of models called statistical and mechanical, though their usefulness lies in a different direction. For the statistical and mechanical models see: Lévi-Strauss, *Scope of Anthropology*, 27; *The Savage Mind*, 232–33; Hugo G. Nutini, "Some Considerations on the Nature of Social Structure and Model Building: A Critique of Claude Lévi-Strauss and Edmund Leach," *American Anthropologist*, 67:3 (June 1965), 707–31; Fredrik Barth, *Models of Social Organization*, Royal Anthropological Institute Occasional Paper, 23 (Glasgow: Robert MacLehose for Royal Anthropological Institute, 1966), v. 1–2, 12–13, 22–23, 31–32.

28. Alan Lomax, *Folk Song Style and Culture*, A.A.A.S. Publication, 88 (Washington: American Assn. for the Advancement of Science, 1968).

29. Armstrong, *The Affecting Presence*, 101–73.

30. Erwin Panofsky, *Gothic Architecture and Scholasticism* (New York: World, 1957). Two works that deal interestingly with artistic correlations in the ancient world are William M. Ivins, Jr., *Art and Geometry: A Study in Space Intuitions* (1946; rpt. New York: Dover, 1964) and H. P. L'Orange, *Art Forms and Civic Life in the Late Roman Empire* (Princeton: Princeton Univ. Press, 1972).

31. See Bloch, *Feudal Society*, I, 59.

32. Panofsky, *Gothic Architecture and Scholasticism*, 2, 20–21; Heinrich Wölfflin, *Renaissance and Baroque*, trans. Kathrin Simon (London: Fontana/Collins, 1971), 76–77.

33. J. L. Fischer, "Art Styles as Cultural Cognitive Maps," *American Anthropoligist*, 63:1 (Feb. 1961), 79–93.

34. DeBow, *Statistical View of the United States*, 321–22. The problem of the census-taker's definition of a family remains, of course, but that is the trouble with the use of old documents.

35. Barnett, *Innovation*, 65, 101.

36. James J. F. Deetz, "Ceramics from Plymouth, 1620–1835: The Archaeological Evidence," in *Ceramics in America: Winterthur Conference Report*, 1972, ed. Ian M. G. Quimby (Charlottesville: Univ. Press of Virginia for the Henry Francis duPont Winterthur Museum, 1973), 18–19, 29–33.

37. See D. H. Lawrence, *Studies in Classic American Literature* (Garden City, N.Y.: Doubleday, 1953), 13–18, 36–37.

38. Here are two recent defenses of pragmatic historiography: Patrick Gardiner, *The Nature of Historical Explana-*

tion (New York: Oxford Univ. Press, 1968), parts II and III; J. H. Hexter, *Doing History* (Bloomington: Indiana Univ. Press, 1971), chs. 2 and 5. These are likable books that ably describe the historian's method; they neglect, though, to defend the results of historical research.

39. See Harris, *Rise of Anthropological Theory*, 220.

40. *Journals and Letters of Philip Vickers Fithian, 1773–1774: A Plantation Tutor of the Old Dominion*, ed. Hunter Dickinson Farish (Williamsburg, Va.: Colonial Williamsburg, Inc., 1943), 35, 148, 150, 226–27.

41. Wertenbaker, *Planters of Colonial Virginia*, 23.

42. Douglas Southall Freeman, *George Washington: A Biography*, I (New York: Scribner's, 1948), 142, 168–70.

43. See William Wirt, *Sketches of the Life and Character of Patrick Henry* (Philadelphia: Thomas Cowperthwait, 1841), 24; Boorstin, *The Americans: The Colonial Experience*, 112–13.

44. Wertenbaker, *Patrician and Plebeian in Virginia*, 207–11.

45. Bridenbaugh, *Myths and Realities: Societies of the Colonial South*, 33.

46. Jefferson, *Notes on the State of Virginia*, 87–93; Fiske, *Old Virginia and Her Neighbors*, II, 191; Wertenbaker, *Planters of Colonial Virginia*, 131. The figures are not in agreement, though they drift compatibly.

47. Wertenbaker, *Planters of Colonial Virginia*, 128–29.

48. *The Aristocratic Journey: Being the Outspoken Letters of Mrs. Basil Hall Written during a Fourteen Months' Sojourn in America, 1827–1828*, ed. Una Pope-Hennessy (New York: Putnam's, 1931), 197.

49. The change is from the saltbox to the central-chimney house with a symmetrical gable plan, whether in a one- or two-story expression, and from a balanced three-opening façade to a geometrically symmetrical five-opening façade. See Kelly, *Early Domestic Architecture of Connecticut*, ch. II, for examples.

50. Henry Glassie, "Evolving Structures of Separation: A Comparison of Architectural Forms in America and Ireland,"

in *Artifactual Studies*, ed. William C. Sturtevant (Washington: Anthropological Society of Washington, in press).

51. One could not ask for better data with which to illustrate these changes than that provided in W. G. Hoskins' superb, *The Midland Peasant: The Economic and Social History of a Leicestershire Village* (London: Macmillan, 1965), the "Excursis on Peasant Houses and Interiors" at the end, and the illustrations at pp. 149, 187, 213, 243. The façade changed from asymmetrical to symmetrical; one entered directly into the early house, but into a cold transitional space in the later one. See the references in ch. VI, footnote 37, for Welsh examples of the same change.

52. It is the change from type S 2 to S 4 excellently set out in R. W. Brunskill, "Traditional Domestic Architecture of the Solway Plain," Diss. Univ. of Manchester (April 1963).

53. See Redfield, *The Little Community*, 108–12, 139–48; Peter Laslett, "The Face to Face Society," in *Philosophy, Politics and Society*, ed. Peter Laslett (Oxford: Basil Blackwell, 1970), 157–84.

54. White, *Medieval Technology and Social Change*, 56–57.

55. Bloch, *Land and Work in Mediaeval Europe*, 49; Hoskins, *The Midland Peasant*, 193–99, 253–55.

56. Von Martin, *Sociology of the Renaissance*, 62–65; Guilio C. Argan, *The Renaissance City*, trans. Susan Edna Bassnett (New York: Braziller, 1969), 14, 25; Max J. Friedlander, *Landscape, Portrait, Still-Life*, trans. R. F. C. Hull (New York: Schocken, 1963), 12, 158–63.

57. Robert K. Merton, *Science, Technology and Society in Seventeenth-Century England* (1938; rpt. New York: Harper, 1970), 76–79, 228–38.

58. John Ruskin, *The Stones of Venice*, II (London: Smith, Elder, and Co., 1853), 154–73; John Ruskin, *Lectures on Art* (New York: John Wiley and Sons, 1888), 99–126; William Morris, *Art and Its Producers, and the Arts and Crafts of Today: Two Addresses Delivered Before the National Association for the Advancement of Art* (London: Longmans, 1901); William Morris, "The Lesser Arts," "The Worker's Share of

Art," in *William Morris: Selected Writings and Designs*, ed. Asa Briggs (Baltimore: Penguin, 1962), 85–105, 140–43; Gropius, *New Architecture and the Bauhaus*, 58–66; Herbert Marcuse, "Art as a Form of Reality," in *On the Future of Art*, ed. Edward F. Fry (New York: Viking, 1970), 126–27.

59. Laslett, *The World We Have Lost*, 13, 16, 18–19, 156, 233; Demos, *A Little Commonwealth*, 187–88.

60. Leslie A. White, *The Science of Culture: A Study of Man and Civilization* (New York: Farrar, Strauss and Giroux, 1970), ch. 13.

Selected Bibliography

This bibliography was subjectively pruned to provide a list of works I feel to be most useful in performing a structural analysis of historical Anglo-American domestic folk architecture. The list was arranged (February 1973) to permit entrance into the "literature" of fields other than one's own.

I. Theory

FUNDAMENTAL PROCEDURES

This most personal section of the bibliography, an idiosyncratic selection of works on method, is probably of the least use to the reader, but its presence makes the point that scholarship demands serious and constant examination of presuppositions and fundamental purposes.

Bocheński, J. M. *The Methods of Contemporary Thought*, trans. Peter Caws. New York: Harper, 1968.

Burke, Kenneth. *A Grammar of Motives*. Berkeley: Univ. of California Press, 1969.

Merton, Robert K. *On Theoretical Sociology: Five Essays, Old and New*. New York: Free Press, 1967.

Sartre, Jean-Paul. *Search for a Method*, trans. Hazel E. Barnes. New York: Vintage Books, 1963.

Winch, Peter. *The Idea of a Social Science and its Relation to Philosophy*. New York: Humanities Press, 1971.

STRUCTURALISM IN GENERAL

The current interest in structuralism has led to the production of several general works. Lane's and Ehrmann's books are valuable anthologies; Lane's particularly includes several classic statements. Gardner's is a clear, simply stated introduction. Piaget's book, I feel, is far and away the best general work on structuralism.

Ehrmann, Jacques, ed. *Structuralism*. Garden City, N. Y.: Doubleday, 1970.

Gardner, Howard. *The Quest for Mind: Piaget, Lévi-Strauss and the Structuralist Movement*. New York: Knopf, 1973.

Lane, Michael, ed. *Introduction to Structuralism*. New York: Basic Books, 1970.

Piaget, Jean. *Structuralism*, trans. Chaninah Maschler. New York: Basic Books, 1970.

STRUCTURALISM: LINGUISTICS

Noam Chomsky does not term his theories structural. In American linguistics, generative and transformational theories replaced the theories called structural; still, Chomsky's work is philosophically akin to what is called structuralism in anthropology. Chomsky's writings are necessary and basic to an understanding of generative grammar, and John Lyons' book, *Noam Chomsky* (New York: Viking, 1970), will help the reader come to Chomsky. King's book includes an especially lucid outline of generative grammar, in addition to extending the structuralist procedure into time. The books by Lyons, Barthes, and Jakobson and Halle are also good introductions.

Barthes, Roland. *Elements of Semiology*, trans. Annette Lavers and Colin Smith. Boston: Beacon Press, 1970.

Chomsky, Noam. *Aspects of the Theory of Syntax*. Cambridge: M.I.T. Press, 1970.

———. *Language and Mind*. New York: Harcourt, Brace, and World, 1968.

———. *Syntactic Structures*. Janua Linguarum, 4. The Hague: Mouton, 1969.

Jakobson, Roman, and Morris Halle. *Fundamentals of Language*. Janua Linguarum, 1. The Hague: Mouton, 1971.

King, Robert D. *Historical Linguistics and Generative Grammar*. Englewood Cliffs, N. J.: Prentice-Hall, 1969.

Lyons, John. *Introduction to Theoretical Linguistics*. London: Cambridge Univ. Press, 1968.

STRUCTURALISM: ANTHROPOLOGY

Aspects of anthropological structuralism were in evidence before Claude Lévi-Strauss, and many contemporary anthropologists are using his ideas in their own analysis. A good, representative example would be Victor W. Turner, *The Ritual Process: Structure and Anti-Structure* (Chicago: Aldine, 1969). But I think Lévi-Strauss is his own theory's best and most careful practitioner, and I would prefer for the reader new to anthropological structuralism to begin with him. His subtly interpenetrating, concentric style makes his ideas sometimes difficult of access. For some people his writings are annoying; for others, like myself, they are metaphorically rich: his thinking can be helpful even when it is incom-

pletely understood. Beginning at the wrong point in Lévi-Strauss' corpus may make it especially hard on the person approaching him. An introductory program for the English reader who wishes to comprehend Lévi-Strauss' analysis of myth—the vein through his thought that is richest for the student of autonomous objects—might follow this order: *Tristes Tropiques, The Scope of Anthropology, Structural Anthropology* (part I), *Totemism, The Savage Mind, Structural Anthropology* (parts II, III), *The Raw and the Cooked, From Honey to Ashes*. He considers *The Savage Mind* a digressive pause; I consider it crucially pivotal.

Lévi-Strauss, Claude. *From Honey to Ashes, Introduction to a Science of Mythology*, 2, trans. John and Doreen Weightman. New York: Harper, 1973.

———. *The Raw and the Cooked, Introduction to a Science of Mythology*, 1, trans. John and Doreen Weightman. New York: Harper, 1970.

———. *The Savage Mind*. Chicago: Univ. of Chicago Press, 1966.

———. *The Scope of Anthropology*, trans. Sherry Ortner Paul and Robert A. Paul. London: Jonathan Cape, 1967.

———. *Structural Anthropology*, trans. Claire Jacobson and Brooke Grundfest Schoepf. Garden City, N.Y.: Doubleday, 1967.

———. *Totemism*, trans. Rodney Needham. Boston: Beacon Press, 1963.

———. *Tristes Tropiques: An Anthropological Study of Primitive Societies in Brazil*, trans. John Russell. New York: Atheneum, 1970.

So important—or fascinating—is Lévi-Strauss that numerous essays have been written on him. Somehow most of these works seem inadequate, even incorrect to me. I list them with the caveat that though many provide some insight, many may also mislead. The papers by Nutini, Scholte, and Caws included in the Hayes' volume are especially interesting, and the article by Rossi seems to be the best thing yet written. *The Structural Study of Myth and Totemism* contains Lévi-Strauss' own "The Story of Asdiwal."

Hayes, E. Nelson, and Tanya Hayes, eds. *Claude Lévi-Strauss: The Anthropologist as Hero*. Cambridge: M.I.T. Press, 1970.

Leach, Edmund. *Claude Lévi-Strauss*. New York: Viking, 1970.

Leach, Edmund, ed. *The Structural Study of Myth and Totemism*. A.S.A. Monographs, 5. London: Tavistock, 1971.

Paz, Octavio. *Claude Lévi-Strauss: An Introduction*, trans. J. S. Bernstein and Maxine Bernstein. London: Jonathan Cape, 1970.

Rossi, Ino. "The Unconscious in the Anthropology of Claude Lévi-Strauss." *American Anthropologist*, 75:1 (Feb. 1973), 20–48.

STRUCTURALISM: FOLKLORE

Lévi-Strauss' structural studies of the narrative have been called "paradigmatic." They have concentrated on the reversible relations that yield meaning. Folklorists have tended to isolate "syntagmatic" structures—irreversible relations that yield shape. Vladimir Propp's book remains the classic folkloristic study. Brémond and Dundes have been among those who have interestingly extended Propp's concepts. In the Marandas' anthology, the paper by A. Julien Greimas is a particularly useful statement.

Brémond, Claude. "Morphology of the French Folktale," *Semiotica*, II:3 (1970), 247–76.

Dundes, Alan. *The Morphology of North American Indian Folktales*. Folklore Fellows Communications, 195. Helsinki: Suomalainen Tiedeakatemia, 1964.

Maranda, Pierre, and Elli Köngäs Maranda, eds. *Structural Analysis of Oral Tradition*. Univ. of Pennsylvania Publications in Folklore and Folklife, 3. Philadelphia: Univ. of Pennsylvania Press, 1971.

Propp, V. *Morphology of the Folktale*, ed. and trans. Laurence Scott and Louis A. Wagner. American Folklore Society, Bibliographical and Special Series, 9; Indian Univ. Research Center in Anthropology, Folklore, and Linguistics, 10. Austin: Univ. of Texas Press, 1968.

COMPOSITION AND INNOVATION

These works are not explicitly structuralist, and some of them were conceived in opposition to structuralism, but all of them hold suggestions for the expansion of structuralist concerns. The object that manifests structure was the result of the application of a dynamic of composition; the works by Lowes, Lord, and Hansen consider the nature of composition, and thus may be related to theories of mental process such as those of Lévi-Strauss and Chomsky. The object is a vehicle for communication; the works by Duncan, Goffman, Hall, Labov, Sommer, and especially Hymes present important aspects of the communicating process of fitting form to context. Evaluating the result of the interplay of object and context requires a theory for innovation, and the books by Barnett and Kuhn are especially helpful to that end.

Barnett, H. G. *Innovation: The Basis of Cultural Change*. New York: McGraw-Hill, 1953.

Duncan, Hugh Dalziel. *Symbols in Society*. New York: Oxford Univ. Press, 1972.

Goffman, Erving. *Behavior in Public Places: Notes on the Social Organization of Gatherings*. New York: Free Press, 1969.

———. *Interaction Ritual: Essays on Face-to-Face Behaviour*. Hammondsworth: Penguin, 1972.

———. *The Presentation of Self in Everyday Life*. Garden City, N. Y. Doubleday, 1959.

Hall, Edward T. *The Hidden Dimension*. Garden City, N. Y.: Doubleday, 1969.

———. *The Silent Language*. Greenwich, Conn.: Fawcett, 1964.

Hansen, William F. *The Conference Sequence: Patterned Narration and Narrative Inconsistency in the Odyssey*. Univ. of California Publications: Classical Studies, 8. Berkeley: Univ. of California Press, 1972.

Hymes, Dell. "Directions in (Ethno-) Linguistic Theory," in *Transcultural Studies in Cognition,* ed. A. Kimball Romney and Roy Goodwin D'Andrade. *American Anthropologist*, 66:3, 2. Menasha, Wis.: American Anthropological Assn. (1964), 6–56.

———. "Introduction: Toward Ethnographies of Communication," in *The Ethnography of Communication*, ed. John J. Gumpers and Dell Hymes. *American Anthropologist*, 66:6, 2. Menasha, Wis.: American Anthropological Assn. (1964), 1–34.

Kuhn, Thomas S. *The Structure of Scientific Revolutions*, International Encyclopedia of Unified Science, II:2. Chicago: Univ. of Chicago Press, 1970.

Labov, William. *The Social Stratification of English in New York City*. Washington: Center for Applied Linguistics, 1966.

Lord, Albert B. *The Singer of Tales*. New York: Atheneum, 1965.

Lowes, John Livingston. *The Road to Xanadu: A Study in the Ways of the Imagination*. New York: Vintage Books, 1959.

Sommer, Robert. *Personal Space: The Behavioral Basis of Design*. Englewood Cliffs, N. J. Prentice-Hall, 1969.

II.   Theories of Artifactual Analysis

DESIGN

People actively engaged in designing things have written several exceedingly important essays on the theory of artifacts. All of these listed are very suggestive works, but I would like to draw attention in particular to Alexander's book and to Norberg-Schulz's remarkable *Intentions in Architecture*.

Fitch, James Marston. *American Building, 2: The Environmental Forces That Shape It*. Boston: Houghton Mifflin, 1972.

Greenough, Horatio. *Form and Function: Remarks on Art, Design, and Architecture*, ed. Harold A. Small. Berkeley: Univ. of California Press, 1966.

Klee, Paul. *On Modern Art*, trans. Paul Findlay. London: Faber, 1969.

———. *Pedagogical Sketchbook*, trans. Sibyl Moholy-Nagy. New York: Praeger, 1965.

Le Corbusier. *The Modulor: A Harmonious Measure to the Human Scale Universally Applicable to Architecture and*

Mechanics, trans. Peter De Francia and Anna Bostock. Cambridge: M.I.T. Press, 1968.

Norberg-Schulz, Christian. *Existence, Space, and Architecture*. New York: Praeger, 1971.

———. *Intentions in Architecture*. Cambridge: M.I.T. Press, 1968.

Pye, David. *The Nature of Design*. New York: Reinhold, 1967.

Shahn, Ben. *The Shape of Content*. New York: Vintage Books, 1960.

Simon, Herbert A. *The Sciences of the Artificial*. Cambridge: M.I.T. Press, 1969.

ARCHAEOLOGY

Next to the designer himself, the anthropological archaeologist has been the artifact's major teorist. Deetz's *Invitation* is a succinct, readable, excellent introduction to anthropological archaeology. The anthologies edited by Deetz and Chang include many important papers; the reader should be directed especially to Lewis R. Binford's contributions to Deetz's volume. The paper by Fontana *et al.* is a delight. Ivor Noël Hume's book is a good introduction to the solid, if theoretically timid, work of nonanthropological historical archaeologists.

Chang, K. C., ed. *Settlement Archaeology*. Palo Alto: National Press Books, 1968.

Deetz, James. *Invitation to Archaeology*. Garden City, N. Y.: Natural History Press for the American Museum of Natural History, 1967.

———, ed. *Man's Imprint from the Past: Readings in the Methods of Archaeology*. Boston: Little, Brown, 1971.

Fontana, Bernard L., J. Cameron Greenleaf, *et al.* "Johnny Ward's Ranch: A Study in Historic Archaeology." *The Kiva*, 28:1–2 (Oct.–Dec. 1962), 1–115.

Noël Hume, Ivor. *Historical Archaeology*. New York: Knopf, 1969.

ANTHROPOLOGY

With the exception of those who are archaeologists, anthropologists have evinced little interest in the artifact; still, several important studies of art have been published. Among other important papers, Jopling's anthology reprints J. L. Fischer's "Art Styles as Cultural Cognitive Maps."

Armstrong, Robert Plant. *The Affecting Presence: An Essay in Humanistic Anthropology.* Urbana: Univ. of Illinois Press, 1971.

Biebuyck, Daniel R., ed. *Tradition and Creativity in Tribal Art.* Berkeley: Univ. of California Press, 1969.

Boas, Franz. *Primitive Art.* 1927; rpt. New York: Dover, 1955.

Bunzel, Ruth L. *The Pueblo Potter: A Study of Creative Imagination in Primitive Art.* 1929; rpt. New York: Dover, 1972.

Fontana, Bernard L., William J. Robinson, Charles W. Cormack, and Ernest B. Leavitt, Jr. *Papago Indian Pottery.* Seattle: Univ. of Washington Press for the American Ethnological Society, 1962.

Gerbrands, Adrian. *Wow-ipits: Eight Asmat Wood-Carvers of New Guinea.* The Hague: Mouton, 1967.

Helm, June, ed. *Essays on the Verbal and Visual Arts: Proceedings of the 1966 Annual Spring Meeting.* Seattle: Univ. of Washington Press for the American Ethnological Society, 1967.

Jopling, Carol F., ed. *Art and Aesthetics in Primitive Societies.* New York: Dutton, 1971.

For those who are not anthropologists, yet who would like some feeling for the field, A. L. Kroeber's *Anthropology* (New York: Harcourt, Brace, 1948) is a classic introduction. Robert Redfield's *The Little Community* (Chicago: Univ. of Chicago Press, 1960) presents the anthropological tradition of holism with clarity. The culturally relative anthropoligical approach to art is well set out in Alan P. Merriam, *The Anthropology of Music* (Evanston, Ill.: Northwestern Univ. Press, 1964). The journals *American Anthropologist* and *Current Anthropology* illustrate the trends in anthropological thinking.

FOLKLORE

It is reasonable that the student of patterns in tradition would study folk artifacts as well as folk oral literature. In Europe students of folk culture have long attended to material traditions, but interest in the artifact is recent among American folklorists. Although folkloristic scholars of the artifact have produced many good studies, their theoretical intentions have generally remained submerged in description. These works will serve as an introduction to the folklore (or folklife or regional ethnology) approach to the artifact (or material culture).

Bogatyrev, Petr. *The Functions of Folk Costume in Moravian Slovakia,* trans. Richard G. Crum. Approaches to Semiotics, 5. The Hague: Mouton, 1971.

Erixon, Sigurd. "Regional European Ethnology." *Folkliv,* 2–3 (1937), 89–108; 3 (1938), 263–94.

Evans, E. Estyn. *Irish Folk Ways.* New York: Devin-Adair, 1957.

Fenton, Alexander. "An Approach to Folk Life Studies." *Keystone Folklore Quarterly,* XII:1 (Spring 1967), 5–21.

Gailey, Alan, and Alexander Fenton, eds. *The Spade in Northern and Atlantic Europe.* Belfast: Ulster Folk Museum and Institute for Irish Studies, Queen's Univ., 1970.

Glassie, Henry. *Pattern in the Material Folk Culture of the Eastern United States.* Univ. of Pennsylvania Publications in Folklore and Folklife, 1. Philadelphia: Univ. of Pennsylvania Press, 1969.

———. "Structure and Function, Folklore and the Artifact." *Semiotica,* VII:4 (1973), 313–51.

Jenkins, J. Geraint. *The English Farm Wagon: Origins and Structure.* Reading: Oakwood Press for Univ. of Reading, Museum of English Rural Life, 1961.

———, ed. *Studies in Folk Life: Essays in Honour of Iorwerth C. Peate.* London: Routledge and Kegan Paul, 1969.

Yoder, Don. "The Folklife Studies Movement." *Pennsylvania Folklife,* 13:3 (July 1963), 43–56.

An idea of folklore as a modern discipline can be taken from Richard M. Dorson, ed., *Folklore and Folklife: An Introduction* (Chicago: Univ. of Chicago Press, 1972); Alan Dundes, ed., *The Study of Folklore* (Englewood Cliffs, N. J.: Prentice-Hall,

1965); Jan Harold Brunvand, *The Study of American Folklore: An Introduction* (New York; Norton, 1968); and from these journals: *Journal of American Folklore, Journal of the Folklore Institute, Folk Life, Ulster Folklife, Ethnologia Europaea.*

GEOGRAPHY

Cultural and historical geographers have been interested in the artifact as a means to dividing space and as a component in the cultural system of environmental modification. The former interest is best stated in Kniffen's essay, the latter in Rapoport's book. The interests are combined in good local or regional studies, such as those of Evans, Wacker, Weiss, and Sauer.

Evans, E. Estyn. *Mourne Country: Landscape and Life in South Down.* Dundalk: Dundalgan Press, Inst. of Irish Studies, Queen's Univ., Belfast, 1967.

Kniffen, Fred. "Folk Housing: Key to Diffusion." *Annals of the Association of American Geographers,* 55:4 (Dec. 1965), 549–77.

Lewis, Peirce F. "The Geography of Old Houses." *Earth and Mineral Sciences,* 39:5 (Feb. 1970), 33–37.

Rapoport, Amos. *House Form and Culture.* Foundations of Cultural Geography Series. Englewood Cliffs, N. J.: Prentice-Hall, 1969.

Sauer, Carl O. *The Geography of the Ozark Highlands of Missouri.* Geographic Society of Chicago Bulletin, 7. Chicago: Univ. of Chicago, 1920.

Wacker, Peter O. *The Musconetcong Valley of New Jersey: A Historical Geography.* New Brunswick, N. J. Rutgers Univ. Press, 1968.

Weiss, Richard. *Häuser und Landschaften der Schweiz.* Erlenbach: Eugen Rentsch, 1959.

An introduction to cultural geography may be found in Philip L. Wagner and Marvin W. Mikesell, eds., *Readings in Cultural Geography* (Chicago: Univ. of Chicago Press, 1967). Another good place to begin is John Leightly, ed., *Land and Life: A Selection from the Writings of Carl Ortwin Sauer* (Berkeley: Univ. of California Press, 1969). The major journals are the *Geographical Review* and *Annals of the Association of American Geographers.*

ART HISTORY

The art historian's customary attention to extraordinary monuments, his tacit acceptance of progressive schemes, and his proclivity to uncontrolled generalizations frequently make his works good reading, but poor aids to the formulation of theories. Still, there are many art historical works of different kinds that require the attention of the student of artifacts because of sparkling commentary (as in the case of Ruskin, Kubler, Malraux, Greenberg, or Read), because of the correlation of art works with other expressions of culture (Panofsky, L'Orange, and Kouwenhoven), or because of close historical-descriptive scrutiny of a movement or class of object (Madsen and Montgomery). The universalizing application of Gowans's method stops me, but the introduction of his book is an important statement, conceptually comparable with the writings of anthropological students of art.

Gowans, Alan. *On Parallels in Universal History Discoverable in Arts and Artifacts: An Outline Statement.* Univ. of Victoria Monograph Series: History in the Arts, 6. Victoria, B. C.: Univ. of Victoria, 1972.

Greenberg, Clement. *Art and Culture: Critical Essays.* Boston: Beacon Press, 1969.

Kouwenhoven, John A. *The Arts in Modern American Civilization.* New York: Norton, 1967.

Kubler, George. *The Shape of Time: Remarks on the History of Things.* New Haven: Yale Univ. Press, 1967.

L'Orange, H. P. *Art Forms and Civic Life in the Late Roman Empire.* Princeton: Princeton Univ. Press, 1972.

Madsen, S. Tschudi. *Art Nouveau,* trans. R. J. Christopherson. New York: McGraw-Hill, 1967.

Malraux, André. *Museums Without Walls: The Voices of Silence,* trans. Stuart Gilbert and Francis Price. Garden City, N. Y.: Doubleday, 1967.

Montgomery, Charles F. *American Furniture: The Federal Period, in the Henry Francis du Pont Winterthur Museum.* New York: Viking, 1966.

Panofsky, Erwin. *Gothic Architecture and Scholasticism.* New York: World, 1957.

Read, Herbert. *Art and Alienation: The Role of the Artist in Society.* New York: Viking, 1969.

——. *Art and Industry.* Bloomington: Indiana Univ. Press, 1964.

——. *Icon and Idea: The Function of Art in the Development of Human Consciousness.* New York: Schocken Books, 1967.

Ruskin, John. *The Stones of Venice.* 3 vols. London: Smith, Elder, 1851–53.

III. History

METHOD

Many descriptions are avaliable of historiographic method. Some good examples follow.

Bloch, Marc. *The Historian's Craft,* trans. Peter Putnam. New York: Vintage Books, 1953.

Butterfield, Herbert. *The Whig Interpretation of History.* New York: Norton, 1965.

Gardiner, Patrick. *The Nature of Historical Explanation.* London: Oxford Univ. Press, 1968.

Hexter, J. H. *Doing History.* Bloomington: Indiana Univ. Press, 1971.

Hoskins, W. G. *Local History in England.* London: Longmans, 1965.

Comments upon the problems of history by scholars whose main commitment is to disciplines other than history are useful in judging normative historiography. Marvin Harris' *The Rise of Anthropological Theory: A History of Theories of Culture* (New York: Thomas Y. Crowell, 1968), though somewhat polemical, includes a history of anthropological studies of history. The position of one influential folklorist can be found in two selections of essays by Richard M. Dorson: *American Folklore and the Historian* (Chicago: Univ. of Chicago Press, 1971) and *Folklore: Selected Essays* (Bloomington: Indiana Univ. Press, 1972), chap. 8 and 9.

PRACTICE

Studies of history are better than methodological essays for providing the reader with a sense of the possibilities of historical research. Below are listed works I value especially highly because they share intensity (Hoskins is a good example), careful methods (Macfarlane, Merton, and Montell), and sociocultural sophistication (Bloch, Demos, and Laslett).

Bloch, Marc. *Feudal Society,* trans. L. A. Manyon. 2 vols. Chicago: Univ of Chicago Press, 1968.

——. *French Rural History: An Essay on Its Basic Characteristics,* trans. Janet Sondheimer. Berkeley: Univ. of California Press, 1970.

Demos, John. *A Little Commonwealth: Family Life in Plymouth Colony.* New York: Oxford Univ. Press, 1970.

Greven, Philip J., Jr. *Four Generations: Population, Land and Family in Colonial Andover, Massachusetts.* Ithaca, N. Y.: Cornell Univ. Press, 1970.

Hoskins, W. G. *The Midland Peasant: The Economic and Social History of a Leicestershire Village.* London: Macmillan, 1965.

Laslett, Peter. *The World We Have Lost: England Before the Industrial Age.* New York: Scribner's, 1965.

Macfarlane, Alan. *Witchcraft in Tudor and Stuart England: A Regional and Comparative Study.* New York: Harper, 1970.

Marx, Leo. *The Machine in the Garden: Technology and the Pastoral Ideal in America.* New York: Oxford Univ. Press, 1967.

Merton, Robert K. *Science, Technology and Society in Seventeenth Century England.* New York: Harper, 1970.

Montell, William Lynwood. *The Saga of Coe Ridge: A Study in Oral History.* Knoxville: Univ. of Tennessee Press, 1970.

Thompson, E. P. *The Making of the English Working Class*. New York: Vintage Books, 1963.
White, Lynn, Jr. *Medieval Technology and Social Change*. New York: Oxford Univ. Press, 1969.

There is a distinct class of study that falls between history and geography. These historical studies of landscapes are of great use to the student of the artifact.

Clark, Andrew Hill. *Three Centuries and the Island: A Historical Geography of Settlements and Agriculture in Prince Edward Island, Canada*. Toronto: Univ. of Toronto Press, 1959.
Evans, E. Estyn. *The Personality of Ireland: Habitat, Heritage and History*. Cambridge: Cambridge Univ. Press, 1973.
Hoskins, W. G. *The Making of the English Landscape*. Hammondsworth: Penguin, 1970.
Jordan, Terry G. *German Seed in Texas Soil: Immigrant Farmers in Nineteenth-Century Texas*. Austin: Univ. of Texas Press, 1966.
Lemon, James T. *The Best Poor Man's Country: A Geographical Study of Early Southeastern Pennsylvania*. Baltimore: Johns Hopkins Univ. Press, 1972.
Taylor, Christopher. *Dorset*. London: Hodder and Stoughton, 1970.

VIRGINIA

A regular assumption of the historian is that there will be writings to study. Some societies obsessively document themselves, preserving wills, rolls, and accounts in great numbers. Others do not, which makes it much harder to do historical research—or good historical research—in an area like Middle Virginia than in an area like eastern Massachusetts. Not only are early records scanty, there are not even full local histories written by Victorian amateurs. The student of a place like Middle Virginia will find only thin, poor local histories. He will find some useful first-hand accounts of

explorers, travelers, and early settlers, so that, oddly, the seventeenth and early eighteenth centuries can be known better from documents than the late eighteenth, nineteenth, and early twentieth centures. He will find some professional historical writings that, no matter how stringently they battle stereotyping, still speak in fuzzy generalities about most people and speak with precision only about upper-class men.

VIRGINIA: FIRST-HAND ACCOUNTS

Arber, Edwin, and A. G. Bradley, eds. *Travels and Works of Captain John Smith*. 2 vols. Edinburgh: John Grant, 1910.
Beverley, Robert. *The History and Present State of Virginia*, ed. Louis B. Wright. Chapel Hill: Univ. of North Carolina Press for the Institute of Early American History and Culture at Williamsburg, Va., 1947.
Burnaby, Andrew. *Travels through the Middle Settlements in North-America in the Years 1759 and 1760. With Observations Upon the State of the Colonies*. Ithaca, N.Y.: Cornell Univ. Press, 1960.
Cook, Ebenezer. *The Sot-Weed Factor: Or, a Voyage to Maryland. A Satyr*, in *Early Maryland Poetry*, ed. Bernard C. Steiner. Maryland Historical Fund Publication, 36. Baltimore: Maryland Historical Society, 1900.
Farish, Hunter Dickinson, ed. *Journals and Letters of Philip Vickers Fithian, 1773–1774: A Plantation Tutor of the Old Dominion*. Williamsburg, Va.: Colonial Williamsburg, 1943.
Hakluyt, Richard, ed. *The Principal Navigations, Voyages, Traffiques, and Discoveries of the English Nation*. 12 vols. Glasgow: James MacLehose, 1903–1905. Vol. 8 is the important one for Virginia.
Jefferson, Thomas. *Notes on the State of Virginia*. Boston: Wells and Lilly, 1829.
Jones, Hugh. *The Present State of Virginia From Whence Is Inferred a Short View of Maryland and North Carolina*, ed. Richard L. Morton. Chapel Hill: Univ. of North Carolina Press for the Virginia Historical Society, 1956.

VIRGINIA: HISTORIANS

These works improve as we near the present, but the impression they leave tallies perfectly with neither the first-hand accounts nor with architectural analysis.

Boorstin, Daniel J. *The Americans: The Colonial Experience*. New York: Vintage Books, 1958.

Bridenbaugh, Carl. *Myths and Realities: Societies of the Colonial South*. Baton Rouge: Louisiana State Univ. Press, 1952.

Fiske, John. *Old Virginia and Her Neighbors*. 2 vols. Boston: Houghton Mifflin, 1899.

Wertenbaker, Thomas J. *The Planters of Colonial Virginia*. Princeton: Princeton Univ. Press, 1922.

IV. Traditional Architecture

ENGLAND

The serious interest in English traditional architecture dates into the nineteenth century. Addy's early work should be remembered. Brunskill's handbook is very useful, and Barley's work is particularly excellent.

Addy, Sidney Oldall. *The Evolution of the English House*. Social England Series. London: Swan Sonnenschein, 1898.

Barley, M. W. *The English Farmhouse and Cottage*. London: Routledge and Kegan Paul, 1961.

Briggs, Martin S. *The English Farmhouse*. London: Batsford, 1953.

Brunskill, R. W. *An Illustrated Handbook of Vernacular Architecture*. New York: Universe Books, 1970.

Innocent, C. F. *The Development of English Building Construction*. 1916; rpt. Newton Abbot: David and Charles, 1971.

Smith, J. T. "Timber-Framed Building in England: Its Development and Regional Difference." *Archaeological Journal*, CXXII (1965), 133–58.

ENGLAND: LOCAL STUDIES

Over the past century a great many works dealing with the domestic architecture of an English county or locality have been published. Although many of them include good illustrations and commentary, I have chosen to list only recent and excellent works; that by Wood-Jones is a superb model study.

Brunskill, R. W. "The Clay Houses of Cumberland." *Transactions of the Ancient Monuments Society*, 10 (1962), 57–80.

Charles, F. W. B. *Medieval Cruck-Building and Its Derivatives: A Study of Timber-Framed Construction based on Buildings in Worcestershire*. Society for Medieval Archaeology Monograph Series, 2. London: Society for Medieval Archaeology, 1967.

Eden, P. "Smaller Post-medieval Houses in Eastern England," in *East Anglian Studies*, ed. Lionel M. Munby. Cambridge: W. Heffer (1968), 71–93.

Hewett, Cecil Alec. *The Development of Carpentry: 1200–1700: An Essex Study*. Newton Abbot: David and Charles, 1969.

Peters, J. E. C. *The Development of Farm Buildings in Western Lowland Staffordshire up to 1880*. Manchester: Manchester Univ. Press, 1969.

Stell, Christopher. "Pennine Houses: An Introduction." *Folk Life*, 3 (1965), 5–24.

Wadhams, M. C. "The Development of Buildings in Witham from 1500 to circa 1880." *Post-Medieval Archaeology*, 6 (1972), 1–41.

Wood-Jones, Raymond B. *Traditional Domestic Architecture in the Banbury Region*. Manchester: Manchester Univ. Press, 1963.

WALES

The bibliography on Welsh folk architecture is short but noble. Peate's is an excellent pioneering study; Fox and Raglan's is the first of the exemplary modern studies of British traditional domestic architecture; and the study by Smith and Jones is excellent.

Fox, Sir Cyril, and Lord Raglan. *Monmouthshire Houses*. 3 vols. Cardiff: National Museum of Wales, 1951–54.

Jones, S. R., and J. T. Smith. "The Houses of Breconshire." *Brycheiniog*, IX (1963), 1–77; X (1964), 69–183; XI (1965), 1–149; XII (1966/67); 1–91.

Peate, Iorwerth C. *The Welsh House: A Study in Folk Culture*. London: The Honourable Society of Cymmrodorion, 1940.

SCOTLAND

Considerably less information is available on Scottish folk architecture than on that of the other areas of the British Isles. A beginning can be made with chap. 7 of T. W. West, *A History of Architecture in Scotland* (London: Univ. of London Press, 1967), chaps. VII and VIII of I. F. Grant, *Highland Folk Ways* (London: Routledge and Kegan Paul, 1961), and in these works devoted to folk housing.

Gailey, Alan. "The Peasant Houses of the South-west Highlands of Scotland: Distribution, Parallels and Evolution." *Gwerin*, III:5 (June 1962), 227–42.

Sinclair, Colin. *The Thatched Houses of the Old Highlands*. Edinburgh: Oliver and Boyd, 1953.

IRELAND

Irish architecture has not been handled with the systematic care accorded that of England. The students of Irish houses have, however, often admirably considered the house as a part of culture. Information on folk house types can be found in E. Estyn Evans' *Irish Folk Ways* (New York: Devin-Adair, 1957), in Kevin Danaher's *The Pleasant Land of Ireland* (Cork: Mercier Press, 1970), and in many good articles, especially in the journal *Ulster Folklife*. Among the basic articles are:

Campbell, Åke. "Irish Fields and Houses: A Study of Rural Culture." *Béaloideas*, V:1 (1935), 57–74.

———. "Notes on the Irish House." *Folkliv*, 2–3 (1937), 205–34; 2 (1938), 173–96.

Evans, E. Estyn. "Donegal Survivals." *Antiquity*, XIII:50 (June 1939), 207–22.

———. "The Ulster Farmhouse." *Ulster Folklife*, 1 (1955), 27–31.

Gailey, Alan. "The Thatched Houses of Ulster." *Ulster Folklife*, 7 (1961), 9–18.

Ó Danachair, Caoimhín. "The Combined Byre-and-Dwelling in Ireland." *Folk Life*, 2 (1964), 58–75.

———. "Three House Types." *Ulster Folklife*, 2 (1956), 22–26.

AFRICA

Much of the information on African traditional architecture is scattered through ethnographies and geographical studies. Much of the work concentrating on architecture is limited to decoration or construction. There are, though, some good, complete works—the three included here are all excellent—and the future should hold more.

Beguin, Jean-Pierre, *et al. L'Habitat au Cameroun*. Paris: Office de le Recherche Scientifique Outre-Mer, 1952.

Prussin, Labelle. *Architecture in Northern Ghana: A Study of Forms and Functions*. Berkeley: Univ. of California Press, 1969.

Walton, James. *African Village*. Pretoria: J. L. van Schaik, 1956.

NORTH AMERICA

There are many good histories of American domestic architecture, though these deal mostly with the fashionable few and often slide into error when they attempt to consider folk building. There are also many awful books on American domestic architecture; they are not listed.

Fitch, James Marston. *American Building: The Historical Forces That Shaped It*. New York: Schocken, 1973.

Gowans, Alan. *Images of American Living: Four Centuries of Architecture and Furniture as Cultural Expression*. Philadelphia: Lippincott, 1964.

Kniffen, Fred, and Henry Glassie. "Building in Wood in the Eastern United States: A Time-Place Perspective." *The Geographical Review*, LVI:1 (Jan. 1966), 40–66.

Morrison, Hugh. *Early American Architecture from the First Colonial Settlements to the National Period*. New York: Oxford Univ. Press, 1952.

Reps, John W. *Town Planning in Frontier America*. Princeton: Princeton Univ. Press, 1969.

Whiffen, Marcus. *American Architecture Since 1780: A Guide to the Styles*. Cambridge: M.I.T. Press, 1969.

NORTH AMERICA: LOCAL STUDIES

Most of the local studies of American domestic architecture are of limited value, being picture books portraying local expressions of national and international styles. Still, architectural historians, geographers, and folklorists have produced many studies that incorporate good information, although the architectural historians tend to maintain an interest in only a few sorts of buildings, and there is a tendency to superficiality of architectural recording among both folklorists and geographers. The excellent *Journal of the Society of Architectural Historians* has, unfortunately, carried few papers on American traditional architecture. The modest journal *Pioneer America* contains an abundance of invaluable data on folk architecture.

Blair, Don. *Harmonist Construction: Principally as Found in the Two-Story Houses in Harmonie, Indiana, 1814–1824*. Indiana Historical Society Publications, 23:2. Indianapolis: Indiana Historical Society, 1964.

Brumbaugh, G. Edwin. "Colonial Architecture of the Pennsylvania Germans." *Pennsylvania German Society Proceedings*, XLI (1933), 1–60, plates 2–105.

Bucher, Robert C. "The Continental Log House." *Pennsylvania Folklife*, 12:4 (Summer 1962), 14–19.

Bunting, Bainbridge, Jean Lee Booth, and William R. Sims, Jr. *Taos Adobes: Spanish Colonial Territorial Architecture of the Taos Valley*. Publication 2. Santa Fe: Fort Burgwin Research Center, Museum of New Mexico Press, 1964.

Candee, Richard M. "A Documentary History of Plymouth Colony Architecture, 1620–1700." *Old-Time New England*, LIX:3 (Jan.–March 1969), 59–71; LIX:4 (Spring 1969), 105–11; LX:2 (Fall 1969), 37–53.

Connally, Ernest Allen. "The Cape Cod House: an Introductory Study." *Journal of the Society of Architectural Historians*, XIX:2 (May 1960), 47–56.

Cotten, Fred R. "Log Cabins of the Parker County Region." *West Texas Historical Association Year Book*, XXIX (Oct. 1953), 96–104.

Dornbusch, Charles H., and John K. Heyl. *Pennsylvania German Barns*. Pennsylvania German Folklore Society, XXI (1956). Allentown: Schlechter's, 1958.

Fife, Austin E. "Stone Houses of Northern Utah." *Utah Historical Quarterly*, 40:1 (Winter 1972), 6–23.

Fitchen, John. *The New World Dutch Barn: A Study of Its Characteristics, Its Structural System, and Its Probable Erection Procedures*. Syracuse, N.Y.: Syracuse Univ. Press, 1968.

Forman, Henry Chandlee. *The Architecture of the Old South: The Medieval Style, 1585–1850*. Cambridge: Harvard Univ. Press, 1948.

Garvan, Anthony N. B. *Architecture and Town Planning in Colonial Connecticut*. New Haven: Yale Univ. Press, 1951.

Glassie, Henry. "The Double-Crib Barn in South Central Pennsylvania." *Pioneer America*, I:1 (Winter 1969), 9–16; I:2 (July 1969), 40–45; II:1 (Jan. 1970), 47–52; II:2 (July 1970), 23–34.

———. "Eighteenth-Century Cultural Process in Delaware Valley Folk Building." *Winterthur Portfolio*, 7. Charlottesville: Univ. Press of Virginia for the Henry Francis du Pont Winterthur Museum, 1972, 29–57.

———. "The Pennsylvania Barn in the South." *Pennsylvania Folklife*, 15:2 (Winter 1965–66), 8–19; 15:4 (Summer 1966), 12–25.

————. "The Types of the Southern Mountain Cabin," in *The Study of American Folklore*, ed. Jan H. Brunvand. New York: Norton (1968), 338–70.

————. "The Variation of Concepts Within Tradition: Barn Building in Otsego County, New York," in *Man and Cultural Heritage*, ed. H. J. Walker and W. G. Haag. Geoscience and Man, 5. Baton Rouge: Louisiana State Univ., in press.

Heimsath, Clovis. *Pioneer Texas Buildings: A Geometry Lesson*. Austin: Univ. of Texas Press, 1968.

Isham, Norman M., and Albert F. Brown. *Early Connecticut Houses: An Historical and Architectural Study*. 1900; rpt. New York: Dover, 1965.

Kelly, J. Frederick. *Early Domestic Architecture of Connecticut*. 1924; rpt. New York: Dover, 1963.

Kniffen, Fred. "Louisiana House Types." *Annals of the Association of American Geographers*, XXVI (1936), 179–93.

————. "The Physiognomy of Rural Louisiana." *Louisiana History*, IV:4 (Fall 1963), 291–99.

Lancaster, Clay. *Ante Bellum Houses of the Bluegrass*. Lexington: Univ. of Kentucky Press, 1961.

Long, Amos, Jr. *The Pennsylvania German Family Farm*. Publications of the Pennsylvania German Society, VI. Breinigsville: The Pennsylvania German Society, 1972.

Niederer, Frances J. *The Town of Fincastle, Virginia*. Charlottesville: Univ. Press of Virginia, 1966.

Perrin, Richard W. E. *Historic Wisconsin Buildings: A Survey of Pioneer Architecture, 1835–1870*. Publications in History, 4. Milwaukee: Milwaukee Public Museum, 1962.

Peterson, Charles E. "The Houses of French St. Louis," in *The French in the Mississippi Valley*, ed. John Francis McDermott. Urbana: Univ. of Illinois Press (1965), 17–40.

Rempel, John I. *Building with Wood and Other Aspects of Nineteenth-Century Building in Ontario*. Toronto: Univ. of Toronto Press, 1967.

Ridlen, Susanne S. "Bank Barns in Cass County, Indiana." *Pioneer America*, IV:2 (July 1972), 25–43.

Rodgers, Ava D. *The Housing of Oglethorpe County, Georgia: 1790–1860*. Tallahassee: Florida State Univ. Press, 1971.

Séguin, Robert-Lionel. *Les Granges du Québec du XVIIe au XIXe Siècle*. Musée National du Canada Bulletin, 192. Ottawa: Ministère du Nord Canadien et des Ressources Nationales, 1963.

Wacker, Peter O. "New Jersey's Cultural Landscape Before 1800." *Proceedings of the Second Annual Symposium of the New Jersey Historical Commission*. Newark: New Jersey Historical Society (1971), 35–62.

Welsch, Roger L. *Sod Walls: The Story of the Nebraska Sod House*. Broken Bow, Neb.: Purcells, 1968.

Whiffen, Marcus. *The Eighteenth-Century Houses of Williamsburg*. Williamsburg, Va.: Colonial Williamsburg, 1960.

Wilhelm, E. J., Jr. "Folk Settlement Types in the Blue Ridge Mountains." *Keystone Folklore Quarterly*, XII:3 (Fall 1967), 151–74.

Wilson, Eugene M. "The Single Pen House in the South." *Pioneer America*, II:1 (Jan. 1970), 21–28.

Zelinsky, Wilbur. "The New England Connecting Barn." *The Geographical Review*, XLVIII:4 (Oct. 1958), 540–53.

RECORDING TECHNIQUES

The easiest criticism to level at studies of traditional architecture is that of theoretical anemia, but even sheerly descriptive accounts have commonly been ruined by sloppy recording. Buildings must be exactingly measured and studied in detail, and they must be precisely located on the land. Only then is description complete, and only then can the analyst move past description and begin saying something of significance about the buildings. Here are some works that outline recording procedures.

Brunskill, R. W. "A Systematic Procedure for Recording English Vernacular Architecture." *Transactions of the Ancient*

Monuments Society, 13 (1965–66), 42–126. In 1973, Brunskill developed an important addition: "Recording the Buildings of the Farmstead," mimeo.

Fenton, Alexander. *The Recording of Crofts and Houses*. Edinburgh: School of Scottish Studies, National Museum of Antiquities, n.d.

McKee, Harley J. *Recording Historic Buildings: The Historic American Buildings Survey*. Washington: U.S. Dept. of the Interior, National Park Service, 1970.

Peterson, Charles E. "The Technology of Early American Building." *Newsletter of the Association of Preservation Technology*, I:1 (1969), 3–17.

Renk, Thomas B. "A Guide to Recording Structural Details of Historic Buildings." *Historical Archaeology*, III (1969), 34–48.

Roberts, Warren E. "Fieldwork: Recording Material Culture," in *Folklore and Folklife: An Introduction*, ed. Richard M. Dorson. Chicago: Univ. of Chicago Press (1972), 431–44.

Index

Folk Housing in Middle Virginia has been composed on the Mergenthaler VIP in the Caledonia type design. Korinna Bold type was selected for display. The book was designed by Bill Cason, composed by Graphic Composition, Inc., Athens, Georgia, printed by Thomson-Shore, Inc., Dexter, Michigan, and bound by John H. Dekker & Sons, Grand Rapids, Michigan.

THE UNIVERSITY OF TENNESSEE PRESS
Knoxville